READER'S DIGEST

ON THE ROAD USA

NORTH-SOUTH ROUTES

Reader's Digest

The Reader's Digest Association, Inc.
Pleasantville, New York / Montreal

ON THE ROAD USA

Project Editor	Carroll C. Calkins
Project Art Editor	Gilbert L. Nielsen
Art Editor	Perri DeFino
Project Coordinator	Don Earnest
Associate Editors	Noreen B. Church, Diana Marsh (Copy Desk), Thomas A. Ranieri
Assistant Editor	D. Diefendorf
Project Research Editor	Hildegard Anderson
Research Editors	Shirley Miller, Maymay Quey Lin
Art Associate	Morris Karol
Associate Picture Editor	Richard Pasqual
Project Secretary	Jason Peterson

Contributors

Editor	Margaret Perry
Writers	Shelley Aspaklaria, Robert Brown, David Caras, Laura Dearborn, Diane Hall, Signe Hammer, Guy Henle, Archie Hobson, John Kiely, Anne Lubell, Susan Macovsky, Mona Malone, Richard Marshall, Barbara Rogan, Tim Snider, Richard Sudhalter, Robert Thurston, Carol Weeg, Joseph Wilkinson, Elaine Williams, Donald Young
Copy Editor	Harriett Bachman
Researchers	Mary Hart, Nathalie Laguerre, Mary Lyn Maiscott, Raissa Silverman, Kelly Tasker
Art Associates	Joseph Dyas, Bruce McKillip
Picture Researcher	Marian Paone
Indexer	Sydney Wolfe Cohen

Reader's Digest General Books

Editor in Chief	John A. Pope, Jr.
Managing Editor	Jane Polley
Art Director	David Trooper
Group Editors	Norman B. Mack, Susan J. Wernert, Joseph L. Gardner (International), Joel Musler (Art)
Chief of Research	Monica Borrowman
Copy Chief	Edward W. Atkinson
Picture Editor	Robert J. Woodward
Rights and Permissions	Pat Colomban
Head Librarian	Jo Manning

How to use this book

First, be sure you have the right volume. This is the North–South book, with the odd-numbered interstates. The even-numbered East–West routes are in the other volume.

The map on the next two pages shows all the routes in this book and refers you to detailed maps on which numbered brackets indicate segments of each interstate.

When you turn to any two-page section in this volume, you'll see a green line along the outer side of each page. It represents the segment of interstate covered on those two pages. The boxed exit numbers on the lines are keyed to descriptions of the points of interest. The small numbers between the exit boxes indicate the distance (to the nearest mile) between exits. The total number of miles covered by a two-page section is shown at the bottom of each page. Where interstates intersect, you'll find cross-references to the appropriate section—whether in this volume or the other one.

The book works two ways

When going south, leaf through the book from front to back. When going north, leaf through from back to front. When there are two exit numbers for one destination, the first exit given is for drivers headed south; the second, for drivers headed north.

Most entries describe such sites as parks, museums, and natural wonders. But cities are included when they are on or near an interstate. A city's highlights are mentioned; for maps and further information, contact the tourist bureau that's listed. Virtually all the attractions are 30 minutes or less from the interstate exit. And when some spectacular destination—like the Grand Canyon or Mt. Rainier—is within reasonable reach, we have included it in a box entitled "If You Have Some Extra Time."

We have made every effort to provide accurate information. Our driver-reporters visited each site; our researchers contacted each place to double-check their reports. But you may still encounter surprises. A site may change the dates it's open, adopt a new admission policy—or close altogether. Exit numbers also change, and some interstate segments, scheduled to be completed by our publication date, may not be finished. But the detailed maps in the front of the book and the mileage between exits shown on the green lines should help keep you oriented. We trust that any inconvenience will be more than compensated for by the hundreds of suggestions for restful and rewarding things to see and do within easy range of the interstates.

—*The Editors*

About the directions and other information

Mileage at the beginning of an entry is rounded to the nearest half-mile; no mileage is given for a drive of 5 minutes or less. Driving time is approximate and may vary with conditions. In a city entry, mileage and time (to the tourist bureau) appear when the city is not on the interstate. In directions the word *Route* (abbreviated Rte., as in Rte. 101) is used for all numbered noninterstate highways and roads—U.S., state, and local. At the end of an entry, the dates given are inclusive; thus Mon.–Fri. and May–Sept., mean Monday *through* Friday and May *through* September. If admission fees are not mentioned, they are not required. Symbols (below) appear when relevant.

Picnicking Camping Trailers Hiking Swimming Fishing Wheelchairs

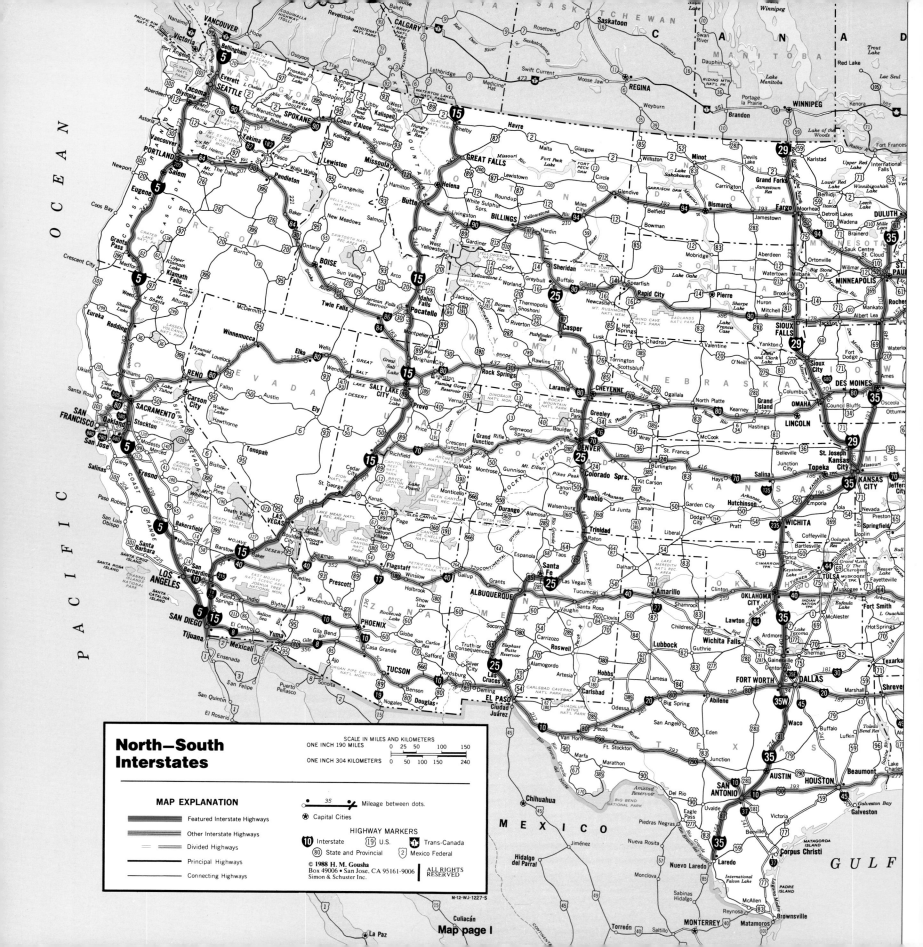

North–South Interstates

MAP EXPLANATION

SCALE IN MILES AND KILOMETERS
ONE INCH 190 MILES   0 25 50   100   150
ONE INCH 304 KILOMETERS   0 50 100 150   240

35 Mileage between dots.

Capital Cities

HIGHWAY MARKERS
10 Interstate   19 U.S.   Trans-Canada
80 State and Provincial   2 Mexico Federal

Featured Interstate Highways
Other Interstate Highways
Divided Highways
Principal Highways
Connecting Highways

M-12-WJ-1227-S

Map page I

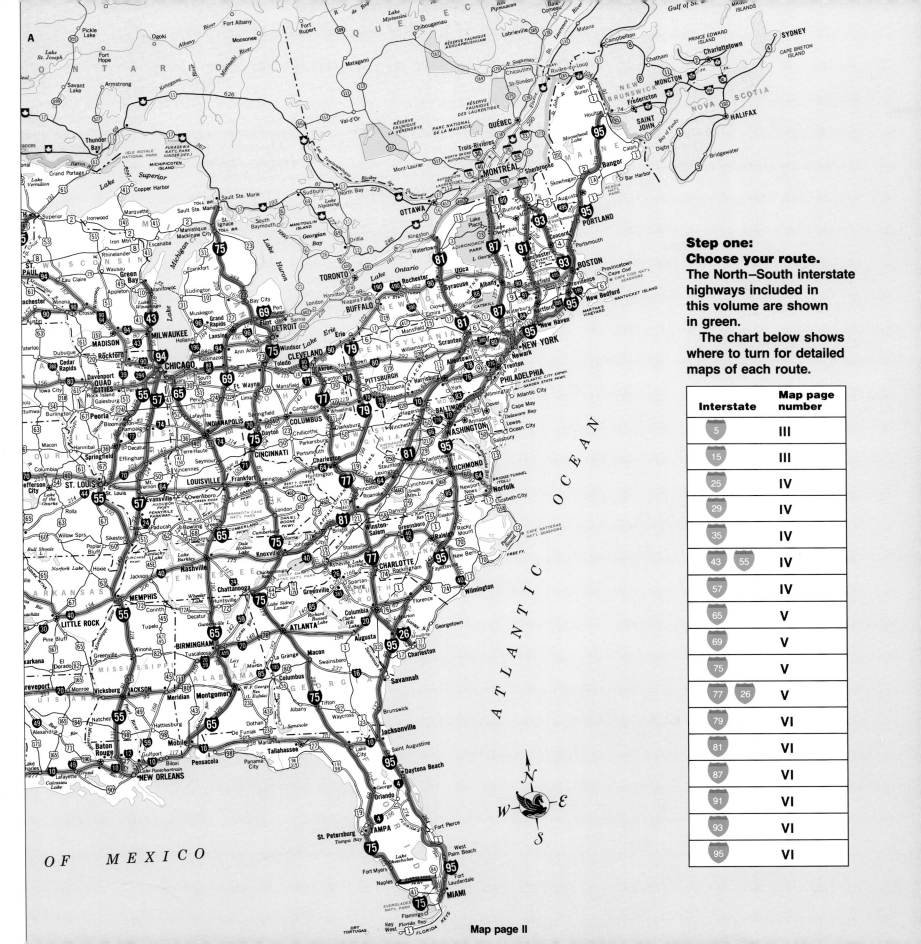

Map page II

Step one:
Choose your route.
The North–South interstate highways included in this volume are shown in green.

The chart below shows where to turn for detailed maps of each route.

Interstate	Map page number
5	III
15	III
25	IV
29	IV
35	IV
43 55	IV
57	IV
65	V
69	V
75	V
77 26	V
79	VI
81	VI
87	VI
91	VI
93	VI
95	VI

Step two:
Choose a section of the route. Each interstate has been divided into segments indicated by numbered red brackets.

Each number represents a two-page section in the book. Turn to the appropriate numbered section to find the points of interest (and exit numbers) on the bracketed stretch of highway you plan to drive.

The interstates highlighted below are included on map pages III and IV. The others are on map pages V and VI.

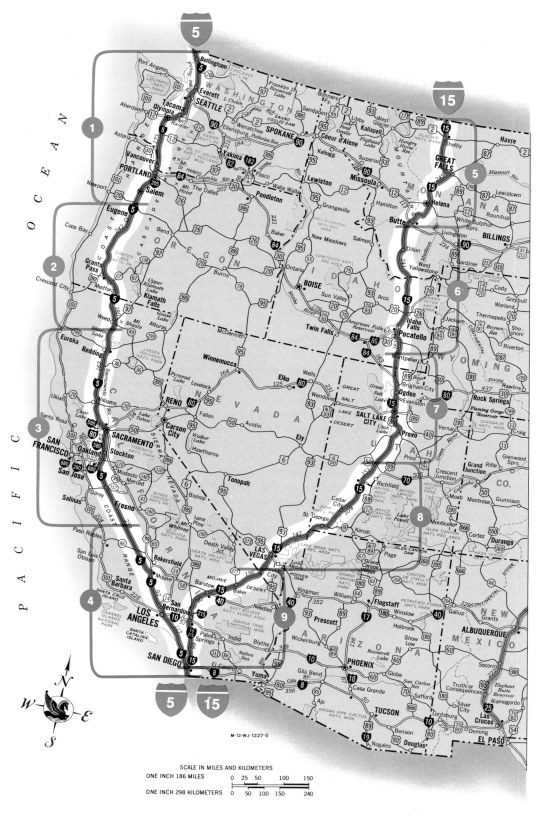

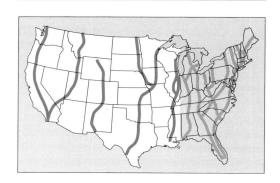

SCALE IN MILES AND KILOMETERS

ONE INCH 186 MILES

| 0 | 25 | 50 | 100 | 150 |

ONE INCH 298 KILOMETERS

| 0 | 50 | 100 | 150 | 240 |

M-12-WJ-1227-S

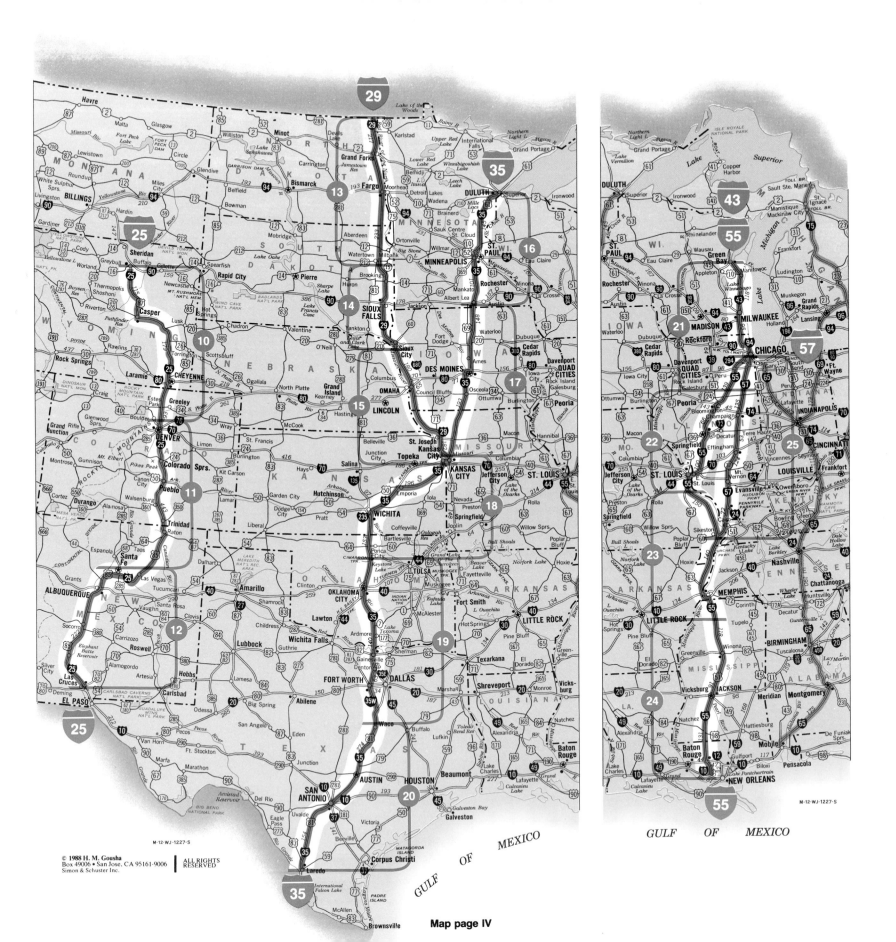

Map page IV

Step two:
Choose a section of the route. Each interstate has been divided into segments indicated by numbered red brackets.

Each number represents a two-page section in the book. Turn to the appropriate numbered section to find the points of interest (and exit numbers) on the bracketed stretch of highway you plan to drive.

The interstates highlighted below are included on map pages V and VI. The others are on map pages III and IV.

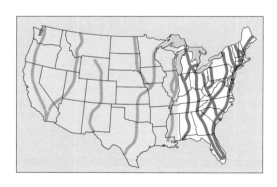

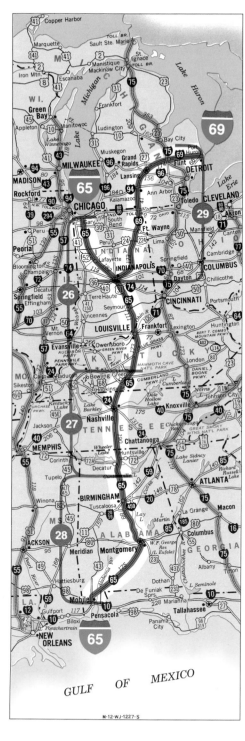

SCALE IN MILES AND KILOMETERS
ONE INCH 186 MILES   0 25 50   100   150
ONE INCH 298 KILOMETERS 0   50 100 150   240

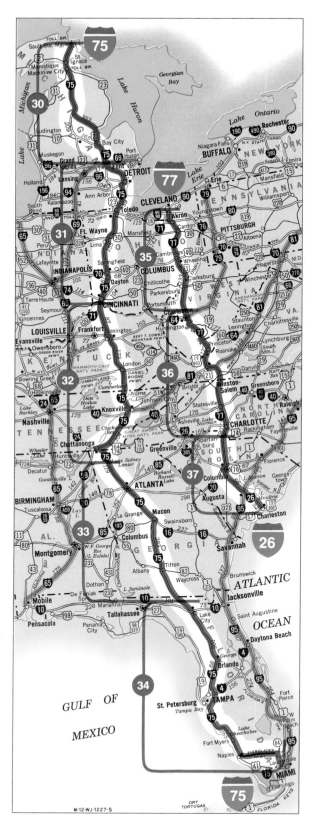

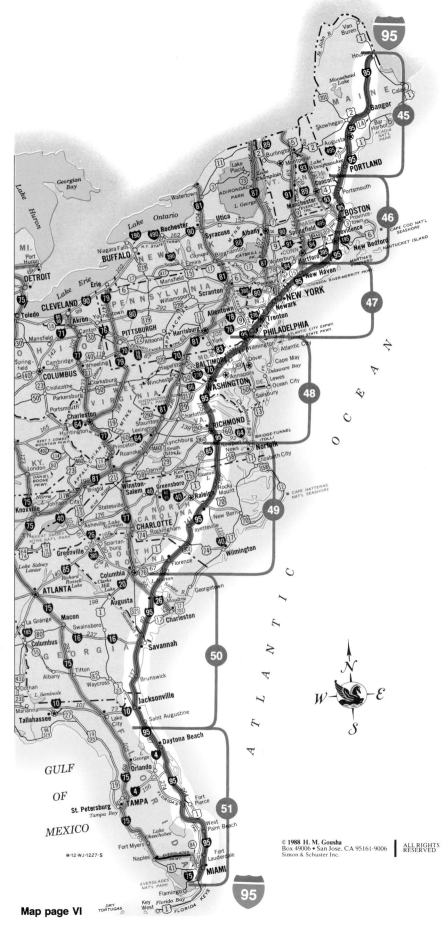

Map page VI

CANADA
U.S.A.
WA
276

23

253

2

250

18

231

42

189

23

See
E–W book,
sec. 1.

166

39

127

16

111

6

276 Peace Arch State Park

2 min. Follow signs. The imposing masonry arch, with one support in each country, commemorates the lasting peace between Canada and the United States. It was built by volunteer labor from each country, and children donated the first funds for the creation of the surrounding park with its fine views of Semiahmoo Bay. Broad lawns spread across the border, and formal flower beds provide bright accents of color. *Open year-round.*

276. *A graceful monument in a tranquil setting celebrates a peaceful border.*

253 Bellingham, WA 98227

Visitors/Convention Bureau, 904 Potter St. (206) 671-3990. More than 25 parks affirm this community's appreciation of its beaches, lakes, and woodlands. The splendor of the San Juan Islands can be viewed from a hilltop arboretum, and island cruises and whale-watching trips are offered by the local marina. Handsome brick buildings memorialize the 1890's lumber boom. The Whatcom Museum of History and Art is a fine example of Victorian architecture.

250 Chuckanut Drive
231

Exit 250: south on Rte. 11. Exit 231: north on Rte. 11. This scenic route (allow 35 minutes to drive its 21 miles) adds about 30 minutes to the time it would take on the interstate—if you don't stop. But be forewarned: there are some tempting trails, overlooks, and picnic areas along the way. At the northern end this curving drive hugs forested cliffs that provide spectacular views of the San Juan Islands across the Bellingham, Chuckanut, and Samish bays. Watch, too, for the distinctive red bark of the broad-leaved Pacific madrones among the lush green of the conifers. At the southern end the drive straightens and runs through fertile farmlands, where barns, in various interesting stages of collapse, may foretell the future of the handsome new and old farm buildings still standing.

189 Boeing 747/767 Division Assembly Plant Tour

4 mi./7 min. West on Rte. 526. The plant, an 11-story structure covering 62 acres, is by volume one of the largest buildings in the world. Boeing 747's and 767's are assembled here, and eight of each can be accommodated at the same time. The tour begins with a slide show of the company history and a 6-minute film on the assembly of a 767, then goes on to the viewing balcony, from which you can see the work under way. On the flight line you'll get a close look at the gigantic, gleaming finished products. *Open Mon.–Fri. Children under 12 not admitted.*

166 Seattle, WA 98101

Convention and Visitors Bureau, 1815 7th Ave. (206) 447-4200. Here on seven hills, almost surrounded by water, is one of America's most dramatic settings for a city. The Space Needle in Seattle Center provides stunning views of Puget Sound, Lake Washington, and (weather permitting) the distant Olympic Range, Cascade Range, and the majesty of Mt. Rainier. Downtown attractions include the waterfront, Pioneer Square, and Pike Place Market, where the display of fresh fruits and vegetables has become an art form.

111 Tolmie State Park

5 mi./10 min. West on Marvin Rd. Unlikely as it may seem, the main attractions here are snorkeling and scuba diving around the wooden barges submerged to create an artificial reef to attract fish and other sea life. The white buoys offshore mark the barges' location. There is good fishing for flounder and ling cod. At low tide you can also dig for butter, horse, and razor clams. For land-oriented visitors there is an interesting hour-long walk through the forest of some 30 species of trees—mostly firs, maples, and alders. *Open daily Apr.–Sept.; Wed.– Sun. Oct.–Mar.*

105 Olympia, WA 98507

Visitor Convention Bureau, 1000 Plum St. (206) 357-3370. The chief business here is government, as evidenced by the beautifully landscaped grounds and the massive masonry dome of the capitol dominating the skyline. A few blocks to the south is the State Capital Museum, where the state's Indian heritage and pioneer past are memorialized. Priest Point Park, the public market, and the waterfront are other popular destinations.

166. *The Space Needle features an observation deck and revolving restaurants.*

77 Rainbow Falls State Park

16 mi./20 min. West on Rte. 6. The peaceful stillness of this wooded parkland is punctuated by the song of the small cascade that gives the park its name. The waters spill over a wide shoulder of projecting rock, sometimes forming a colorful rainbow in the morning sun.

Swimming, fishing, boating, and hiking through the forest of towering trees entice visitors, who share the woodland with elks, deer, and raccoons. Ducks and gray herons often gather in the river here. A swinging footbridge and several log cabins contribute to the peaceful rustic setting. *Open year-round.*

49 Mount St. Helens National Monument Visitor Center

5 mi./10 min. East on Rte. 504. The mysteries of the Mt. St. Helens cataclysmic eruption that changed the Pacific Northwest skyline in the spring of 1980 are graphically explained at this center, where you can walk through a model of a volcano and look down into a simulated magma chamber. A seismograph constantly monitors the real mountain's activity.

Situated on the shores of scenic Silver Lake, the center is about 60 miles from the mountain, which can be seen on clear days.

A short nature trail follows the lakeshore, where bald eagles, ducks, great blue herons, and other water birds congregate, especially in the mornings and evenings. *Open daily except Thanksgiving Day and Christmas.*

299 Portland, OR 97204

Convention and Visitors Association, 26 SW Salmon St. (503) 222-2223. The favored flowers in the City of Roses are at their best in Washington Park from mid-May to late November. Here, too, is a superb Japanese garden, a forestry center, a museum of science and industry, and some inviting picnic areas. The zoo is famous for its Asian elephants. Other attractions include a unique block-wide landscaped water fountain, a magnificent mansion, museums of Oregon's history and art, and a museum of advertising.

278 Champoeg State Park

6 mi./10 min. West on Ehlen Rd.; bear right on Champoeg Rd. Although the town of Champoeg was washed away by the raging waters of the Willamette in 1861, the site is still of historic significance. For it was here that American settlers on the West Coast formed their first provisional government. Exhibits and films recall this event and the lives of local Indians, explorers, and trappers as well. This beautiful 600-acre park with a spacious rolling landscape of shady lawns and forested campsites is a pleasant place to relax. There are also playfields, and cycling and fishing are popular. Sheep from the neighboring farms often graze on the park grounds. *Open year-round. Admission charged weekends Memorial Day–Labor Day.*

253 Salem, OR 97301

Convention and Visitors Association, 1313 Mill St. SE. (503) 581-4325. The gilded statue of the pioneer standing atop the capitol pays tribute to those who first cleared the wilderness in the Oregon country. By the mid-1800's churches and homes were established, and some interesting examples of these, along with a woolen mill, are maintained in Mission Mill Village. Nearby are the Bush House and the Deepwood Estate, which reveal the taste for beauty and elegance that developed in the 19th century. And historic buildings grace the Willamette University campus.

248 Enchanted Forest Theme Park

3 min. East on Delaney, right on Enchanted Way; follow signs. Among the storybook favorites encountered in three dimensions in this amusement park are Snow White and the Seven Dwarfs, Humpty-Dumpty, the Three Bears, and Alice in Wonderland. There's a slide that goes down through the Old Lady's Shoe, and a bobsled ride on Ice Mountain. Pathways through the pleasant wooded site lead to a haunted house, a castle, a gingerbread house, and a mining town. Children of a certain age are indeed likely to be enchanted. *Open mid-Mar.–Sept. Admission charged.*

If You Have Some Extra Time:

Mount Rainier National Park

127 *60 mi./75 min.* Should you happen to be on the road when "the mountain is out," as they say in Washington, you will see how Mt. Rainier dominates the skyline and why this dormant volcano has become a major point of reference from the shores of Puget Sound to central Washington.

If you would like to experience the mountain up close, allow about 2 hours to get from the interstate to the visitor center at Paradise. A stop at the Kautz Creek Mudflow, just inside the entrance to the park, is of ecological interest. In 1947 a great swatch of forest was devastated, and the road was buried under 20 feet of mud and debris. Here you can see how the forest is regenerating itself.

At the Longmire Visitor Center the mountain looms even larger against the sky but is still at a distance. It is not until you drive the 10-mile stretch of zigzag road to the aptly named Paradise Visitor Center that the full impact of Mt. Rainier hits you. From here you'll have a stunning panoramic view of evergreen forests, alpine meadows, glacier fields, and the ice-capped 14,410-foot summit rising grandly above it all.

From Paradise you can walk the trails, where in summer more than 30 kinds of wildflowers light up the landscape. You may also glimpse mountain goats, deer, marmots, and birds of many kinds. *How to get there: Exit 127, south on Rte. 7 to Elbe; follow signs on Rte. 706 to park entrance. Open year-round. Admission charged.*

105

28

77

28

49

58

WA

OR

299

21

278

25

253

5

248

32

5

216

216 Linn County Historical Museum, Brownsville

4 min. East on Rte. 228, left on Main St., right on Park Ave. Linn County, which originally extended to the Rocky Mountains and south to California, has lost a little in size; but, as evidenced by the museum and historic houses here, a lively sense of the past is retained. It's not surprising that the museum, in a turn-of-the-century bungalow-style depot, with four railroad cars, a circus train, and a caboose, has a large collection of railroadiana. A prairie schooner that brought some early settlers to the Brownsville area establishes the pioneer presence, and the period settings of replicas of a barbershop, a millinery salon, a general store, a bank, and a telephone switchboard recall the mid-19th century. The nearby Moyer House, built in 1881, can be toured on request. A self-guiding walking tour covers other historic buildings. *Open Tues.–Sat., P.M. Sun., and holidays May–Sept.; Thurs.–Sat. and P.M. Sun. except holidays Oct.–Apr. Admission free but donations encouraged.* 🚐 ♿

119. *The Bengal tiger's cool appraisal encourages the use of a telephoto lens.*

199 / 195 Armitage State Park

Exit 199: 4 mi./7 min. West on Van Duyn Rd., left on Coberg Rd. Exit 195: 3.5 mi./7 min. West on Belt Line Rd., right on Coberg Rd. This small and well-kept park is on the McKenzie River, a favorite of fishermen and boaters. There's picnicking in the shade of the redwoods, maples, and firs, recreation areas on the spacious lawns, and hiking along the 1½-mile winding trail that follows the edge of the river. The McKenzie joins the Willamette, another famous Oregon river, about 2 miles downstream from here. *Open year-round. Admission charged on weekends and holidays.* 🏕 🚶 🐟 ♿

194 Eugene, OR 97401

Convention and Visitors Bureau, 305 W. 7th Ave. (800) 452-3670; (800) 547-5445 outside OR. The pleasant tree-shaded campus of the University of Oregon is an attraction in itself, and the Museum of Art has an extensive collection of Oriental art. Also on campus is the Museum of Natural History. The city's pioneer and Victorian eras are represented in the Lane County Historical Museum. Rhododendrons are featured in Hendricks Park, while Owens Municipal Park is noted for its roses.

119 Wildlife Safari, Winston

5 mi./8 min. West on Rte. 42, right on Lookingglass Rd. to Safari Rd.; follow signs. There are about 100 species, some threatened or endangered, among the 600 animals and birds that roam freely in this spacious and attractive setting. The 2½-mile self-guiding auto route leads through the Asian section, which has Bengal tigers, yaks, and deer, along with rheas, emus, and other unusual birds. The African area includes hippo ponds, the world's largest antelope, lions, and Cape buffaloes. Zebras, elephants, cheetahs, wildebeests, Bactrian camels, and rhinos are among the other exotic animals you may also see at close range. At the Safari Village you'll find a petting zoo for children, as well as animal shows and elephant rides. *Open year-round. Admission charged.* 🏕 🚐 🚶 ♿

76 Wolf Creek Tavern

2 min. West from exit. The route that I-5 follows between Portland and Sacramento is much like that of the original stagecoach road in the 1860's. The trip took 6 days then, and some 60 stage stops along the way supplied a change of horses as well as food and lodging for passengers. The Wolf Creek Tavern has provided virtually continuous service for more than 100 years. It is an operating restaurant and hostelry, but a self-guiding tour of the premises is encouraged. In the ladies' parlor, the men's sitting room, and the main staircase, all beautifully restored, one can savor an intimate sense of a bygone era. *Open daily except first 2 weeks in Jan.* 🏕 ♿

61. *Kayaks and the large tour boat are dwarfed by Hellgate's rocky ramparts.*

61 Hellgate Canyon and Indian Mary Park

9.5 mi./25 min. West on Merlin-Galice Rd. to Hellgate Overlook. Two adjacent sites—Hellgate Canyon and Indian Mary Park—reveal contrasting aspects of the scenic Rogue River. At Hellgate, where it rushes through the rocky narrows, the river is popular with white-water boatmen and rafters, whom you may see in action. At the park the river widens, slows its pace, and becomes inviting to fishermen and swimmers. The perspective from water level dramatizes the canyon's formations of folded rock, sheer cliffs, and forested slopes. In the shady recesses of the park, the native trees and shrubs have been agreeably supplemented with species from many other states and nations. *Open year-round.* 🏕 ⛺ 🚐 🚶 🦫 🐟

40/27 Jacksonville National Historic Landmark

Exit 40: 11.5 mi./15 min. South on Old Stage Rd. Exit 27: 6 mi./15 min. West on Barnett Rd., right on Riverside Ave., left on Main St. (Rte. 238); follow signs. During the gold boom in the mid-19th century, Jacksonville survived fire, flood, and epidemic. But when the gold began to run out and the railroad bypassed the town, it went into decline. In recent years more than 80 buildings, dating from the 1850's up to 1916, have been restored and refurbished, and the town has become a national historic landmark.

The handsome courthouse, from about 1883, houses a museum, and there's a bank in the impressive U.S. Hotel, built in 1880. Pioneer Village (admission charged), north of town, features such early-day necessities as a smokehouse, a country schoolhouse, a saloon, and Applegate Valley's first store and post office. The large collection of horse-drawn vehicles includes a hearse, a stagecoach, and several covered wagons. *Open year-round.* ⛩

19/11 Lithia Park, Ashland

Exit 19: 3 mi./10 min. Right on Valley View Rd., left on Rte. 99 to Ashland; follow signs. Exit 11: 5 mi./10 min. North on Rte. 99 to Ashland; follow signs. The 100-acre Lithia Park takes its name from the area's naturally carbonated mineral water (you can taste it in the park's fountain). Created in 1893 as a hub of culture and entertainment, the park, now an outstanding example of American landscape architecture, is the scene of evening band concerts, ballet performances, and silent films in its open-air theater.

Quiet forest paths follow Ashland Creek through the park, which is located in a canyon at the base of Mt. Ashland. Lithia Park also has a Japanese garden, duck ponds, tennis courts, and a formal rose garden. An excellent booklet describes more than 90 kinds of shrubs and trees, including towering silver maples, Russian olives, and a wide variety of Japanese maples, found on the Woodland Trail. This tranquil place can excite the senses and calm the spirit. *Open year-round.* ⛩🚶♿

CMS. *Just beyond the forested ridge the interstate cuts a swath between Siskiyou Lake in the foreground and Mt. Shasta's majestic profile in the distance.*

CY Siskiyou County Museum, Yreka

Central Yreka exit. 3 min. West to Main St.; follow signs. Most of the essential tools, equipment, materials, firearms, and miscellaneous goods required to survive (and prosper) in the early days of the county are thoughtfully displayed in this excellent museum, a replica of an 1854 ranch hotel.

Prehistoric times are represented by marine fossils and mastodon bones. There are early Indian artifacts, as well as those of the Chinese, who came to this area in the mid-1850's, when gold was discovered. The country store, the blacksmith's shop, and the millinery and music shops are much as they were in pioneer days. A separate building houses the museum's collection of vintage horse-drawn vehicles. *Open Mon.–Sat., P.M. Sun. Memorial Day–Labor Day; Tues.–Sat. rest of year.* ♿

CMS Mount Shasta Scenic Drive

Central Mt. Shasta exit. 5 min. East on Lake St., left on Pine St., right on W. Alma St., left on Everitt Memorial Hwy. The 14-mile roadway through the Shasta-Trinity National Forest takes you up the mountain to the 7,750-foot level, past outstanding views of sweeping valleys and purple mountain peaks. At the roadway's end Mt. Shasta seems close enough to touch.

If you wish to extend your stay, pitch a tent at either McBride Springs or Panther Meadows campground. Hiking trails leading to the mountain's 14,162-foot summit begin where the scenic drive stops. *Open year-round up to Bunny Flat (12 mi.); last 2 mi. closed in winter because of snow.* ⛩🏕🚐🚶

CAS Castle Crags State Park

Castella exit. 2 min. West from exit. Formed some 170 million to 225 million years ago as granite became heated and forced its way up through the earth's surface, these jagged mountain peaks, carved by glaciers, soar to a height of some 6,000 feet. A 2-mile drive from the park's entrance will take you to an overlook for a spectacular panorama of these and other mountain peaks etched against the skyline.

Camping, picnicking, swimming, hiking, and trout fishing are especially delightful in this thickly forested park, where the fragrance of the evergreen trees fills the crystal-clear air. *Open daily except during heavy snows.* ⛩🏕🚐🚶🏊🎣

61

21

40

13

27

8

19

8

11

OR
CA

32

CY

35

CMS

10

CAS

38

5

See map page III.

CV Shasta Dam and Lake

Central Valley–Shasta Dam exit: 6 mi./20 min. West on Rte. 151. With a spillway three times higher than Niagara Falls and two-thirds of a mile across, the dam was built between 1938 and 1949 to store surplus winter runoff for summer irrigation and for flood control in the Sacramento and San Joaquin valleys. It traps the waters of the McCloud, Pit, and Sacramento rivers, forming Lake Shasta—one of the nation's most diversified recreation areas—and creating one of California's largest power plants. The dam's visitor center has an observation theater overlooking the spillway.

With marinas, hiking trails, a camping and picnic area, superb fishing sites, and some 345 houseboats available for rent, the lake is a magnet for vacationers seeking active refreshment as well as relaxation. *Open year-round.*

CR Shasta State Historic Park

Central Redding Hwy. exit: 8 mi./15 min. West on Rte. 299. During California's 1850 gold rush, when all roads north of San Francisco stopped at Shasta City, a boomtown that shipped out as much as $100,000 in gold each week, it became known as the Queen City of the North. Its prosperity lasted approximately 18 years, until a new north-south stage route, and later the railroad, bypassed it. The city's ruins, now preserved in this park, evoke life in the region during the mid-1800's. The museum, formerly the county courthouse, has the original jail cells and contains a fine collection of artifacts, books, and art related to California. A tree-shaded picnic area is popular with visitors. *Open daily except Thanksgiving Day, Christmas, and New Year's Day. Admission charged.*

RB William B. Ide Adobe State Historic Park

Red Bluff/N. Main St. exit: 5 min. South on N. Main St., left on Adobe Rd. Red Bluff/S. Main St. exit: 4 mi./10 min. North on S. Main St., right on Adobe Rd. William B. Ide was a leader of the Bear Flag Rebellion, an 1846 revolt by American settlers in California against their Mexican rulers. Ide built his adobe house overlooking the scenic Sacramento River around 1850 and established a ferry that became an important link on the California-Oregon Trail. He also served the county as a judge and, on one occasion, as court clerk, prosecutor, and defense attorney—on the same case. In the well-restored house a wide range of period household items and farm tools is on display. The park provides a pleasant picnic spot, and you can fish for trout and salmon. *Open year-round.*

CV. *Snowmelt from Mt. Shasta and adjacent peaks contributes to the waters of the lake.*

O/C Bidwell Mansion State Historic Park, Chico

Orland/Chico exit: 21 mi./30 min. East on Rte. 32 to Chico, left on Sacramento Ave., right on the Esplanade. The charm and elegance of another era are recalled in this parklike estate. In 1865 John Bidwell, farmer, statesman, and humanitarian, started to build his three-story, 26-room mansion on the 22,000-acre Rancho Arroyo Chico in order to successfully woo and win the socially prominent, idealistic Annie Ellicott Kennedy of Washington, D.C. The shaded lawns, the footbridge over Arroyo Creek, and groves of towering oaks and sycamores invite strolling. *Open daily except Thanksgiving Day, Christmas, and New Year's Day. Admission charged.*

ROUTE 20 Colusa – Sacramento River State Recreation Area

9 mi./15 min. East on Rte. 20. Despite its humble origins (it was once a city dump), this 63-acre park with a half-mile sandy beach, junglelike river forest, and boat-mooring facilities, now appeals to anglers, picnickers, campers, boaters, and sunbathers. A looped trail leads from the day-use area to the forest and beach. The Sacramento River offers good fishing, including king salmon, steelhead, sturgeon, catfish, and striped bass. A variety of birds inhabit the recreation area. *Open year-round. Admission charged.*

J Sacramento, CA 95814

J St. exit: Convention & Visitors Bureau, 1421 K St. (916) 442-5542. The gold rush that made this city a boomtown and the state capital is memorialized in the Old Sacramento Historic District and Sutter's Fort State Historic Park. The fort—the first restored in the U.S.A.—has many original shops and historic artifacts. An Indian museum in the park features the handiwork of those who found their way to this region without the lure of gold. The Crocker Art Museum, with its opulent Victorian gallery, features old masters' drawings, Oriental art objects, contemporary paintings, and photographs. Car and rail buffs will enjoy the California Towe Ford Museum and the California State Historic Railroad Museum.

See E–W book, sec. 17.

25

EM

28

ROUTE
120

42

ROUTE
140

13

ROUTE
152

76

COA

64

5

If You Have Some Extra Time: Yosemite National Park

ROUTE 140 **91 mi./2 hr.** As you enter the stone corridor of the Yosemite Valley, you are sure to be overwhelmed by the magnificence of the granite domes, vertical cliffs, sculptured spires, and dazzling waterfalls. Elsewhere in the park—as if this were not enough—there are alpine meadows, limpid lakes, creeks and rivers, and scores of mountain peaks. Three superb stands of sequoia trees, including the Mariposa Grove, with its 2,700-year-old Grizzly Giant soaring up to a height of 209 feet, provide awe-inspiring views for both you and your camera. Of the six major waterfalls in the park, Bridalveil, with its gossamer veil, is the loveliest, and Yosemite, with its three-part cascade, is the most dramatic, especially during the heavy runoff in May. In spring, wildflowers carpet the meadows, and in fall the park blazes with colorful foliage.

Stop off at the visitor center for the slide program and information about the very impressive range of plants, birds, and animals to be found in the park. Trail maps available there show the many options for exploration.

The road to Glacier Point—open from Memorial Day, or earlier if plows can get through, until the first heavy snow in November—leads to a breathtaking panorama of the valley and the peaks of the Sierra Nevada. From this perspective the scale of these mountains is made dramatically clear. The entire range, about 400 miles long and 50 to 80 miles wide, is a single block of granite. In this context the valley that seems so overwhelming when you are on its floor is no more than a minor crack in that incredible mass of rock. *How to get there: Rte. 140 exit, east on Rte. 140 to park entrance. Open year-round. Admission charged.*

EM ## Micke Grove Park and Zoo, Lodi

Eight Mile Rd. exit: 7 mi./11 min. East on Eight Mile Rd., left on Micke Grove Rd. At this attractive and varied 65-acre park, you'll find a museum with an extensive collection of farming tools and equipment; a zoo featuring the bald eagle and the rare snow leopard; a nature trail with signs noting the effect of agriculture on land and wildlife; an amusement park with a small merry-go-round and a miniature train ride; indoor and outdoor picnic areas; and a Japanese garden designed by the onetime superintendent of the Imperial Palace Garden in Tokyo. *Park open year-round; zoo open daily except Christmas; museum open P.M. Wed.–Sun. except Thanksgiving Day, Christmas Eve, Christmas, and New Year's Day. Admission charged.*

J. *The leisurely pace of the past can be enjoyed in Sacramento's Historic District.*

ROUTE 120 ## Caswell Memorial State Park

13 mi./16 min. East on Rte. 120, right on Manteca Rd., left on W. Ripon Rd., right on Austin Rd. A hundred years ago, the riverbanks and plains of the Central Valley were dominated by towering oak trees native only to California. A 138-acre slice of that magnificent hardwood forest is preserved at this park, which contains some "weeping oaks" that are 100 feet tall and 6 feet in diameter. Throughout the park you'll spot rabbits, foxes, and muskrats, and in the nearby Stanislaus River there are bluegill, bass, catfish, sturgeon, buffalo carp, and salmon. The history of the area is recounted in a shelter at the head of the Oak Forest Nature Trail. *Open year-round. Admission charged.*

ROUTE 152 ## San Luis Reservoir State Recreation Area

6 mi./10 min. West on Rte. 152. These three man-made lakes, which cover more than 16,000 acres, are a welcome sight for travelers. Swimming, boating, and water-skiing are the main activities. Fishermen find this is a good spot for striped bass, bluegill, and crappie. Perched on a knoll at the end of a massive earth-filled dam is the Romero Visitors' Center, run by the California Department of Water Resources. It provides a sweeping view of the dam, the San Luis

Reservoir, and the mountains beyond. One exhibit tells the story of the California State Water Project, which, together with the Central Valley Project, is one of the world's largest public works enterprises. *Park open year-round; visitor center open daily except Thanksgiving Day, Christmas, and New Year's Day. Admission charged for park.*

COA ## R. C. Baker Memorial Museum, Coalinga

Coalinga exit: 11 mi./13 min. West on Jayne Ave., left on Elm Ave. This charming museum tells the story of oil and coal discovery in a small western boomtown during the days of the wild frontier. Coalinga's Spanish-sounding name is actually a contraction of Coaling Station A, a rail coal-loading site around which the town grew. The museum, named for the man whose oil tool company once occupied the building, displays an amazing assortment of items. A sampling of things you'll see might include 300 pieces of barbed wire; the jaw, teeth, and tusks of a fossilized elephant; a prehistoric snail; an Arabian saddle; an early telephone booth; old Christmas cards; a pair of beaded moccasins; oilfield equipment; period clothing and furniture; and photos of the damage inflicted upon Coalinga by a major earthquake in 1983. *Open Mon.–Sat. and P.M. Sun. except holidays.*

See E–W book, sec. 48.

STO Tule Elk State Reserve

Stockdale Hwy. exit: 5 min. West on Stockdale Hwy., left on Morris Rd., right on Station Rd. Enormous herds of tule elk that once roamed California were reduced almost to extinction by hunters and by the conversion of marshland to farmland in the 19th century. This grassland reserve now shelters 32 of the rare animals. Visitors can view the elk, some with impressive racks of antlers, from a tree-shaded picnic area. The animals congregate at two nearby watering holes rimmed with marsh plants, where they come to wallow in the water and cool off—one of their favorite activities. *Open year-round.*

STO Kern County Museum, Bakersfield

Stockdale Hwy. exit: 20 mi./28 min. East on Stockdale Hwy., left on Chester Ave. The county's pioneer life is vividly displayed here in more than 50 buildings, including a rough-hewn log cabin, a one-room schoolhouse with a potbellied stove, a dentist's office with an early X-ray machine, a ranch house and cook wagon, and a train depot with telegraphic equipment. The museum features Indian artifacts, dioramas of animals and birds native to the area, historical photographs, and exhibits of trade tools. At the nearby Lori Brock Children's Museum (a separate entity with the same hours) youngsters can take part in various hands-on educational experiences. *Both museums open daily except Thanksgiving Day, Christmas, and New Year's Day. Admission charged.*

FT Fort Tejon State Historical Park

Ft. Tejon exit: 1 min. West from exit; follow signs. Territorial expansion and the discovery of gold in the 1850's called for army troops to patrol the frontier. The assignment went to the 1st Dragoons, who dressed somewhat like French Legionnaires. Visitors can inspect their sparsely furnished barracks, the officers' residence, and the cramped orderlies' quarters. A tree-shaded brook borders the museum, which provides a graphic representation of life in the army, the ways of the Indians in the area, and the story of the Camel Corps, led by Lt. Edward F. Beale. *Open daily except Thanksgiving Day, Christmas, and New Year's Day. Admission charged.*

MAG Six Flags Magic Mountain, Valencia

Magic Mountain Pkwy. exit: 1 min. Follow signs. From a breathtaking stand-up roller coaster ride to shooting the rapids in a raft, this theme park has plenty of excitement. Several rides loop above the park, and flowers, trees, and blossoming vines line the walkways. Looney Tunes characters stroll about, and children can ride a pirate ship or spin in a birdcage in Bugs Bunny World. There are games, a petting zoo, performing dolphins and sea lions, and demonstrations of crafts. *Open daily late May–mid-Sept.; weekends and school holidays, mid-Sept.–late May except Christmas. Admission charged.*

PAS Los Angeles, CA 90071

I-10 *Pasadena Frwy. exit (south): Visitor Information Center, 505 S. Flower St., Level B. (213) 689-8822.* The maze of freeways in and around L.A. can frustrate even the most unflappable driver, but a little aggravation is a small price to pay for this vast city's considerable charms. Mulholland Drive in the Hollywood Hills or the 27-story City Hall Tower downtown provide spectacular views of the city. Hollywood Boulevard has changed since the old days, but Mann's Chinese Theater is a plush reminder of the glamour that was. For a look at modern-day moviemaking, take the Universal Studios tour. If you prefer still pictures, sample the outstanding collections at the Los Angeles County Museum of Art. Griffith Park, the largest municipal park in the country, has over 4,000 hilly acres to explore. The Los Angeles Zoo has 2,500 animals, and the 165-acre Descanso Gardens boasts an astonishing variety of blossoming plants.

ROUTE 710 The Queen Mary and the Spruce Goose, Long Beach

17 mi./21 min. South on Rte. 710. Now permanently berthed at Long Beach, the *Queen Mary* was among the grandest of the great ocean liners. The lifestyles of the privileged who crossed the Atlantic on it are reflected in its opulent art deco ballrooms, staterooms, and promenade deck. Displays also recall its troop-carrying days during World War II. On the lower decks you can see one of the ship's engine rooms and a large collection of intricately crafted models of ships, including many famous ones. The other major attraction here is now called by its nickname. The *Spruce Goose*, an enormous wooden airplane with a 320-foot wingspan, was a pet project of the eccentric millionaire Howard Hughes. Flown only once, the white aircraft now sits dramatically over a mirrorlike reflecting pool, with its roomy cargo bay, flight deck, and cockpit open for viewing. Also here is a village of shops and restaurants. *Open year-round. Admission charged.*

HAR Disneyland, Anaheim

Harbor Blvd. exit: 5 min. Follow signs. "The greatest piece of design in the United States" is how a noted designer once described Disneyland. This 76-acre theme park may also be one of the America's

HAR. *Who better than Disney could create a working replica of a riverboat?*

greatest pieces of enchantment. You can shake hands with the Seven Dwarfs, take a jungle cruise down a murky lagoon, see swashbuckling pirates in action, sip a soda at an old-fashioned turn-of-the-century ice cream parlor, and pose for snapshots with Mickey Mouse, Donald Duck, and other Disney characters. Horse-drawn buggies and sleek monorails provide transportation to the seven theme areas: Adventureland, Frontierland, Fantasyland, Tomorrowland, New Orleans Square, Bear Country, and Main Street U.S.A.—all perfectly maintained and spotlessly clean. *Open year-round. Admission charged.*

74. *Fountains and gardens echo the mission's unpretentious style and charm.*

ROUTE 74 | Mission San Juan Capistrano

2 min. West on Rte. 74; follow signs. Although best known for the swallows that return each March 19, this charming mission is worth a visit any time of year. The ruins of the old stone church built in 1797 by Father Junípero Serra are adorned with great vines of bougainvillea. Still standing is his long rectangular chapel with elaborate murals and an extravagant baroque altar. The bells of Capistrano hang in wall arches next to the church, and the surrounding courtyards are graced with fountains and planted with lilies and palms. Stone vats for tallow making, a smelter, and dyeing, weaving, and candlemaking shops reflect the villagelike atmosphere of an early California mission. *Open year-round. Admission charged.*

ROUTE 78 | Lawrence Welk Museum, Escondido

20 mi./30 min. East on Rte. 78, left on I-15, right on Deer Springs Rd.; follow signs. Sidewalks paved with musical instrument shapes lead to this museum in a theater lobby in a luxurious retirement community named for the popular bandleader. A recreation of the Welk bandstand and stage set dominates a room lit with crystal chandeliers. Welk's long career is chronicled in photos, letters, gold records, and awards, including the ballroom-dancing years from the 1920's through the 1950's. You'll see his first accordion and scenes from his television show. *Open year-round.*

CV | Torrey Pines State Reserve

Carmel Valley Rd. exit: 3 mi./8 min. West on Carmel Valley Rd., left on N. Torrey Pines Rd.; follow signs. This beautiful, rugged coastal reserve is named for the rare Torrey pines that grow on the hilltops. It rises from a long, sandy beach and a series of canyons to a clifftop plateau. The canyons are densely covered with succulents, laurel sumac, and sage, and are veined with sandy footpaths. From Red Butte, with its needle-sharp rock formations, you can watch for migrating whales from December through March and enjoy magnifi-

CV. *Contorted shapes of the Torrey pines reveal the unremitting power of the wind.*

cent ocean views any time of year. Two trails lead down to the beach. Swimming is permitted, but be careful: rip currents are present, and the waves can be rough. The adobe visitor center serves as a living museum and the starting point for ranger-guided nature walks. *Open year-round. Admission charged.*

ROUTE 209 | Cabrillo National Monument, San Diego

10 mi./20 min. South on Rte. 209; follow signs. Juan Rodríguez Cabrillo was the first European to explore this section of the Pacific Coast, and it was this windswept finger of land that greeted him when he sailed into the harbor here. Today, at this park named in his honor, he wouldn't recognize the view to the east: a panorama of ocean freighters against a backdrop of San Diego's white skyscrapers. But to the west is the vast unchanged Pacific, where whale watching is now popular from late December to mid-March. Exhibits in the visitor center concentrate on the peninsula's natural features and Indian artifacts as well as Spanish explorers. There is also a restored lighthouse; and a 2-mile round-trip nature trail, edged by chaparral, runs alongside the harbor. *Open year-round.*

ROUTE 163 | San Diego Zoo

5 min. North on Rte. 163; continue on Richmond St.; follow signs. With a population of 3,200, representing some 800 species from around the world, this fine zoo is a veritable United Nations of the animal kingdom. If you have time, take the 40-minute guided bus tour for orientation, then return to your favorite spots on foot or by means of outdoor escalators and moving walkways. You'll see Australian koalas, highland gorillas, miniature deer, giant anteaters, Mongolian wild horses, and the world's largest collection of parrots and parrotlike birds. The children's zoo, scaled to four-year-olds, features a nursery where baby mammals are bottle-fed, bathed, and diapered. There are elephant and camel rides, animal shows, an overhead Skyfari, "behind the scenes" group tours, and special facilities for the disabled. *Open year-round. Admission charged.*

22

HAR

35

ROUTE 74

30

ROUTE 78

16

CV

9

See E–W book, sec. 56.

ROUTE 209

8

3

See N–S book, sec. 9.

ROUTE 163

15

End I-5

15

CANADA
·—·—·—·—·—·—·
U.S.A.
MT

35

363

5

358

78

280

10

270

61

If You Have Some Extra Time: Glacier National Park

363 **90 mi./2 hr.** The name is exactly appropriate. Not only are glaciers a dominant aspect of the park today; they and their predecessors over millions of years are its creators. The irresistible force of moving ice sculpted the cliffs, spires, and ridges, shaped the slopes where forests thrive, and leveled the land for the prairies and meadows. Some 50 remaining glaciers still feed more than 200 lakes and 1,450 miles of streams and rivers.

The St. Mary Visitor Center at the east entrance has explanatory exhibits and information about the many interesting varieties of flora and fauna to be found here.

The Going-to-the-Sun Road, the park's only east-west crossing, is open from about June to mid-November. If you have time for it, this 50-mile drive is one of the most spectacular in the country. At least try to take the first 5 miles to the parking turnoff, from which Triple Divide Peak is visible to the southeast. The runoff flows to three oceans: the Arctic, the Pacific, and the Atlantic.

About 13 miles farther west, at Logan Pass, the road crosses the Continental Divide. From the visitor center here there's a 3-mile round-trip self-guiding nature trail and boardwalk across brooks and meadows to an unforgettable view overlooking Hidden Lake. This reserve of more than a million acres is worthy of an extended visit. There are some 15 inviting campgrounds to stay in and many miles of trails for hiking and horseback riding. But even a brief encounter with such a magnificent wilderness is better than none at all. *How to get there: Exit 363, west from Shelby on Rte. 2, then right on Rte. 89 to the eastern park entrance. Open year-round, but eastern roads are usually closed owing to heavy snow mid-Nov.–mid-Apr. Admission charged.*

---

358 **Williamson Park**

4 min. East from exit, right on Marias Valley Rd.; follow signs. Nestled in the scenic Marias River Canyon and shaded by stands of cottonwoods, this beautiful little park is a popular picnic spot. Hikers enjoy exploring the canyon walls, and there is a playground for children. A local hillside serves as an informal rifle range, no doubt to the consternation of the large deer population. The river can be a busy place with its swimmers, boaters, and anglers (catfish, northern pike, and walleye are the most frequent catches). Since only primitive camping is permitted, this bucolic riverside park is ideal for those who want to get away from it all. *Open Apr.–Sept. Admission charged.*

280 **Charles M. Russell Museum and Studio, Great Falls**

5 min. East on Central Ave. W. (becomes 1st Ave. N.), left on 13th St. N. The Old West is preserved in Charles Russell's paintings, which depict scenes from the lives of the Plains Indians and the American cowboy. Born in 1864, Russell was one of the most important and prolific of the western painters, producing over 4,500 works. This outstanding cultural complex includes Russell's log cabin studio, with his easel and brushes, clay figurines, and the Indian, Mexican, and cowboy guns and artifacts that appear in his paintings. A museum houses 7,500 works by Russell and his contemporaries, a Browning firearm collection, and Edward Curtis's Indian photographs. The artist's restored house, built around 1900, may be viewed only in the summertime. *Open daily May–Sept.; Tues.–Sun. Oct.–Apr. except Thanksgiving Day, Christmas, New Year's Day, and Easter. Admission charged.*

280 **Giant Springs State Park, Great Falls**

9 mi./20 min. East on Central Ave. W. (becomes 1st Ave. N.), left on 15th St., right on River Dr. The centerpiece of this beautiful 100-acre riverside park is Giant Springs—one of the world's largest, discharging 134,000 gallons of water per minute. It was discovered by Meriwether Lewis during his portage around the Great Falls in 1805. Plaques tell of Lewis and Clark's portage and the dangers they faced from storms and grizzly bears. Today the major pastimes are picnicking, hiking, and casting in the Missouri for trout. The springs' constant 52° F temperature and its pure water make it ideal for growing trout. A self-guiding tour of the fish hatchery includes audio programs about fish production, growth, and management. *Open year-round.*

270 **Ulm Pishkun State Monument**

7 mi./20 min. West on access road; follow signs. This high, sheer cliff jutting up from 50 to 80 feet above the prairie was used as early as A.D. 500 by primitive hunters. At the *pishkun*—an Indian word for a cliff or corral where they killed buffalo—large herds were stampeded over the cliff to their deaths. The carcasses provided food for the winter, hides for clothing and shelter, and bones for tools. The jump was abandoned after the mid-1800's, when buffaloes became scarce. Today you'll see the centuries-old piles of bones and tepee rings from Indian encampments. Signs explain the history of the buffalo jump and the daily life of prairie dogs, which have a sizable town here near the picnic area. *Open daily mid-Apr.–mid-Oct.*

209 Gates of the Mountains

5 min. East on access road. While exploring the Missouri River in the summer of 1805, Meriwether Lewis referred to this canyon that the river flows through as the Gateway to the Rocky Mountains and noted that some of the cliffs appeared to be on the verge of tumbling over on him. Cruise boats have been plying the waters of the canyon for more than a century, and today it appears much the same as it did in Lewis's day—a rugged land of limestone bluffs crumpled and folded by the earth's inner pressure, punctuated by caves, and etched with ancient Indian petroglyphs.

The cruises provide an excellent opportunity to see wildlife. Rocky Mountain goats inhabit the cliffs, and bighorn sheep visit salt licks at the river's edge. More than 100 species of birds have been sighted. The cruise boat stops at the Meriwether Campground—the very spot where the Lewis party made camp. You can stay here and explore the backcountry for a few hours, or a few days, and catch a later boat back. *Cruises daily Memorial Day–Labor Day. Fee charged.*

209. *The drama of the cliffs that Lewis saw is now somewhat muted by the trees.*

192 Norwest Bank Helena Museum of Gold

5 min. West on Rte. 12, left on Last Chance Gulch St. What better place for a gold museum than in a bank? Henry Elling, the bank's first president, came here in 1898 with his collection of gold nuggets. The collection has grown over the years to include samples from 18 Montana gulches and from California and Alaska. Gold in many of its native forms is on display here—from pumpkin seed and sheet gold to flakes and gold in quartz. Of some 700 nuggets, the largest, from Alaska, has a troy weight of 46 ounces. "Character" nuggets, sculpted by nature into unusual shapes, are valued by collectors, and the museum has a fine assortment of them, including cowboy boots, buffalo skulls, and Jimmy Durante. A collection of prized gold coins includes $4 "Stellas," with a mid-1980's value of $1,500 each; Lewis and Clark commemorative dollars, minted in 1904–05; and a mid-19th-century octagonal $50 piece, which is also known as a California slug. *Open Mon.–Fri. except holidays.*

192 Frontier Town

19 mi./25 min. West on Rte. 12. Frontier Town was created by the late John Quigley. In the 1940's he selected a 20-acre site atop the 6,320-foot-high MacDonald Pass and, working mostly by himself for some 30 years, built this town of logs and rocks. You'll see a frontier fort, a jail, a bank, a general store, a chapel, and other buildings furnished with antiques. The complex contains 46 rooms, 54 log doors, and more than 260 tons of stonework. Quigley also made wood carvings and log furniture, hewing a bar top from a 50-foot-long Douglas fir log. The 75-mile view of the Helena Valley and distant mountains is spectacular. *Open daily Apr.–Oct. Admission charged.*

164 Elkhorn

19.5 mi./30 min. South on Rte. 69, left on Elkhorn Rd.; follow signs. Off the beaten track but worth the visit, this old mine site is the genuine article, and it presents some colorful opportunities for photographers. Elkhorn was a late-19th-century boomtown, with a peak population of about 2,500. The Elkhorn Mine produced some 9 million ounces of silver, 8,500 ounces of gold, and 4 million pounds of lead. Today, along with 30 or 40 timeworn buildings, there are still mine tailings, equipment rusting in the forests, and abandoned shafts in this privately owned ghost town nestled amid mountains and thick fir forests. Trailheads lead into the surrounding Deerlodge National Forest, where rugged mountain hiking, camping, trout fishing, snowmobiling, and cross-country skiing are popular. *Open year-round.*

126 Copper King Mansion, Butte

124 *5 min. Exit 126: east on I-115, left on Montana St., left on Granite St. Exit 124: north on Montana St., left on Granite St.* This luxurious 32-room mansion is an outstanding example of Victorian architecture. It was built in the 1880's by William Andrews Clark, a U.S. senator and a multimillionaire entrepreneur with interests in real estate, banking, and oil as well as copper companies. The opulently furnished home has frescoed ceilings, Tiffany glass windows, hand-carved woodwork, ornate chandeliers, and an organ with 825 pipes. On the 1½-hour guided tour, you'll see fine examples of period art and glassware, dolls, toys, and women's fashions. *Open year-round. Admission charged.*

64 Beaverhead County Museum, Dillon

63 *Exit 64: 2 min. South on Montana St. Exit 63: 4 min. North on Atlantic St., left on Bannack St.* This county was the site of Montana's first gold rush. Later on, ranching, timber, farming, and the mining of other minerals became the linchpins of the economy. In this large structure the county's diverse and colorful past is reflected in exhibits that include Indian artifacts, boomtown memorabilia, branding irons and farming implements, gold and mining paraphernalia, weapons from both world wars, and collections of china, crystal, glass, silver, and watches. Several mounted animals are excellent examples of taxidermy. *Open daily May–Aug.; P.M. Mon.–Fri. Sept.–Apr.*

209
17
192
28
164
38
See E–W book, sec. 2.
90
126
2
124
90
64
1
63
4
15

59. *The three R's were dispensed here, sometimes to the tune of a hickory stick.*

59 | Bannack State Park

25 mi./30 min. West on Rte. 278, left on access road; follow signs. This park has a surprising main attraction—a ghost town. Bannack, which was Montana's first territorial capital, sprang up in 1862 when gold was discovered in Grasshopper Creek. In addition to saloons, dance halls, and stores, the town had two hotels, a billiard parlor, a Chinese restaurant, and a Masonic temple with public school. A self-guiding tour covers some two dozen sites, and the visitor center has exhibits on Bannack's past. *Open year-round.*

44 | Clark Canyon Reservoir

3 min. West on Rte. 324. Some 10 miles long and 3 miles wide, this extensive lake created by damming the Red Rock River is popular for outdoor activities of all kinds. A sandy shore close to several campgrounds draws bathers and picnickers, and fishermen from boat and shore angle for trout and ling cod, known to grow rapidly in these waters. Hunting for waterfowl is an attraction in fall, while ice fishing and snowmobiling are popular pastimes in the winter. A monument on the north shore marks the site where Lewis and Clark camped and traded with Indians when they changed from boats to horses to continue exploring the vast new territories that America had acquired in the West. *Open year-round.*

44. *Light snow and thin ice add a wintry dimension to a Montana March morning.*

172 | U.S. Sheep Experiment Station

2 min. East on access road; follow signs. Five thousand to 10,000 sheep, depending on the season, are kept here, some in corrals, others on the range pastures of the station. Jointly run by the U.S. Department of Agriculture and the University of Idaho College of Agriculture, this research facility is not well known, despite its excellent facilities for visitors. A guided tour includes lambing pens, shelters, and displays of different breeds of sheep. Depending on the season, you may see lambs being born (2,500 each year), sheep sheared, or guard dog and predator-control experiments. *Open Mon.–Fri. except holidays.*

143 | Beaver Dick Recreation Area

15 mi./20 min. East on Rte. 33. This small wayside park is named after "Beaver Dick" Leigh, an English-born mountain man who married a Shoshone Indian woman and lived in this area until 1899. He was well known as a guide, outfitter, and picturesque character. The park adjoins the Henry Fork of the Snake River, where anglers like to try for trout and whitefish. A spacious lawn, a covered picnic shelter, and a children's playground make it an appealing spot for a family outing.

Three miles to the west are the Menan Buttes, two glassy cones of lava rising 800 feet above the plain. A roadside marker explains how they were formed. *Open daily Apr.–Oct.*

118 | Idaho Falls of the Snake River

2 min. East on Broadway, left on Memorial Dr. Here in the heart of Idaho Falls, the magnificent waterfalls of the Snake River are surrounded by the picturesque buildings of the city and the lush greenery of nearby parks. The watery spectacle combines natural cascades with a 1,500-foot-wide man-made dam, which diverts water from the river to irrigate 7,000 acres of land. Adjacent to the falls, the east and west banks of the river have picnic tables, playgrounds, and signboards that explain the hydroelectric projects and the history of the dam. Several parks, including one on an island, provide opportunities for swimming, boating, trout fishing, jogging, and sunbathing. *Open year-round.*

118 Bonneville Museum, Idaho Falls

3 min. East on Broadway. The passing parade of history in eastern Idaho has included Indians, trappers, prospectors, pioneers, farmers, and ranchers. This museum in a former public library in Idaho Falls chronicles them all with artifacts, interpretive panels, photographs, and other memorabilia. Displays cover the history of Idaho Falls, gold panning, harvesting Idaho potatoes, ranching, and atomic energy. There is also a complete kitchen from Idaho Falls' early days and mounted specimens of local wildlife. *Open Mon.–Sat. Admission free but donations encouraged.*

118 Tautphaus Park, Idaho Falls

5 min. East on Broadway, right on Yellowstone Hwy., left on 17th St., right on Rollendet St. Eighty acres of lawns and large stands of pine and cottonwood in this pleasant city park provide an ideal setting for a stroll, a picnic, a cookout on a grill, or a game on one of the spacious playfields. For children, an amusement park offers swings, an arcade, pitch-and-putt golf, a Ferris wheel, and other diversions. Everyone will enjoy the park's zoo, which houses ostriches, trumpeter swans, goats, elk, deer, zebras, llamas, and other inhabitants. *Park open year-round; zoo open daily June–Aug., weekends only Sept.–Oct. Admission charged for zoo.*

93 Bingham County Historical Museum, Blackfoot

2 mi./7 min. East on Bergner Ave. (Judicial St.) into Blackfoot, left on N. Shilling St. Built in 1905 by a prominent merchant, this 15-room lava-rock and lumber house was once the center of Blackfoot's social life. Today it houses a remarkably varied assortment of antiques and Idaho memorabilia. Some of the items are expected: guns and ammunition from the black-powder days, red velvet-upholstered furniture, Indian relics, and a 13-star American flag. But you'll also find a rocker handmade by Mor-

mon leader Brigham Young, a hand-carved English piano, a hand-loomed Liberty rug that tells the story of America in pictures, an unusually fine doll collection, 200 miniature kerosene lamps and lanterns, a Quaker afghan rug, and equipment from the local mental hospital, including its first electric shock machine. *Open P.M. Wed.–Fri. Feb.–Nov. except holidays.*

69 67 Bannock County Historical Museum, Pocatello

Exit 69: 2 mi./10 min. West on Clark St., left on 1st Ave., then right on Center St. Exit 67: 3 mi./10 min. North on S. 5th St., left on Benton St., right on Garfield St. In the days before the railroad, the Shoshone Indians lived here on 1.3 million acres, including the land on which the city of Pocatello now stands. The strongest aspect of this small museum is its depiction of two implacable rivals: the established Indian tribes and the irresistible iron horse that ultimately uprooted them. The Indian photo archive is particularly poignant, recording a people determined and proud yet defenseless against the inevitable. Beadwork and leatherwork can be seen here, as well as samples of Indian food and its preparation. Railroad memorabilia include wheels, wrenches, oilcans, uniforms, and hundreds of photos. *Open P.M. Tues.–Sat. except holidays.*

67 Ross Park, Pocatello

3 min. North on S. 5th St., left on Fredregill Rd., left on S. 2nd St. A choice of pleasures is offered on this rolling, tree-shaded site. On the lower level are the baseball fields, playgrounds, a swimming pool, and a band shell where concerts are given on Sunday evenings in the summer.

Pleasureland Amusement Park, located on the slopes, offers a variety of booths and rides and a zoo with such permanent residents as buffaloes, grizzly bears, sandhill cranes, swans, and golden eagles. During the summer animals from other zoos in the area are occasional visitors.

A full-scale replica of Old Fort Hall, a trading post established in 1834, sits on the bluff above the zoo. It served the early fur traders and was a well-known landmark on

the Oregon Trail. Log cabins, a blacksmith's shop, covered wagons, and Indian tepees recall the history of the fort. *Open daily June–mid-Sept.; Tues.–Sat. Apr.–May. Admission charged.*

47 Lava Hot Springs Foundation

11 mi./15 min. East on Rte. 30. Geologists estimate that the springs have been at a level 110° F for 50 million years, evidence of the region's continuing volcanic history. A self-supporting state agency operates hot mineral pools (masseurs available) and, on the other side of town, two large swimming pools, one of them Olympic size with a 33-foot-high diving board. The waters— non-

47. *The surrounding dry hills make the town swimming pools even more inviting.*

sulfurous, odor-free, and soothing—draw more than 250,000 visitors yearly for pleasure and for treatment of arthritis and other ailments. It's a resort surrounded by parks, tennis courts, golf courses, and the trout-rich Portneuf River, which is enjoyed by anglers year-round. Also worth a look are the sunken flower gardens, planted on the lava terraces of an extinct volcano and in fullest bloom from August to October. *Open year-round.*

15

17

ID
UT

50

84

See
E–W book,
sec. 16.

364

14

360

14

346

19

3

327

325

17

17 Weston Canyon

15 mi./30 min. Southeast on Rte. 36. The rugged rock formations in this scenic 1½-mile-long canyon stand out in remarkable contrast to the rolling stretches of scrub brush, sage, maple, and cedar in the surrounding Caribou National Forest. Even though there are no marked trails, you can enjoy the scenery on short hikes, and Weston Canyon Reservoir offers a tempting selection of largemouth bass, perch, and trout. In winter, snowmobiling and ice fishing are popular. *Open year-round.*

364 Box Elder Tabernacle, Brigham City

5 min. East on Rte. 91, left on Main St. Built on a site selected by Brigham Young himself, this imposing 1,200-seat Mormon landmark is as much a work of art as a historic building. The structure, which still bears Brigham City's original name, was started in the 1860's and then rebuilt in 1896–97 after a fire left only the stone walls standing. Gothic in design, it is a masterpiece of fine workmanship, with arched windows and doors, slender buttresses with graceful pinnacles, and a majestic steeple. Inside there are some fine examples of inlaid and carved woodworking and decorative painting techniques. *Tours daily May–Oct.*

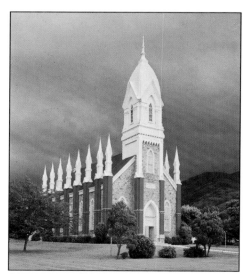

364. *Heavenly aspirations are impressively symbolized by the dramatic spires.*

360 Willard Bay State Park

1 min. West from exit. A scant quarter-mile from the interstate, this park bustles with boaters, swimmers, and fishermen taking advantage of a 9,900-acre man-made lake. The freshwater lake, which has marinas at both its north and south ends, was reclaimed from the salt marshes of the Great Salt Lake. On the land, Russian olive, elm, and poplar trees shade camping areas. The park is a haven for birds, and more than 200 species have been sighted. Many can be spotted in the early morning along the lake's dike. The sign at Exit 354 leads to the park's older, less interesting southern section. *North marina open year-round; south marina open daily Apr.–Oct. Admission charged.*

346 Ogden, UT 84401

Golden Spike Empire, 2501 Wall Ave. (801) 399-8288; (800) 255-8824 outside UT. In the railroad era, towns in which the steam trains stopped were likely to prosper. Ogden's Mediterranean-style station is an imposing monument to the commercial impact of the iron horse. It is now the centerpiece of the 25th Street Historic District, where commercial buildings of bygone days have been converted to modern use. Among the displays in the station are model railroads, classic cars, a gem collection, firearms, and a gunsmith's shop.

Ft. Buenaventura State Park, a reconstruction of a fort established by pioneer Miles Goodyear, recalls the life and times of the mountain men. Visitors with a scientific bent will enjoy the local planetarium and the Natural Science Museum.

327 / 325 Lagoon Amusement Park and Pioneer Village

Exit 327: 3 min. South on Lagoon Dr.; follow signs. Exit 325: 3 min. North on Lagoon Dr.; follow signs. In this 100-year-old amusement park, you'll find everything from traditional arcade games to a merry-go-round with real hand-carved animals, Dracula's Castle, gardens and fountains, and an opera house that features Broadway musicals. Rides include bumper cars, a Tilt-A-Whirl, and an 85-foot-high double-loop roller coaster called the Fire Dragon. Pioneer Village, with century-old buildings brought from various parts of Utah, contains a jail, a two-story log cabin, a Pony Express station, and a narrow-gauge railroad. Guns, dolls, carriages, and Ute Indian beadwork are among the items on display. *Open daily Memorial Day–Labor Day; weekends only Apr.–May and Sept. Admission charged.*

310 Salt Lake City, UT 84101

Convention & Visitors Bureau, 180 S. West Temple. (801) 521-2822; (800) 831-4332 outside UT. No other city in America owes so much to one group of people. Since its founding in 1847 by Brigham Young, who told his hardy band of followers: "This is the place," Salt Lake City has been largely the creation of the Mormons (members of the Church of Jesus Christ of Latter-day Saints). The city is built around Temple Square, where the dominant structure is the Temple, with its six Gothic spires. The Temple is closed to the public. But visitors are welcome at the impressive, acoustically excellent Tabernacle, where the world-famous choir can be heard Sunday mornings and Thursday nights, and public organ recitals are given weekdays at noon and at 4 P.M. on Saturdays and Sundays.

The state capitol, the Pioneer Memorial Museum, and the Council Hall draw tourists to Capitol Hill. In Pioneer Trail State Park there are some interesting renovated historic buildings; other attractions include the State Arboretum and Liberty Park.

301 Bingham Canyon Mine

14 mi./20 min. West on Rte. 48; follow signs. The world's first open-pit copper mine, and America's largest man-made excavation, is an awesome 2½ miles across and half a mile deep. From the visitor center on the mine's rim, you can see drilling, blasting, and loading, as well as electric shovels that lift 55 tons at a scoop into trucks as big as houses. A pamphlet explains how 12 pounds of copper are produced from 1 ton of ore. An audio program explains the day-to-day operation of the mine. *Open daily mid-Apr.–Oct.*

275. *Few of the many falls of the same name so clearly fulfill the description.*

287 Timpanogos Cave National Monument

10 mi./20 min. East on Rte. 92. Three caverns connected by a man-made tunnel are the centerpiece of this 250-acre park on the rugged slopes of the Wasatch Mountains.

The cave system is known for its profusion of helictites that grow up, down, and even sideways—seemingly defying gravity. The main feature of the largest cave is a 2-ton stalagmite called the Great Heart of Timpanogos. Other cave areas such as the Cavern of Sleep, Father Time, and the Jewel Box also contain stalactite, stalagmite, and flowstone formations. The 3-hour tour begins with a 1½-mile hike to the cave entrance at an elevation of 6,730 feet. Programs given at the visitor center explain the ecology of this beautiful canyon, the evolution of the caves, and the history of the area. *Open daily except Thanksgiving Day, Christmas, and New Year's Day; cave tours mid-May–mid-Oct. Admission charged.*

275 Bridal Veil Falls

8 mi./20 min. East on Rte. 189. The world's steepest passenger tram ascends 1,228 feet, at a 45° angle, to the summit of Cascade Mountain. The glass-bottomed car provides breathtaking views of the falls as you glide above them. At the mountaintop a quarter-mile trail reaches the head of the spring-fed falls, where the water begins its tumultuous 600-foot cascade. Another trail offers scenic views of the Utah Valley to the west. If you are leery of steep rides, you might like to know that there's never been an accident here in more than a million passenger-miles. *Open daily mid-May–mid-Oct. Admission charged.*

268 Utah Lake State Park

5 min. West on Center St.; follow signs. This freshwater lake, a feeding ground for ducks and geese, covers 96,900 acres. Fishermen come for the walleyed pike, bass, catfish, bluegill, and trout. Docks, ramps, and beaches provide full access to warm-weather boating and swimming. An outdoor ice rink is popular with skaters in winter. Hikers can stretch their legs on a trail that starts in the park and follows a stream for 45 miles up a nearby canyon. *Open year-round. Admission charged.*

266 Provo, UT 84601

Convention and Visitor Bureau, 899 S. University Ave. (801) 374-8687. Brigham Young University, founded here in 1875, has become a cultural and educational center for the community as well as the students. The art gallery, the fine arts center, with its unusual collection of music and old instruments, the planetarium, a life-science museum, and the Museum of Peoples and Cultures are among the most interesting university facilities open to the public.

Utah in the mid-1800's is recalled in the Pioneer Museum collections of art and artifacts and in the McCurdy Historical Doll Museum's display of more than 3,000 dolls in theme settings.

202 Yuba State Park

5 min. East on access road; follow signs. A scenic landscape is the backdrop for the various attractions at an unusual jade-green lake, which is the largest of several reservoirs along the Sevier River and owes its color to a high concentration of minerals. You'll find many inviting places to picnic, camp, or just contemplate the diverse scenery. Boat ramps at Yuba Dam and at Painted Rocks provide access to water sports and fishing along both sides of this 22-mile reservoir. During the cold winter months the park is popular with snowmobilers and hardy anglers who fish through the ice for perch, northern pike, and catfish. *Open year-round. Admission charged.*

266. *With surrounding mountains and tree-filled streets, nature stakes a claim in Provo.*

Section **7** (264 miles)

See map page III.

310

9

See E–W book, sec. 18.

301

14

287

12

275

7

268

2

266

64

202

39

See
E–W book,
sec. 26.

167 / 163 Territorial Statehouse State Park, Fillmore

Exit 167: 3 min. South on Rte. 99 to Capitol Ave. Exit 163: 3 min. North on Rte. 99 to Capitol Ave. The oldest surviving government building in Utah was commissioned by Brigham Young and designed by the architect of Salt Lake's Mormon Temple. But the full plan for a cruciform-shaped building with a central Moorish dome was abandoned when the territorial legislature moved to Salt Lake City. Today the structure is a museum housing 19th-century room settings, tools, antique clothing, quilts, weapons, musical instruments, household objects, and a large collection of Paiute Indian relics. *Open year-round. Admission charged.*

I-70 Fremont Indian State Park

16 mi./25 min. East on I-70 to Exit 17, north on access road, right on Park Rd. Mule deer, kit foxes, and marmots roam the red rocks and sage wilderness of Clear Creek Canyon, where Indians of the Fremont culture lived from A.D. 500 to 1400. The visitor center contains interpretive exhibits and Indian artifacts unearthed here, but real adventure lies in exploring the canyon. Look for petroglyphs along the quarter-mile Art Rock Trail; the more rugged Discovery and Overlook trails provide fascinating insights into the Fremonts' use of natural resources. A concessionaire offers horse-and-wagon and horseback-riding trips to the backcountry. Clear Creek's waters attract fishermen. *Open year-round. Admission charged.*

112 / 109 Old Beaver County Courthouse Museum, Beaver

Exit 112: 5 min. South on Rte. 160, left on Center St. Exit 109: 5 min. North on Rte. 160, right on Center St. In the mid-1800's, Brigham Young sent a group of Mormons to settle the wilderness that is now Beaver County. Many of the county's current residents are descended from these pioneers, whose sturdy stone buildings still survive—in fact, more than 115 are listed in *The National Register of Historic Places.* Prominent among them is the Old Beaver County Courthouse, which now houses a museum where the area's pioneers are remembered. This brick structure of about 1877, with a charming clock tower, rests on a massive foundation of volcanic rock. *Open P.M. Tues.–Sat. Memorial Day–Labor Day.*

59 Iron Mission State Park

3 min. East on Rte. 56, left on Rte. 91. Horse-drawn vehicles are the focus of this park, which features a bullet-scarred stagecoach from Butch Cassidy's territory and wagons of all uses and descriptions culled from all over Utah. The site is named for the Mormon mission that in 1851 joined a group of British miners in their quest for iron ore. The beginning of the iron industry in the area is commemorated by a diorama in the park museum. *Open daily except Thanksgiving Day, Christmas, and New Year's Day. Admission charged.*

59 Cedar Breaks National Monument

24 mi./30 min. East on Rte. 56, right on Rte. 91, left on Rte. 14, left on Rte. 148. Cedar Breaks is a 3-mile-long natural amphitheater that cuts 2,000 feet deep into the side of the Markagunt Plateau. Tiered layers of red, yellow, and violet in the rock of the Wasatch Formation, accented by the deep green of pine, juniper, and fir, create a series of dramatic compositions. The high country atop the plateau is known for its ancient bristlecone pines, which grow to be thousands of years old, golden aspen groves, spruce forests, and seasonal extravaganzas of wildflowers. You can view all this splendor from overlooks along a 5-mile scenic drive. *Open late May–late Oct. Admission charged.*

40 Kolob Canyons of Zion National Park

1 min. East from exit. Zion National Park proper is a vast and justly popular place, but one of its most dramatic areas is also one of the least visited: the Finger Canyons of northern Zion Park (also called the Kolob Canyons, from a Mormon term). Just beyond the visitor center a 5-mile spur road winds upward through Taylor Creek Canyon, Lee Pass, and Timber Creek Canyon. Turnoffs, scenic picnic spots, and well-marked trails afford beautiful vistas of the red Navajo sandstone monoliths that tower over deep, narrow box canyons. Hikers who venture on a challenging 6-mile walk will see majestic Kolob Arch, firmly

75. *Contrasting blue skies accentuate the red of Elephant Rock's ancient sandstone.*

buttressed by 700-foot-high red sandstone cliffs; its 310-foot span makes it possibly the longest freestanding arch in the world. *Open year-round but may be inaccessible in winter.* 🌲🚶♿

6 Snow Canyon State Park

7 mi./15 min. North on Rte. 18; follow signs. Named for a pair of prominent pioneer brothers, Lorenzo and Erastus Snow, this 6,500-acre park contains two distinct lava flows, one from 3 million years ago and the other from 1,000 years. The pristine sand dunes and stratified red sandstone cliffs up to 750 feet tall may look familiar: they have appeared in several Hollywood westerns. Here, too, you'll see lava caves, Indian petroglyphs, natural ponds that once served as Indian watering holes, yuccas and Joshua trees, and the occasional coyote, mule deer, owl, or blue jay. *Open year-round. Admission charged.*

🌲⛺🚐🚶♿

6 Historic Jacob Hamblin Home, Santa Clara

7 mi./15 min. North on Rte. 18, left on Sunset Blvd. (becomes Santa Clara Dr.). Jacob Hamblin was a passionate convert to Mormonism, and he was a remarkable man in many ways. Confirmed in 1854 by Brigham Young as a missionary to the Indians, he expanded his role to become a peacemaker among the Paiute, Navajo, and Hopi tribes and between the Indians and white settlers. In 1870 he advised a government team surveying the Grand Canyon. Somehow he found time to marry four women, father 24 offspring, and adopt several Indian children. His 1863 sandstone house is now restored and maintained by the Mormons, whose guides convey a vivid sense of pioneer life. *Open daily except Thanksgiving Day and Christmas.*

75 Valley of Fire State Park

15 mi./25 min. East on Rte. 169. The colorful rock sculptures of Nevada's oldest state park define a remarkable landscape distinct from the rest of the Mojave Desert. Established in 1935, the park was named for its predominantly red rocks, though vis-

itors might well imagine that the name derives from noontime temperatures of up to 120° F. In the summer it's best to visit in the early morning hours, when the wind-carved rocks glow red, lavender, and gold and shadows accentuate the textures and convoluted shapes of the hardened sand dunes from the Jurassic period. That's also when the park's animal inhabitants—coyotes, jackrabbits, kit foxes, lizards, snakes, and the rare desert tortoise—are astir. A signed trail leads past 1,000-year-old petroglyphs (carved by Anasazi Indians) to a natural rock basin. There are numerous other scenic trails, overlooks, and gravel roads. The air-conditioned visitor center has interpretive geological and historic exhibits. *Park open year-round but may be inaccessible after rainstorms; visitor center open daily except Christmas and New Year's Day.* 🌲⛺🚐🚣♿

33 Red Rock Canyon Recreation Lands

15 mi./25 min. West on Rte. 160, right on Rte. 159; follow signs. Rarely are thrust fault lines as clearly delineated as those of the 65-million-year-old Keystone Thrust Fault, where gray limestone has pushed up and over the younger red Aztec sandstone. A 13-mile loop drive provides stunning roadside vistas and access to a variety of short trails into the canyons. It's only a short walk to Lost Creek, site of a perpetual spring and a seasonal waterfall, and 2 miles round-trip to a ruined homestead in Pine Creek Canyon. If you hike, carry water and beware of flash floods. Wild burros, descendents of pack animals abandoned by prospectors, thrive in this arid environment. *Open year-round but may be inaccessible in winter.* 🌲🚶♿

27 Clark County Southern Nevada Museum, Henderson

17 mi./22 min. Northeast on Rte. 146, right on Boulder Hwy., left on Museum Dr. A new exhibition hall houses the main collection of this local historical museum. Artifacts are placed in context by a time line that traces human habitation in the area back 10,000 years, from the prehistoric hunters of mammoths and great bison, through the Anasazi and Southern Paiute

If You Have Some Extra Time:

Hoover Dam

27

33 mi./45 min. This great arc of concrete set in the rocky narrows of Black Canyon is a spectacular expression of mankind's determination to control a raging river. In 1928 Congress approved a project to dam the Colorado River to generate electricity, control flooding, and distribute water for agricultural, industrial, and domestic use. When the dam was finished in 1935, the impounded water created Lake Meade, an inland sea 110 miles long with more than 800 miles of shoreline.

The elegant proportions of the dam in its rugged setting are a remarkable synthesis of natural and man-made beauty. The structure, 660 feet thick at the bottom, 45 feet thick at the top, and 1,244 feet across, is a national historic landmark. Guided tours penetrate deep into the heart of the monolith, and one can feel the throb of the mighty turbines and generators that link the dam to thousands of southwestern households. *How to get there: Exit 27, northeast on Rte. 146 (Lake Meade Dr.), right on Rte. 93 (Boulder Hwy.) to dam. Open year-round. Admission charged.*

people, to the early Mormon settlers. In addition, the museum's Heritage Street features a restored 1912 California-style bungalow, a mining-town cottage, a 1931 train depot, a replica of a frontier printshop, and other historic structures. Outdoor exhibits include a ghost town and a Paiute camp. *Open daily except Christmas, New Year's Day, and possibly other holidays. Admission charged.* 🌲🚶♿

CR—GT. *Not fancy, but silver worth millions came up through shafts like this.*

CR | Calico Ghost Town
GT

4 mi./5 min. Calico Rd. exit: North on Calico Rd.; follow signs. Ghost Town Rd. exit: North on Ghost Town Rd.; follow signs. Perched on a ridge above the undulating Mojave Desert, this town is named for the multicolored rocks that enriched silver miners during the 1880's. The town virtually died after the price of silver dropped in 1896, but today it bustles with activity. You can tour a silver mine, ride on an ore train, camp out in the canyon below the town, or picnic in the desert. At the reconstructed firehouse you can inspect a handsome old-time pump wagon trimmed with gleaming brass appointments. Modern shops are located nearby in the period buildings. *Open daily except Christmas. Admission charged.*

BAR | California Desert Information Center, Barstow

Barstow Rd. exit: 2 min. North on Barstow Rd. Whether you are about to cross the great Mojave Desert or have already done so, a stop here will enhance your appreciation of the region and its plant and animal life. Noteworthy among the displays are preserved specimens of desert rattlers (surprisingly small in size) and other creatures to watch out for when exploring on foot. Should you plan to venture onto desert roads in a four-wheel-drive vehicle, the center will provide you with a detailed map of the Mojave. On view part of the year is the Old Woman meteorite, the second largest ever found in the United States (the remainder of the year the Smithsonian has the real meteorite, while the center displays a replica). Weighing over 6,000 pounds, it was discovered in 1975 in the Old Woman Mountains in the eastern Mojave. Across the street from the center is a park with picnic tables. *Open daily except Christmas and New Year's Day.*

PAL | Roy Rogers—Dale Evans Museum, Victorville

Palmdale Rd. exit: 5 min. West on Palmdale Rd., right on Kentwood Blvd., right on Civic Dr. The corridors of this museum are lined with nostalgic family photos and memorabilia portraying Roy Rogers and his wife and costar, Dale Evans, from childhood through their long entertainment careers. Rogers's favorite horse, Trigger, has been mounted in a lifelike rearing position, wearing the saddle used in all Roy Rogers movies. Nearby stands Dale's buckskin gelding, Buttermilk. The museum displays costumes, parade saddles, and movie props. One of Rogers's cars, a yellow convertible, and his big-game trophies, shown in dioramas of African and Alaskan wildlife, take you beyond the cowboy image; so do the honors awarded the couple for humanitarian and professional work. *Open daily except Thanksgiving Day and Christmas. Admission charged.*

ROUTE 138 | Silverwood Lake State Recreation Area

12 mi./20 min. East on Rte. 138; follow signs. At the southern edge of the Mojave Desert, you'd hardly anticipate such a dramatic and refreshing change of scene. This park, tucked away in the San Bernardino National Forest, has a remarkably beautiful setting. Lush green mountains rise sharply from a shimmering sapphire lake, which offers a variety of water sports; and its sprawling, 13-mile shoreline harbors a number of inviting picnic spots, including three reachable only by boat. There are miles of paths for hiking and biking. Miller Canyon is a more secluded area, where bears are commonly seen.

The drive to the park is rewarding in itself. Although steep and curvy in stretches, Route 138 offers spacious views of the lake and mountains. *Open year-round. Admission charged.*

ROUTE 60 | The Mission Inn, Riverside

12 mi./20 min. East on Rte. 60, right on Rte. 91, right at 7th St. exit. A national historic landmark, the Mission Inn is steeped in Old World charm. The block-long building is an enchanting blend of baroque Spanish and Moorish architectural motifs—towers, a dome, scalloped arches, carved pillars, and a cloistered garden. Although it resembles an old Spanish mission, the inn was built in the 20th century for hotel owner Frank Miller over a 30-year period. Miller wanted it to be part hotel, part museum, and he filled it with Spanish, Mexican, and Oriental art and antiques. Many famous people have visited Mission Inn, including several U. S. presidents. Among the highlights seen on a guided tour is the exquisite St. Francis Chapel, which is adorned with Louis Comfort Tiffany stained-glass windows. *Open year-round. Admission charged for tours.*

ROUTE 60 | Prado Regional Park

14 mi./20 min. West on Rte. 60, left on Euclid Avenue. This quiet, lovely oasis is a soothing place in which to unwind. The park's 1,200 acres of gently rolling terrain are carpeted with manicured lawns kept

15

CR
3
GT
9
40 BAR

See
E–W book.
sec. 36.

32

PAL

20

ROUTE
138

24

See
E–W book.
sec. 48.

10

ROUTE
60

emerald-green by sprinklers. Ducks and swans glide on the tranquil 56-acre lake, and neat blacktop lanes wind around to picnic spots, shaded pavilions, ballfields, and camping areas. Groves of eucalyptus and the hazy outline of mountains accentuate the beauty. Riding trails encircle the park, and horses can be rented. The park is next to a national wildlife refuge and is visited by cranes, herons, and other waterfowl. *Open daily except Christmas. Admission charged.*

ROUTE 74 | Lake Elsinore State Park

5 min. West on Rte. 74. Fronting on a large, beautiful lake rimmed with mountains, this California park is ideal for families. The spacious sandy beach is studded with young palms and has pleasant picnic facilities. Rowboats and water bikes are rented, and anglers can try for bass, catfish, bluegill, carp, and crappie. The tree-shaded camping areas are inviting, and young children will enjoy the playground facilities and wading area. *Open year-round. Admission charged.*

PAL | Pala Mission

Pala Road exit: 6.5 mi./12 min. East on Pala Rd. (Rte. 76), left on Rte. 16. Located on the Pala Indian Reservation, this is the only *asistencia,* or sub-mission, in California that has continuously ministered to the Indian people since its founding. The Pala Mission, established by Franciscan friars in 1815, is operated today by Comboni missionaries from Italy. The restored chapel, with its white walls, beamed ceiling, and tile roof, is moving in its simplicity. Indian designs with religious symbols are painted on the interior walls. The original bells in the cemetery-garden bell tower still ring out reassuringly to the villagers. A small museum contains church items and Indian artifacts. *Open Tues.–Sun. Admission free but donations encouraged.*

DS | Lawrence Welk Museum, Escondido

Deer Springs Rd. exit: 5 min. East on Deer Springs Rd.; follow signs. In a luxurious retirement community named for the pop-ular bandleader, sidewalks paved with musical instrument shapes lead to this theater lobby and museum. A re-creation of the Welk bandstand and stage set dominates a room lit by crystal chandeliers. Photographs, letters, gold records, and many awards chronicle Welk's long career, including the ballroom-dancing years from the 1920's to the 1950's. You'll see his first accordion and scenes from broadcasts of his television shows. *Open year-round.*

FR | Mission Basilica San Diego de Alcala

Friars Road exit: 5 min. East on Friars Rd., right on Rancho Mission Rd., left on San Diego Mission Rd. Known as the Mother of Missions, this was the first of the early California missions and was built by Father Junípero Serra in 1769. The mission's tall white walls enclose an inner sanctuary of gardens and candle-lit shrines. A *campanario* with bells in its arches stands guard at the church's main entrance. Inside, the decor is surprisingly simple: a red tile floor, exposed beams, and a rough-hewn wooden altar. The cavelike rooms where the friars lived are equally stark, but

FR. *White walls, red tile, and green plants add charm to a place of the spirit.*

the religious vestments and vessels on display are richly ornate. Other exhibits detail the mission's history and, amid the hibiscus and other tropical plants, give color to the main courtyard. In the mission garden there is a wishing well reputed to bring answers to prayers. *Open year-round. Admission charged.*

I-8 | San Diego Zoo

8 mi./15 min. West on I-8, left on Rte. 163 to Park Blvd. exit; follow signs. With a population of 3,200, representing some 800 species from around the world, this fine zoo is a veritable United Nations of the animal kingdom. If you have time, take the 40-minute guided bus tour for orientation, then return to your favorite spots on foot or via outdoor moving walkways and escalators. You will see highland gorillas, Australian koalas, miniature deer, giant anteaters, Mongolian wild horses, and the world's largest collection of parrots and parrotlike birds. The children's zoo is scaled to four-year-olds and features a nursery where baby mammals are bottle-fed, bathed, and diapered. You'll also find elephant and camel rides, animal shows, behind-the-scenes group tours, and special facilities for the handicapped. *Open year-round. Admission charged.*

I-8 | Cabrillo National Monument

15 mi./30 min. West on I-8, left on Rte. 209; follow signs. Juan Rodríguez Cabrillo was the first European to explore this section of the Pacific Coast, and it was this wind-swept finger of land that greeted him when he sailed into the harbor here. Today, at the park named in his honor, he wouldn't recognize the view to the east: a panorama of ocean freighters against a backdrop of San Diego's white skyscrapers. But to the west is the vast unchanged Pacific, where whale-watching is now popular from late December to mid-March. Exhibits in the visitor center concentrate on the peninsula's natural features, local Indian artifacts, and Spanish explorers. There is also a restored lighthouse; and a nature trail, edged by chaparral, runs along the harbor. *Open year-round.*

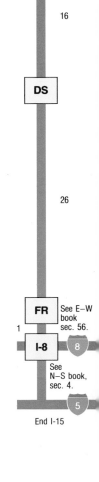

I-90

See E–W book, sec. 3.

299

117

182

42

29

140

111

I-90 | Fort Phil Kearny National Historic Site

15 mi./20 min. North on I-90 to Exit 44, northwest on Rte. 193; follow signs. Constructed in 1866 in violation of the U.S. treaty with the Sioux nation, Ft. Kearny was held under continual siege by Chief Red Cloud and his warriors until it was abandoned in 1868 and was later destroyed by fire. Today the visitor center displays an outline of the fort and the barracks, along with reproductions of army weapons and bows and arrows. Information panels in an adjacent cabin tell the dramatic story of the Wyoming Indian wars and the Bozeman Trail, and describe life on the reservation and frontier. *Open daily June–mid-Oct.*

299 | Jim Gatchell Memorial Museum, Buffalo

5 min. West on Rte. 16; follow signs. Pioneer druggist Jim Gatchell, who dealt frequently with the Indians of the Sioux and Cheyenne tribes, amassed a large collection of their artifacts. Treasures include headdresses, beadwork, and arrowheads. Also on display are guns and shell casings believed to have been used at the Battle of the Little Bighorn, rifles and spent cartridges from the fabled Johnson County shooting war, ore and fossil samples, and the switchboard of the Occidental Hotel, an inn immortalized by Owen Wister's *The Virginian,* a best-selling 1902 novel about a cowhand. *Open daily June–Labor Day. Admission free but donations encouraged.*

182 | Edness Kimball Wilkins State Park

4 min. North on Rte. 253 (Hat Six Rd.), right on Rte. 20/26. These 315 acres near the old Oregon Trail, where the North Platte River reflects the aged cottonwoods along its edges, seem far removed from the busy world. Plans for the park include nature trails, shaded bicycle paths, a riding trail, and additional picnicking areas. The park contains four river-fed ponds that provide pleasant swimming and canoeing in warm weather and ice skating in winter. During the summer members of the Audubon Society often come to bird-watch. *Open year-round.*

140 | Wyoming Pioneer Memorial Museum, Douglas

4 min. East on exit road, right on W. Center St. Almost every object that has ever been used, found, or lost in the West seems to be on display at this remarkably complete museum. Winchesters, six-shooters, Indian arrowheads and spearpoints, tomahawks and war clubs, fossils, furniture, buffalo skulls, branding irons, carriages, cars, swords, and saddlebags—the collection is almost overwhelming. Among the priceless objects are a bugle from Custer's last battle and a hand-made water canteen used by mountain man Jim Bridger at Ft. Laramie. The more artistic displays feature ladies' ornate silk fans and fine glassware and crystal. *Open Mon.–Fri. and P.M. weekends Memorial Day–Oct.; Mon.–Fri. Nov.–Memorial Day except Thanksgiving Day, Christmas, and New Year's Day.*

140 | Fort Fetterman State Historic Site

8 mi./12 min. North on Rte. 93. Soldiers considered duty at this Wyoming outpost a hardship. Pounded mercilessly by savage winter gales, the North Platte River valley was a barren place where fresh produce was a rarity, female companionship all but unknown, and desertion a regular occurrence. Yet the post survived from 1867 until 1882 as a major staging point for supplies and military operations against the Plains Indians. Today's restoration includes the officers' quarters—which house a small museum displaying uniforms and insignia, Indian regalia, and swords and firearms—and the ordnance shed, used now to display farm and military wagons. The fort overlooks scenic rolling hills. *Open daily Memorial Day–Labor Day.*

111 | Glendo State Park

5 min. East into Glendo; follow signs. This park, one of Wyoming's largest, entices vacationers who come to enjoy the idyllic setting, with its rock outcroppings, pine-shaded hills, and lake with 78 miles of shoreline and sandy beaches. Campers can pitch tents anywhere in the park's 10,197 acres, and there's plenty of room for hiking. Boating, water- and jet-skiing, swimming, and fishing are also popular here. *Open year-round.*

92 | Oregon Trail Ruts—Register Cliff State Sites, Guernsey

16 mi./20 min. East on Rte. 26, right on Wyoming St. In the 1800's thousands of Mormons, cattlemen, sheep farmers, and gold seekers followed the Oregon Trail. As

140. *Modern transportation has reduced travel time, but the horizon remains unchanged.*

If You Have Some Extra Time: Rocky Mountain National Park

257A **257B** **35 mi./50 min.** The awe-inspiring scale of this aptly named park in northern Colorado, with more than 100 rugged rocky peaks rising above 10,000 feet, is impressively portrayed in a large relief map at the headquarters building at Beaver Meadows, where you can also see a movie that gives a colorful overview of the highlights.

To see the most spectacular scenery, as well as some of the native animals, take Trail Ridge Road, the nation's highest continuous paved highway, which winds along up to 12,183 feet and crosses the Continental Divide. For about 11 miles the road traverses an area of treeless tundra comparable to that of the Arctic Circle. A walk on Tundra Nature Trail allows close-up inspection of the grass, lichens, and dwarf wildflowers, with long views of the rolling expanse of alpine landscape.

Farview Curve Overlook, a few miles west of the Continental Divide, provides a splendid view and a turnaround for the drive back to Estes Park. You can also continue downhill past Lake Granby to Route 40 and then south to I-70, a distance of about 75 miles.

Trail Ridge Road is closed in winter, from late October until Memorial Day, but the trails and roads open year-round at lower levels reveal other attractions in the park. Just below the tree line, the spruces, firs, and pines are stunted by the ferocious cold and wind; lower down they grow tall and straight, and on the drier slopes lodgepole pines predominate. Lower still are the ponderosa pines, and where these have burned off, quaking aspens thrive, showing their shimmering gold foliage in fall. *How to get there: Exit 257A and Exit 257B, west on Rte. 34. Admission charged.*

---

their wagons lumbered westward, the iron rims cut ruts—many from 4 to 6 feet deep—in this sandstone ridge. At nearby Register Cliff many of these wagon trains, attracted by the camping sites and available water, stopped to rest. The settlers carved their names, dates, hometowns, and destinations in the soft sandstone, leaving a poignant record that still evokes the courage and spirit of these hardy pioneers.

Today, fishermen come to try their luck in the nearby North Platte River, where rainbow and brown trout abound. *Open year-round, weather permitting.*

9 | Cheyenne, WY 82001

Chamber of Commerce, 301 W. 16th St. (307) 638-3388. The phrase "Cheyenne to Deadwood 1876" is still visible on the side of a weather-beaten stagecoach at the Cheyenne Frontier Days Old West Museum, where more than 30 horse-drawn vehicles colorfully recall the days before the automobile. Also shown are an ambulance, a hearse, and sightseeing coaches, along with fancy saddles, rodeo memorabilia, and exhibits on the advent of the railroad and the decline of the Plains Indian tribes.

In Lions Park the solar-heated Cheyenne Botanic Gardens and a lake for swimming, boating, and fishing are especially popular with visitors.

The focus of the Wyoming State Museum is the state's history and frontier life. The museum's exhibits recall the days of the Shoshone and Arapaho Indians, cowboys, pioneer women, and mountain men. Indian beadwork, guns owned by Buffalo Bill Cody, and a diorama of an 1880's cattle roundup are among the highlights.

269 | Lory State Park

15 mi./27 min. West on Rte. 14, right on Rte. 287, left on Rte. 28. This 2,600-acre park lies at the very gateway to the Rockies. From sheltered coves at Horsetooth Reservoir the land sweeps dramatically upward through hogback ridges to Ranger Peak at 7,015 feet. Prairie grass gives way to mountain shrubs and then to stands of ponderosa pine. Some 25 miles of trails offer hikers choices ranging from easy to challenging. From Arthur's Rock, which can be reached by trail, there's a sweeping view of Fort Collins. *Open year-round. Admission charged.*

257B | Centennial Village, Greeley

257A *18 mi./25 min. Exit 257B: east on Rte. 34, left on 14th Ave., left on A St. Exit 257A: proceed as above.* This museum village, opened in 1976 to mark the state's 100th birthday and the nation's

200th, offers a view of life between 1860 and the 1920's. Two adobe structures remained comfortable in the height of summer, while the Swedish-American farm dwelling allayed winter doldrums with a dazzling white interior. Carpenter House has a potbellied stove and tea-leaf china. At Stevens House a pump organ and parlor piano evoke gracious turn-of-the-century living. Other sites include a church, a newspaper office, a firehouse, a carriage house, a blacksmith's shop, and a schoolhouse with ink-stained desks. *Open Mon.– Fri. and P.M. weekends Memorial Day–Labor Day; Tues.–Sat. mid-Apr.–Memorial Day and Labor Day–mid-Oct.*

240 | Longmont Museum

7 mi./10 min. West on Rte. 119, right on Kimbark St. Several exhibits here trace the history of Longmont and the surrounding St. Vrain Valley. The classic Americana on display range from prospector's pans to a high-wheeler or "penny-farthing" bicycle, and from turn-of-the-century washing machines to a jukebox from the early 1960's. The space exhibit celebrates local astronaut Vance Brand with memorabilia from his life in Longmont and from his 1975 Apollo-Soyuz mission. *Open Mon.–Sat. except holidays. Admission free but donations encouraged.*

19
92
83
See E–W book, sec. 19.
9
80
WY
CO
37
269
12
257B 0
257A 0
257B
17
240
See E–W book, sec. 27.
70
30
25

210

54

156B

6

150B

8

142

1

141

3

138

37

101

7

94

210. *As the nearby Rockies recede at night, a man-made range of buildings comes to light.*

210 Denver, CO 80202

Convention & Visitors Bureau, 225 W. Colfax Ave. (303) 892-1112. There is a wealth of museums, parks, and shopping areas in the Mile High City. The Denver Art Museum, covered with a million reflecting tiles, houses a superb Indian collection, with many Mesoamerican pieces. Nearby is the U.S. Mint, where you can watch money being stamped. Among the stately old mansions on Capitol Hill is the popular Molly Brown House, former home of the feisty and "unsinkable" heroine of the *Titanic.* The flavor of Denver's past has been preserved in Larimer Square, with its restored shops, restaurants, arcades, and gaslights. There are some 4,000 acres of parks within the city, one of which, City Park, contains the Denver Museum of Natural History, with its planetarium, and the Denver Zoo.

156B United States Air Force Academy

150B
Exit 156B: 2 min. West on access road. Exit 150B: 2 min. West on access road. Situated just north of Colorado Springs, the nation's youngest service academy (founded in 1954) occupies 18,000 acres of rolling, grassy high prairie, at an elevation of 7,200 feet, with the Rocky Mountains rising dramatically in the background. A map available at the gatehouses leads you on a 14-mile self-guiding auto tour. The famous Cadet Chapel, with its 17 aluminum spires and aircraft-related interior, is a short walk from the visitor center; guided tours are given every half-hour in summer. The chapel's terrace affords an extensive view of the parade ground and other buildings. *Open year-round.* &

142 Colorado Springs, CO 80903

Convention & Visitors Bureau, 104 S. Cascade Ave., Suite 104. (719) 635-7506; (800) 888-4748 outside CO. From almost anywhere in town, the Rocky Mountains are a scenic presence, Pikes Peak in particular. The early history of this fast-growing city of resorts and high-tech industries is recalled at the Pioneers' Museum. The Fine Arts Center features works by American artists, and the Pro Rodeo Hall of Champions and the Museum of the American Cowboy pay tribute to these western skills. Specialists enjoy the comprehensive displays at the American Numismatic Association. Pikes Peak Ghost Town and the Garden of the Gods are, respectively, interesting man-made and natural attractions.

156B–150B. *The Cadet Chapel evokes aspirations of flight as well as spirit.*

141 Garden of the Gods, Colorado Springs

5 mi./9 min. West on Rte. 24; follow signs. This spectacular array of ancient rock outcrops owes its name to a mid-19th-century visitor who, when his companion proclaimed the area suitable for a beer garden, replied that it was more fitting as a "garden of the gods." Fortunately, his vision prevailed, and the 1,300-acre park, which is now a registered natural landmark, has remained unspoiled. The area is unique for its oddly shaped red and white sandstone formations with names like the Kissing Camels, the Three Graces, and the Sleeping Indian. Jutting as high as 300 feet above the ground, these rocks date back some 250 million years or more, when they were sloughed off by the emerging Rocky Mountains. *Open year-round.*　🧺🚶♿

141 Cave of the Winds

6 mi./10 min. West on Rte. 24. Discovered in 1880, this dramatic series of underground caverns in the Front Range of the Rocky Mountains was formed by the rushing waters of an inland sea some 500 million years ago. The guided tour, which covers nearly a mile in 45 minutes, takes you through 21 chambers with such fanciful names as Canopy Hall and Oriental Garden. The cave is surprisingly nonclaustrophobic, since it is well lighted and in general the ceilings are high. Man-made paths make walking easy, but there are a few short steep stairways. *Open daily except Christmas. Admission charged.*　🧺

141 Mount Manitou Incline, Manitou Springs

6.5 mi./20 min. West on Rte. 24, left on Rte. 24 (business), left on Ruxton Ave. If you don't have time for the 3-hour round-trip on the popular Pikes Peak cog railway, this ride in a cable car up an adjoining summit offers an inviting alternative. Starting from a station just across from the Pikes Peak depot, the mile-long incline rises some 2,200 feet into the Pike National Forest. At the top there are panoramic views of Manitou Springs and Colorado Springs, as well as the hiking trail that climbs Pikes Peak. *Open May–Sept. Fare charged.*　🧺🚶

141. *Nature's work, left, in the Garden of the Gods resembles a Giacometti sculpture.*

138 | Will Rogers Shrine of the Sun, Colorado Springs

7 mi./20 min. West on Lake Ave., left on Lake Circle, left on Walnut Ave.; bear right on Miranda Rd., right on Cheyenne Mountain Blvd.; continue on Cheyenne Mountain Zoo Rd. A winding road that begins in the Cheyenne Mountain Zoo takes you to a mountaintop memorial to one of America's best-known humorists. After Rogers was killed in a 1935 plane crash, Spencer Penrose, the monument's benefactor, dedicated the site, with its 80-foot stone tower, to his good friend. The shrine affords views of the Plains to the east, Pikes Peak to the west, and Colorado Springs below. The extensive zoo boasts a major collection of animals, including a large giraffe herd. *Open year-round. Admission charged.*

101 / 94 | The Greenway and Nature Center of Pueblo

Exit 101: 7 mi./8 min. West on Rte. 50, left on Pueblo Blvd. (Rte. 45), right on W. 11th St. Exit 94: 6 mi./10 min. West on Pueblo Blvd. (Rte. 45), left on W. 11th St. Some 20 miles of an inviting trail stretch along the banks of the Arkansas and Fountain rivers in this unique urban park, called the Greenway, set in a lush cotton-wood canyon. On the east the trail leads to the Pueblo City Park (see below); to the west it connects with the full-facility Pueblo State Recreation Area. The Nature Center shows some examples of this semiarid region's flora and fauna. At the Raptor Center, injured birds of prey receive loving care. *Greenway open year-round; Nature Center and Raptor Center open daily except Thanksgiving Day, Christmas, and New Year's Day.*

101 / 94 | Pueblo Zoo and City Park

Exit 101: 6 mi./8 min. West on Rte. 50, left on Pueblo Blvd. (Rte. 45), left on Goodnight Ave. Exit 94: 5 mi./9 min. West on Pueblo Blvd. (Rte. 45), right on Goodnight Ave. The centerpiece of this attractive city park is a charming zoo. In a barnyardlike petting zoo, roosters and rambunctious African pygmy goats run loose, and penned donkeys, sheep, and pigs can be petted. The zoo's other residents include antelopes, monkeys, deer, camels, zebras, prairie dogs, and a small herd of bison. The park also has a pool, free tennis courts, and an amusement minipark with half a dozen or so children's rides. *Zoo and park open year-round; pool open Memorial Day–late Aug.; amusement area open Memorial Day–Labor Day. Admission charged.*

13B | Baca House and Bloom House, Trinidad

3 min. East on Main St. Although these two beautifully restored and authentically refurbished houses are next to each other, there are striking differences. The unpretentious two-story house once owned by Don Felipe Baca, a sheep rancher, has thick adobe walls. The whitewashed interior gives a bright, airy feel. By contrast, the three-story brick mansion built for cattleman and banker Frank Bloom a decade later has wrought-iron railings capping its wraparound porch and mansard roof. The interior is a profusion of Victorian-era patterns and furniture. The Pioneer Museum, in the Baca servants' quarters, displays memorabilia from Trinidad's frontier days. *Open Mon.–Sat. and P.M. Sun. Memorial Day–Labor Day. Admission charged.*

452 | Sugarite Canyon State Park

6 mi./9 min. East on Rte. 72, left on Rte. 526. Near the famed skiing area, this pleasant wooded canyon is one of New Mexico's newest state parks. It was once the home of prosperous coal mines, and their tailings can still be seen on the surrounding cliffs. But nature has reclaimed the canyon, filling it with pines, cottonwoods, and scrub oaks. The park's centerpiece is 120-acre Lake Maloya, which extends across the state line into a Colorado wilderness area. It is popular with local anglers, who come to try for rainbow trout. *Open year-round. Admission charged.*

366 | Fort Union National Monument

7 mi./ 10 min. West on Rte. 477. Built near the juncture of two branches of the Santa Fe Trail, Ft. Union played a vital role in the nation's westward expansion. Beginning in 1851, it was a way station for Missouri entrepreneurs who opened up trade in the Mexican land that later became the U.S. Territory of New Mexico. The fort was abandoned in 1891, when the railroad replaced wagon travel. Today you can see some of the remains—the stone foundations of the enlisted men's and officers' quarters, the crumbling adobe walls of the quartermaster depot, and the remnants of brick chimneys. *Open daily except Christmas and New Year's Day. Admission charged Memorial Day–Labor Day.*

366. *Crumbling symbols of the old West: adobe walls and handmade wheels.*

25

307

299

284

234

40

225

222

175

150

8

15

50

9

3

47

25

See E–W book, sec. 37.

<table>
<tr><td>307</td></tr>
<tr><td>299</td></tr>
</table>

307 | Pecos National Monument

Exit 307: 4 mi./8 min. North on Rte. 63. Exit 299: 8 mi./12 min. East on Rte. 50, right on Rte. 63. The 1¼-mile-long trail that winds among these rock- and grass-covered mounds provides only a suggestion of the Indian settlement that once thrived on this valley ridge in the Sangre de Cristo Mountains. In the mid-1400's the Pecos Pueblo, with its four- and five-story dwellings, was home to some 2,000 Pecos Indians, whose strategic location became a center of trade with the buffalo-hunting Plains Indians to the north and the Indian farmers of the Rio Grande to the south. Visitors can climb down wooden ladders into two restored kivas (circular underground ceremonial rooms). The visitor center, with its displays of Pecos pottery, tools and jewelry, and a film about the pueblo's past, reconstructs the colorful history of the people who once lived here. *Open daily except Christmas and New Year's Day. Admission charged.*

284 | Santa Fe, NM 87501

Convention and Visitors Bureau, 201 W. Marcy St. (505) 984-6760; (800) 528-5369 outside NM. The charm of Santa Fe is derived from its Spanish and Indian past. The adobe Palace of Governors, built in 1610 and said to be the oldest public building in the United States, is now a major repository of southwestern history. The San Miguel Mission, one of the oldest churches in America, was also built in the early 1600's. During the Pueblo uprising of 1680, which drove the Spaniards back to El Paso, the mission was destroyed, but in 1710 it was completely reconstructed. Both structures have managed to retain their original Spanish flavor, despite the many years of conflict that finally ended in 1846 when the U.S. Army raised the American flag and took Santa Fe without resistance.

The Wheelwright Museum has outstanding collections of Indian art. Ethnic crafts from around the world are superbly displayed in the Museum of International Folk Art. The downtown area invites walking, but at an elevation of 7,000 feet, Santa Fe requires a visitor to take it easy at first.

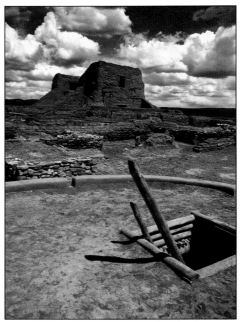

307–299. *Ladder leads to a ceremonial chamber. Mission ruins are in background.*

234 | Sandia Peak Aerial Tramway, Albuquerque

6 mi./10 min. East on Tramway Rd.; follow signs. One of the world's longest aerial tramways carries riders on a trip of 2.7 miles, from Sandia Peak's desert base, over canyons and dense forests, to its verdant top. During the 15-minute ride, which covers a vertical rise of 3,800 feet, you may spot mule deer below and golden eagles circling overhead. From Sandia Peak, part of the Cibola National Forest, you can enjoy a view of more than 11,000 square miles. You'll also find hiking trails and areas for rock climbing and hang gliding. In winter the tram serves as a ski lift, giving access to 25 miles of trails. *Open daily Memorial Day–Labor Day; Thurs.–Tues. and P.M. Wed. Labor Day–Memorial Day. Admission charged.*

225 | Albuquerque, NM 87103

Convention & Visitors Bureau, 305 Romero St. NW. (505) 243-3696; (800) 284-2282 outside NM. The Spanish influence is pleasantly recalled in the Old Town area, with its plaza and the San Felipe de Neri church (1706). The handsome architecture on the University of New Mexico campus has been influenced by the Indian pueblos. Anthropology, geology, and the arts are featured in the city's excellent museums. One of the most intriguing is the New Mexico Museum of Natural History. Here you can step into a volcano or an Ice Age cave and admire a model of a flying quetzalcoatlus with its wingspan of 40 feet. World War II correspondent Ernie Pyle's home is open to the public. The Indian Pueblo Cultural Center details the culture and history of the peoples of New Mexico.

222 | National Atomic Museum, Albuquerque

6 mi./10 min. East on Gibson Blvd., right on Wyoming Blvd. A B-52 bomber used in the last atmospheric nuclear tests, a 280-mm. atomic cannon, and futuristic-looking surface-to-air missiles occupy the grounds outside this museum, which focuses on nuclear weaponry. Exhibits and films illustrate the history of the first atom bomb and include full-size models of its first two designs. Also featured are planes and missiles created to carry atomic weapons, the development of the hydrogen bomb, advances in weapons technology, and safety and testing. Peaceful uses of nuclear technology for medicine, agriculture, and industry are also demonstrated. *Open daily except Thanksgiving Day, Christmas, New Year's Day, and Easter.*

175 | Salinas National Monument, Abó Pueblo Unit

30 mi./35 min. East on Rte. 60, north on Rte. 513. Built by Tompiro Indians before A.D. 1200, Abó grew into one of the largest Pueblo Indian communities in the pre-Spanish Southwest, but was abandoned in the 1670's as a result of disease, drought, and warfare. Today a self-guiding tour tells visitors of the rise and fall of the Pueblo Indian people here. Native religion is represented by the round, partly subterranean spiritual centers called kivas. They form an architectural and cultural contrast to the excavated ruins of the San Gregorio de Abó mission church. The mission's thin sandstone buttressed walls, 40 feet high in places, loom over mounds that cover the sites of houses and other structures of the pueblo. *Open daily except Christmas and New Year's Day. Admission charged.*

150 / 147 San Miguel Mission, Socorro

4 min. Exit 150: south on Loop I-25 (business; Rte. 60), right on Otero St.; follow signs. Exit 147: north on Loop I-25 (business; Rte. 60), left on Otero St.; follow signs. The town of Socorro reportedly was named for the aid ("succor") that Piro Indians were said to have given to Spanish explorers. A wall from the original San Miguel Mission, begun by the Spanish in 1598, is incorporated with the present adobe church, constructed between 1615 and 1626. The chapel wing completed the building in 1853. The interior has hand-carved ceiling beams and pews. You can see other artifacts in the church office. The twin bell towers present a dramatic night-sky silhouette. *Open year-round.*

139 / 124 Bosque del Apache National Wildlife Refuge

Exit 139: 9 mi./15 min. East on Rte. 380, right on Rte. 85. Exit 124: 10 mi./15 min. East on gravel road, left on Rte. 85. Greater sandhill cranes, once in danger of extinction, leap and dance in remarkable displays that can be viewed from the sanctuary's 15-mile loop road. You may also spot a very rare whooping crane, with an 8-foot wingspan, or an endangered bald eagle. Great blue herons are common, as are many shorebirds and songbirds, mule deer, and coyotes. The visitor center has a station for observing wildlife as well as exhibits on natural history. *Refuge open year-round; visitor center open daily Oct.–Mar.; Mon.–Fri. Apr.–Sept. except Christmas and New Year's Day. Admission charged.*

83 Elephant Butte Lake State Park

4 mi./6 min. East on Rte. 52. With 36,733 acres of water and 45,000 of land, the park offers a variety of recreational opportunities: camping, picnicking, sailing, water-skiing (there's a ski jump), and swimming from sandy beaches; fishermen come for catfish, trout, pike, crappie, and black, white, and striped bass. The place called Damsite at the southern end of the lake affords an impressive view of Elephant Butte, the neck of an ancient volcano that is said to resemble an elephant's head rising from the water. A colorful marina rents boats, water skis, and fishing gear. The hiking trails lead past picnic sites shaded by cottonwoods. *Open year-round. Admission charged.*

139–124. *Snow geese find conditions at the Bosque del Apache Refuge to their liking.*

76 Geronimo Springs Museum, Truth or Consequences

3.5 mi./8 min. East on Broadway, left on Pershing St., left on Main St. The soothing 110° F mineral water that bubbles beside this museum attracted Indians long before Geronimo Springs became a spa for white settlers. The museum contains murals of the Indian, the Spanish, the Mexican, and the Anglo cultures, and exhibits of ranching and mining activities. Why the town's name was changed in 1950 from Hot Springs to Truth or Consequences, the title of a radio (and later TV) show, is also explained. *Open Mon.–Sat. and P.M. Sun. except holidays. Admission charged.*

19 Fort Selden State Monument

2 min. West on access road. Set on the banks of the Rio Grande, this fort was established in 1865 to protect settlers from Apaches. The troops also escorted travelers along the Jornada del Muerto ("Journey of Death") desert trail to the north. Exhibits in the visitor center contain uniforms, including the plumed hats and Prussian-style coats of the Buffalo soldiers, a renowned black cavalry unit. The remains of the walls are marked with signs. *Open daily except holidays. Admission charged.*

3 / I-10 La Mesilla Historic Village

Exit 3: 3 mi./8 min. West on University Ave., right on Rte. 28; follow signs. Exit I-10: 4 mi./16 min. West on I-10 to Exit 140, south on Rte. 28; follow signs. This quaint Spanish-style village was Mexican until 1854, when the Gadsden Purchase was signed and the American flag was raised in its plaza. The town's history includes a period of Confederate occupation, a trial of Billy the Kid, and harassment by Geronimo. The mission-style church of San Albino dominates the plaza, and restored adobe buildings house restaurants, gift shops, and art galleries. The Gadsden Museum contains a collection of the folk wood carvings of saints and other religious figures known as *santos. Village open year-round; museum open daily except Thanksgiving Day, Christmas, and Easter. Admission charged for museum.*

3
147
8
139
15
124
41
83
7
76
57
19
16
3
See E–W book, sec. 51.
7
I-10   10
End I-25

215 Pembina State Historic Site

2 min. East on Stutsman St. Built in 1797 by the Northwest Fur Company, Ft. Pembina was the first European settlement in North Dakota. With the building of Ft. Daer in 1812, this region became more military in character. Though picnic sites and playgrounds have long ago replaced Ft. Daer, the area's history is recalled by a visit to the Pembina State Museum. Here one can almost hear the ringing shots of firing practice and the haggling of fur-clad traders. *Museum open P.M. Fri.–Mon. Memorial Day–Labor Day.*

138 Grand Forks County Historical Society

4 mi./9 min. East on 32nd Ave. S, left on Belmont Rd. Built in 1879, this log cabin was the birthplace of wheat king Thomas Campbell, Jr., noted for industrializing his farm. At the turn of the century a huge wing was added, creating the structure known as Campbell House, now used as a museum. Pioneer furnishings and utensils in the cabin contrast with the elegance of ostrich feathers and opera hats in the newer addition. Local history is further recalled in a number of other buildings, including Myra House, a carriage house, a post office, and a schoolhouse. *Museum open year-round; buildings open P.M. daily mid-May–mid-Oct. Admission charged.*

100 KTHI TV Tower, Blanchard

12 mi./14 min. West on Alt. Rte. 200, right on Rte. 18. The 2,063-foot television station KTHI tower, built in 1963, was the world's tallest structure until a tower about 58 feet higher was built in Poland. The KTHI tower can send signals across a 100-mile radius, almost twice the distance of most other towers. Although the tower is stabilized by 27 guy wires, the top sways as much as 10 feet in gusty winds. In 1986 this engineering marvel was considered to be in excellent condition by structural engineers, and there have been no accidents since construction began more than 30 years ago. There are no tours, but visitors are invited to drive to the base of the tower, look up, and be amazed. *Open year-round.*

65 / 63 Bonanzaville, U.S.A., West Fargo

Exit 65: 4 mi./9 min. West on Rte. 10. Exit 63: 4.5 mi./6 min. West on I-94 to Exit 85, east on Rte. 10. Bonanzaville, U.S.A., is a regional museum complex of almost 50 buildings. An aircraft museum, a railroad depot, a collection of dolls, a fire station, and a barn with live animals are some of the attractions. Among the dwellings, you'll find a reproduction of a sod house, log cabins, and early homes, including one that was owned by D. H. Houston, who devised an early type of roll film and a folding camera. The Red River and Northern Plains Regional Museum (headquarters for Bonanzaville) displays collections of military items, toys, models of ships and cars, musical instruments, and one of the most comprehensive American Indian exhibits in this area. *Museum and buildings open Mon.–Fri. and P.M. Sat.–Sun. late May–late Oct.; museum open Tues.–Fri. late Oct.–late May except Thanksgiving Day, Christmas, and New Year's Day. Admission charged.*

63 Plains Art Museum, Moorhead

6 mi./9 min. East on I-94 to Exit 1, north on Rte. 75, left on Main Ave. A Sioux baby bonnet trimmed with dentalia shells, a dance bustle made of feathers and tin, and Ojibwa dance caps of porcupine quills and deer hair are examples of the excellent Native American art in this museum. The collection also includes the work of American impressionist Mary Cassatt, as well as painters Jerry Ott and Luis Jimenez. Many of the items sold in the museum shop were made by area artists and craftsmen. *Open Tues.–Sat. and P.M. Sun. except Thanksgiving Day, Christmas, and New Year's Day. Admission free but donations encouraged.*

37 Fort Abercrombie State Historic Site

7 mi./9 min. East on Rte. 4, right on Rte. 81. Disgruntled over the withholding of goods promised by treaty, the Sioux Indians besieged this fort for nearly 6 weeks in 1862. Military personnel and the settlers who sought protection fended off Indian attacks with 12-pound howitzers until reinforcements arrived and the attacks ceased. The stronghold became a stop for expeditions and frontier-bound pioneers until it was abandoned in 1877. The museum near the fort holds an assortment of local artifacts gleaned from attics, basements, parlors, and private collections. There's an interesting miscellany of portraits of pioneers, painted Norwegian food chests, stone hammers, foot warmers, waffle irons, and a model of the fort. *Fort open year-round; museum open daily June–Aug.; Thurs.–Mon. last 2 weeks in May and first 2 weeks in Sept. Admission charged for museum.*

65–63. *In the 1920's the operator would say "Number, please" and connect the lines.*

207. *The setting sun adds an aura of mystery to the angular lines of Blue Cloud Abbey.*

213 Hartford Beach State Park

18 mi./20 min. East on Rte. 15. The 22,400 acres of Big Stone Lake are the headwaters of the Minnesota River, on the border between Minnesota and South Dakota. In the late 19th and early 20th centuries, pleasure steamers cruised its waters, and hotels catered to vacationers. Wooded bluffs on the lake, their heights topped with prairie and meadow, provide scenic panoramas of Big Stone Island, a nature preserve that can be reached only by boat in summer or across the ice in winter. *Open year-round. Admission charged.*

207 Blue Cloud Abbey

10 mi./15 min. East on Rte. 12. Located on a hill above the Whetstone Valley prairie, this community of 50 or so Benedictine monks welcomes visitors seeking prayer, peace of mind, or simple relaxation. The complex of modern-looking stone buildings was constructed by the monks themselves in the 1950's and 1960's. Also to be found here is the American Indian Culture Research Center, which coordinates the monks' service activities among Indian communities and displays such items as a ceremonial pipe and a model of a burial scaffold. The abbey itself features a glowing stained-glass window and a fine mural depicting the monks' work among the Indians. *Open year-round.*

177 Kampeska Heritage Museum, Watertown

4 mi./8 min. West on Rte. 212, right on Maple St. The museum occupies the main floor, basement, and mezzanine of the former public library, a handsome building with classical columns and ornate woodwork. The exhibits detail the cultural history of Codington County (the first white settlers arrived in the 1870's) and include a series of period rooms furnished in the styles favored locally early in the 20th century. A bank interior with handsome oak and marble furnishings, a well-provisioned general store, and a telephone switchboard also recall the early days in South Dakota. *Open P.M. Tues.–Sun. June–Aug.; P.M. Tues.–Sat. Sept.–May.*

23 Chahinkapa Park, Wahpeton

12 mi./17 min. East on Rte. 13, left on 1st St. Located between the Bois de Sioux River and the Bois de Sioux golf course (its 18 holes lie in two states), this large and appealing city park has facilities for biking, tennis, basketball, swimming, and horseshoes. There are also picnic areas, playgrounds, and a free campground (3-day limit). Chahinkapa Zoo houses bobcats, mountain lions, Scandinavian blue foxes, eagles, peacocks, exotic waterfowl, a miniature horse, and a moose. At Grandpa's Little Zoo, small children can pet the sheep, goats, rabbits, ducks, and donkeys. *Open year-round.*

23 Richland County Historical Museum, Wahpeton

12 mi./17 min. East on Rte. 13, left on 2nd St. The 2,000-page, 508-pound visitors' book with space for 760,000 signatures is the first of the many distinctive items encountered in this museum. The collection of Indian artifacts was assembled by Esther Horne, the great-great-granddaughter of Sacajawea, the Shoshone woman guide who accompanied Lewis and Clark on their famous expedition in 1804–06. The collection includes Sioux dolls, birch-bark boxes, ceremonial clubs, a buffalo-bone breastplate, and various articles of leather clothing with excellent beadwork. A reproduced 1887 claim shack and period rooms feature 19th-century furniture. Exhibits of clothing contain horsehide mittens, elegant hats, fans, baby clothes, and dresses. A collection of World War I memorabilia, farm equipment, and farm-related photographs, and an assortment of miscellaneous items are also displayed. *Open P.M. Fri.– Sun. May–Nov. except Thanksgiving Day.*

232 Roy Lake State Park

23 mi./30 min. West on Rte. 10; follow signs. Artifacts found here reveal that this was the site of a pre-Columbian Indian village, thought to have been the most northerly settlement of a culture that prevailed in the area from A.D. 900 to 1300. The park's two sections, east and west, border the lake, where crystal-clear glacial waters nurture an abundance of perch, bullheads, bluegills, walleyes, and largemouth bass. The park has hiking trails, a beach for swimming and sunning, campgrounds, and a ramp for launching boats. Cabins occupy the tip of the western section. Winter sports enthusiasts can enjoy the trails for cross-country skiing and snowmobiling. *Open year-round. Admission charged May–Sept.*

29
140
8
132
23
109
25
See
E–W book,
sec. 4.
90 I-90
5
79

140 Oakwood Lakes State Park

12 mi./15 min. West on Rte. 30; follow signs. Eight glacial lakes, 3,000 acres of sparkling blue formed during the last ice age, are set amid the lush meadows and woodland that were once, according to legend, an Indian tribal meeting place. Later it became the haunt of trappers and farmers, as evidenced by the Mortimer Cabin, which was built by a fur trader in 1867–70. The structure is furnished crudely, as it might have been when first occupied. In a meadow now reverting to prairie land are Indian mounds. To the south the site of a onetime fort is marked by a solitary log cabin. On Scout Island (actually a peninsula) the ¾-mile Tetonkaha Trail loops through marsh, scrubland, and stands of cottonwoods—favored by bald eagles for roosting and nesting—willows, and bur oaks. From the southern tip of the nature trail you can enjoy some unusually fine lake views. *Open year-round. Admission charged.*

132 McCrory Gardens, Brookings

2 min. West on Rte. 14, right on 20th St. These 70 acres of ornamental gardens, which are maintained by the South Dakota State University Horticulture-Forestry Department, are a delightful resource for those planning their own landscaping. The numerous varieties of annuals, perennials, dwarf conifers, vines, and roses, some of them especially hybridized to withstand the rigors of the South Dakota climate, are all carefully labeled. There are test beds of 140 varieties of Kentucky bluegrasses and perennial ryegrasses. An adjoining arboretum has a good collection of ornamental shrubs and trees. *Open year-round.*

132 State Agricultural Heritage Museum, Brookings

6 min. West on Rte. 14, right on Medary Ave.; follow signs. A colorful account of agriculture on the plains of South Dakota from the 1860's to the present is displayed here. Noteworthy exhibits include a claim shanty built in 1882—20 years after the Homestead Act went into effect—its walls still covered with the original newspaper liners, and a magnificently restored 1915 Case steam-traction engine, resplendent in black, red, and green. Collections of historical photographs and posters bring the past to life; and remarkable exhibits honor the state's leading agronomists and pioneer breeders of hybrid corn, rust-free wheat, and fruit trees hardy enough to withstand the winters here. A small heritage garden contains an impressive living museum of South Dakota's native grasses and staple crops. *Open Mon.–Sat. and P.M. Sun.*

109 Lake Herman State Park

19 mi./25 min. West on Rte. 34. The campground and picnic areas of this 176-acre peninsula park overlook beautiful Lake Herman and are shaded by stands of native oak. The site was frequented by Indians, and occasionally an arrowhead can be found along the trail. The peninsula's first white settler, Herman Luce, lived here, and the log cabin he built in 1871 still stands. There's good hiking, cycling, and cross-country skiing on the nearly 50 miles of trails, and fishing for walleye is popular. Along the Luce Trail, which circles the 15-acre pond at the center of the park, hikers can see hackberry and box elder trees, wild roses, cotoneasters, and Virginia creeper. More than 200 species of birds have been observed in the area. *Open year-round. Admission charged.*

109 Prairie Village

22 mi./30 min. West on Rte. 34; follow signs. To wander through this collection of more than 40 buildings brought from the surrounding area, and now restored, is to come as close as possible to life as it was on the prairie in the late 1800's.

The depot, country store, blacksmith's shop, schoolhouse, dentist's office, barbershop, church, saloon, and jail were staples of most small communities, and the hotel and opera house were not uncommon. Characteristic of the prairie are the claim shanty, the sod house, and a plot of plants and grasses that once grew here. Without water from the windmill, the trademark structure here, life would not have been possible. There's a fine old carousel, locomotive and popcorn wagon—all originally steam-driven—and a number of antique tractors and threshing machines. *Open daily May–Sept. Admission charged.*

I-90 Buffalo Ridge

5 mi./8 min. West on I-90 to Exit 390; follow signs. The buffalo are still at home on the range, although they don't roam as widely as they did in days gone by. Here, alongside Interstate 90, a herd of 40 to 50 bison graze on their 160-acre preserve.

140. *Cottonwoods add golden hues to the skyline and waters of Oakwood Lake.*

109. *All the needs, from shirts to seeds, could be fulfilled at the country store.*

The man-made attraction is a reproduction of a 19th-century western cow town. It has a blacksmith's shop, a gunsmith's shop, an opera house, a stagecoach office, and the all-important jail, among other displays. Models in many of the exhibits will speak contemporary dialogue when activated by a push button. *Open year-round. Admission charged.*

79 Sherman Park, Sioux Falls

5 mi./6 min. East on 12th St., right on Kiwanis Ave. The park, with meadows, ballfields, tennis courts, a skating rink, a children's playground, and shady picnic grounds, lies on the banks of the Big Sioux River. At the northern end is the U.S.S. *South Dakota* Battleship Memorial, a full-size concrete plan of the warship, and a museum of memorabilia. The rest of the park is devoted to the Great Plains Zoo, where a collection of some 300 animals from all parts of the world ranges from the elegantly aloof snow leopard to the appealing Sicilian donkey. The Delbridge Museum of Natural History at the zoo features mounted animals in lifelike dioramas. One exhibit shows what the world looks like to the animals. *Open daily except Christmas. Admission charged.*

38 Union County State Park

5 min. East on Rte. 15, right on Rte. 1C. The park includes the slopes of a glacial moraine and a mixture of woodlands, old meadows reverting to scrub, and prairies. From Parkview Hill, one of the highest points in southeastern South Dakota, there are sweeping views of the area. The Arboretum Trail wanders through plantings of many types of trees that can survive in this climate—for example, the smoke tree, the white poplar, the ponderosa pine, the honeysuckle, and the Kentucky coffee tree. In the fall the trees put on a colorful display and provide berries and seeds for birds and small mammals. *Open year-round but may be inaccessible in winter.*

26 Shrine to Music Museum, Vermillion

8 mi./10 min. West on Rte. 50, left on Pine St., right on Clark St. The delights of this remarkably complete music museum range from violins by the great instrument makers at Cremona—Stradivari, Guarneri, and the Amati family—to sinuously beautiful wood and ivory lutes and such ingenious creations as the "spittoon with bell-ringer and electric igniter" made by Stanley Fritts for his Korn Kobblers band. Other special treasures include European and American keyboard instruments, many of them masterpieces of the cabinetmaker's art, various Italian stringed instruments, nonwestern curiosities, including trumpets made from human leg bones, folk instruments, and a glittering assortment of American band instruments. *Open Mon.–Sat. and P.M. Sun. except Thanksgiving Day, Christmas, and New Year's Day. Admission free but donations encouraged.*

150 Stone State Park

5 mi./8 min. Northwest on Rte. 12. This 1,100-acre park is on the crest and valleys of a loess bluff, one of nature's wonders. Loess is a type of wind-blown soil or loam found mainly in China, the U.S.A., and a few places in Europe. A ridge-top road affords splendid views of the Missouri Valley and heavily wooded hills. Numerous bridle, hiking, cross-country skiing, and snowmobile trails crisscross this unusual terrain once held sacred by the Indians. The self-guiding Carolyn Benne Nature Trail winds through lush wooded-valley vegetation and crosses marshlands and prairies. An informative pamphlet describing the plants on this trail is available. *Open year-round. Admission charged.*

NEB Sioux City Public Museum

Nebraska St. exit: 3 mi./9 min. North on Nebraska St., right on 29th St. Built of pink-colored Sioux Falls quartzite in the early 1890's, the Peirce Mansion first changed hands when the original owner lost his fortune and raffled off the house for $1 a chance. Since then, the mansion has had more than nine different owners and for a while served as a dormitory for student nurses before it became a public museum in 1961. Rooms display pioneer materials, ranging from antique needlework to a furnished log cabin interior, and depict the natural history of the area through displays of birds, animals, fish, and minerals. A number of Indian artifacts are also on display. *Open Mon.–Sat. and P.M. Sun. except holidays. Admission free but donations encouraged.*

41

38

12

26

27

SD

IA

150

3

NEB

36

29

112 | Lewis and Clark State Park

2 min. West on Rte. 175. Named for Meriwether Lewis and William Clark, the first white men to lead an exploratory expedition to the Pacific Northwest, this 286-acre park is located on a horseshoe-shaped lake formed by the Missouri River. Lewis and Clark spent several days here in 1804 observing the plants and animals. Today you can easily do the same on the nature trails. Along with other varieties of plants and animals, you'll see jack pines, diamond willows, wild roses, coyotes, white-tailed deer, and possibly the elusive mink. The adjacent Blue Lake, covering 983 acres, offers a variety of water activities, including swimming, water-skiing, boating, and fishing. A replica of the keelboat that was used on the 1804 expedition sits on the lakeshore. *Open year-round. Admission charged.*

75 | Harrison County Historical Village

5 mi./9 min. East on Rte. 30. The 10 buildings in this complex provide an appealing view of the past in this area of western Iowa. An 1870 tricycle, 100-year-old light bulbs, antique wedding gowns, and a 1540 Spanish pike are among the various articles presented in the main building. The Jail exhibits the first police radio used in the county, the Medical Building displays an early X-ray machine and medicine bottles, and the Chapel has antique Bibles, including a New Testament written in Cherokee. Other buildings display early-day items such as a hickory-frame bicycle, an 1830 McCormick reaper, a 12-pound buffalo gun, and an unusual combination high chair/baby carriage. *Open Tues.–Sat. and P.M. Sun. May–Sept. Admission charged.*

57 3 | The Historic General Dodge House, Council Bluffs

Exit 57: 3 mi./5 min. South on Rte. 192, left on 9th Ave., left on 3rd St. Exit 3: 3 mi./10 min. North on 6th St., right on 5th Ave., right on 3rd St. This three-story Victorian mansion, built in 1869 by Gen. Grenville Dodge, befits the man who once surveyed some 60,000 miles of track and who later presided over 16 railroad companies. The house is elegantly detailed throughout. In the dining room, where two graceful silver tea services are displayed, the general was host to five U.S. presidents and other luminaries. On the ground floor you'll see front and back parlors with fine lace curtains, Austrian crystal chandeliers and pier mirrors at each end. A child's bedroom houses an appealing exhibit of period toys and baby clothes as well as a four-story dollhouse furnished in detail. The third-floor ballroom holds a square rosewood grand piano, a pump organ, and a large music box. *Open Tues.–Sat. and P.M. Sun. except Jan. Admission charged.*

54 | Omaha, NE 68183

Convention & Visitors Bureau, 1819 Farnam St., Suite 1200. (402) 444-4660. There's much more to Nebraska's largest city than the well-known grain and livestock business. It is also rich in parks and museums. The Joslyn Art Museum, an impressive art deco building clad in pink marble, houses fine regional and international collections. A replica of President Lincoln's funeral car, along with other railroad memorabilia, is on view at the Union Pacific Historical Museum. The Great Plains Black Museum features rare photos and displays on black American history, and the Omaha Children's Museum has a variety of hands-on exhibits. Gerald Ford was born here, and his birth site includes exhibits, gardens, and a model of the original house. The Old Market, a shopping area that was once a fruit and vegetable market, has a number of interesting shops, pubs, galleries, restaurants, and boutiques. The famous Boys Town offers self-guiding and conducted tours of its campus.

10 | Waubonsie State Park

6 mi. /8 min. East on Rte. 2, right on Rte. 239. The striking terrain of this spectacular park (named for an Indian chief) is made up of glacial sediment deposited by the wind. The dramatic landscape, with yucca and other dry-land plants, seems to have been magically transported from semiarid areas farther west of these midwestern plains. The geological formations—called loess hills—can be found only here in Iowa, in Missouri, and in China. A striking feature of the topography is the delicately terraced "cat steps" on the western side of the steep, narrow ridges. Other areas of the park are less spectacular, but they are invitingly bright with flowers in spring and colorful foliage in fall. *Open year-round. Admission charged.*

84 | Big Lake State Park

9 mi./12 min. West on Rte. 118, left on Rte. 111. At 615 acres, this is the largest natural lake in Missouri. It is an oxbow lake thought to have been left behind when the meandering Missouri River carved a more direct route downstream. It is now the habitat of beavers and other river creatures, as well as waterfowl attracted to the shallow water and lush marshlands. Pelicans, great blue herons, and in winter, bald eagles are among the more interesting species to be seen here. The lake is deep enough for boating and water-skiing; yet it is shallow enough to offer excellent fishing for catfish, carp, crappie, bass, and bluegill. *Open year-round.*

46 | St. Joseph, MO 64502

Chamber of Commerce, 7th and Felix Sts. (816) 232-4461. This pleasant city has a variety of museums and historical attractions, many of which are within an easy walk of one another. At the Pony Express Museum you'll see how the mail was carried to California for a brief period before the age of the telegraph. The Patee House Museum, once the Pony Express headquarters, now has communications displays, an old train, and a restored city street from the 1800's. Excellent exhibits on American Indians and the history of the West are housed in the St. Joseph Museum, and the Albrecht Art Museum has formal gardens and displays of American art from the past three centuries. Hundreds of antique dolls and toys reside in the city's Doll Museum, and at the Jesse James Home you can visit this famous outlaw's last place of refuge. If you find the outdoors more appealing, there are 1,550 lovely acres of city parks that invite exploration.

20 Pirtle's Weston Vineyards Winery

12 mi./15 min. West on Rte. 92, right on Rte. 45. For those who don't believe that wine is made in Missouri, there's Pirtle's. This establishment produces eight wines made from grapes, an apple wine, and mead, made from honey and described by the owner as man's oldest type of wine. All of these can be tasted and purchased in the upstairs portion of the winery, which was once a Lutheran church. Built in 1867, the brick church now has stained-glass windows made by the vintner and containing the winery's wild rose motif. The cellars, with a capacity of 20,000 gallons, occupy the church's ground floor (this area is not open to the public). *Open Mon.–Sat. and P.M. Sun. except holidays.*

I-70 Kansas City, MO 64107

Convention & Visitors Bureau, 1100 Main St., Suite 2550. (816) 221-5242; (800) 523-5953 outside MO. It may come as a surprise, but this beautifully planned city has more miles of boulevards than Paris and, like Rome, has many beautiful fountains. Its shopping centers, too, are noted for their appealing ambience. The Country Club Plaza, which spreads over 55 acres, is known for its architectural echoes of Seville, Spain, as well as for its shops; Crown Center is an 85-acre city within a city; and at Westport Square some handsome Victorian structures have been turned into shops and restaurants. Among the museums here are the unique Miniature Museum and the Nelson-Atkins Museum of Art, noted for the range of its holdings and special emphasis on works from China and India. Swope Park, which contains the Kansas City Zoo and other attractions, is one of the largest municipal parks in the nation.

I-70. *In a sleek modern setting, "Bronco Buster" recalls Kansas City's rugged past.*

I-70. *This modest home was called the Summer White House from 1945 to 1953.*

I-70 Independence, MO 64050

Truman Home Ticket and Information Center, 223 N. Main St. (816) 254-9929. As might be expected, "the man from Independence," our 33rd president, is well remembered here. There is in fact a Harry S Truman Historic District, a walking tour of which begins at the Truman home (the Summer White House) and winds through a well-preserved neighborhood of brick sidewalks and stately homes. Elsewhere in the city is the Truman Library and Museum, which has a reproduction of his White House office among other exhibits. The restored office and courtroom where Truman began his career is located in the Independence Square Courthouse. There's also a 35-minute audiovisual presentation. Other historic places include the 19-acre Bingham-Waggoner Estate and the Vaile Mansion, a classic example of Victorian architectural exuberance.

I-70 Agricultural Hall of Fame and National Center

18 mi./30 min. West on I-70 to Exit 224, north on Rte. 7; follow signs. An important aspect of Americana is recalled here in this major national institution that is dedicated to American farmers. In the Hall of Rural Living, displays re-create the parlor, sewing room, kitchen, and other elements of the country home of an imaginary grandmother. Her laundry room has manual and early electric washers, and her "back-porch yard" overflows with canning equipment and glassware. In Ye Ol' Town, scenes of rural life include a general store, a telephone exchange, a dentist's office, and a wheelwright's shop. Also noteworthy are the Museum of Farming, a vast warehouse filled with farm equipment, the National Farmers Memorial, with massive bronze-relief panels depicting farmers past, present, and future, and Farm Town U.S.A., which includes a 100-year-old railroad station, a blacksmith's shop, and a restored one-room schoolhouse. *Open daily Apr.–Nov. Admission charged.* &

I-70 Wyandotte County Historical Society and Museum

21 mi./30 min. West on I-70 to Exit 224, north on Rte. 7; follow signs. History here in the heart of the Central Plains starts with the Indians, most notably the Wyandots, an educated people who emigrated from Ohio in 1843 and built a town complete with church, school, and council house. The exhibits in this museum trace life in the region from those days until well into this century. Other displays concentrate on local industries. Transportation is a popular theme, with memorabilia from the railroads and riverboats, which caused this strategically located crossroads to boom, and from the various streetcars that once plied the streets of nearby Kansas City, Kansas. A 1903 steam-driven fire truck is also on display. *Open Tues.–Sun. late Feb.–late Dec. except Thanksgiving Day.*

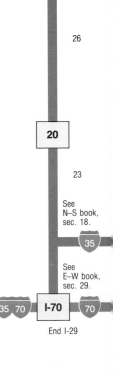

51

84

38

46

26

20

23

See N–S book, sec. 18.

35

See E–W book, sec. 29.

35 70 · I-70 · 70

End I-29

256

235

21

21

214

34

235

49

180

131

I-35 West | I-35 East

256 The Depot, Duluth

1 min. Continue on Michigan St. Duluth's splendid old Union Depot has been transformed into a series of museums, galleries, and a theater. At ground level is Depot Square, a complex of turn-of-the-century shops and the Lake Superior Museum of Transportation. Minnesota's first railway engine, the 1861 brown and yellow *William Crooks,* is resplendent with sparkling steel and brass fixtures and a green boiler. On Level 2 there are displays about early settlers as well as excellent collections of costumes, dolls, and glass. Level 3 features the Heritage Room, with exhibits ranging from Victorian furniture to tin bathtubs, and Level 4 has the Sieur Dulhut Room, which documents the culture of the native Ojibwas and offers a gallery of paintings of Indian life by Eastman Johnson. *Open daily except Thanksgiving Day, Christmas Eve, Christmas Day, New Year's Day, and Easter. Admission charged.*

235 Jay Cooke State Park

6 mi./8 min. East on Rte. 210. The St. Louis River has cut a deep gorge through the rugged terrain here, where the dramatic sound of rushing water contrasts with the stately serenity of the hardwood forest. Beginning near the nature center, the Carlton Trail traverses an enchanting landscape that includes a swinging bridge, tilted slabs of rock sliced by waterfalls, isolated pools, and birch-covered islands in midstream. Oldenburg Point, an overlook on the more elevated Ogantz Trail, affords a scenic view of the river valley. Other trails penetrate the forested interior. Altogether, there are some 50 miles of trails in the park. *Open year-round. Admission charged.*

214 Moose Lake State Recreation Area

1 min. East on Rte. 137. Echo Lake, edged with meadows, marshland, and woods, attracts anglers who try for bass, pike, or panfish. To the north of the lake lie about a thousand acres of pleasant rolling terrain that was once farmland. Today it is planted with pine and spruce to supplement the stands of mature aspen, birch, and maple. One hiking trail follows the edge of the lake, and three others extend into the wooded slopes. *Open year-round. Admission charged.*

180 Kanabec History Center, Mora

19 mi./24 min. West on Rte. 23. Located in a 30-acre park on the Snake River, this museum preserves the history and portrays the lives of the early settlers of Minnesota's heartland. Exhibits include an abundant assortment of homemade furnishings, such as cabinets, cupboards, and tables; early household and agricultural equipment; manuscripts; and photographs. On the grounds you will find a 1904 schoolhouse and an 1899 log structure, along with early farm machinery. Seasonal highlights include quilt shows, craft demonstrations, workshops, and art exhibits. The history center's library has genealogical listings and other family historical data, which are available to the public for research. *Open Mon.–Sat. and P.M. Sun. and holidays. Admission charged.*

131 Carlos Avery Wildlife Area

5.5 mi./9 min. West on Rte. 18. The meadows and marshland of this beautiful, unspoiled wildlife preserve are traversed by sandy roads that may present a challenge in winter and spring to vehicles designed for more civilized surfaces. Nevertheless, the reeds and cattails that alternate with tracts of oak, birch, and aspen create an interesting environment for appreciative observers of nature. Certain parts of the area, which have been designated as wildlife sanctuaries, are not open to the public. *Open year-round.*

17C Minneapolis–St. Paul, MN 55402

Convention & Visitors Association, 15 S. 5th St. (612) 348-4313; (800) 445-7412 outside MN. In summer the parks and waterways clearly dominate the activity here near the headwaters of the Mississippi River. Less obvious are the ways Minnesotans use to cope with the cold. In the dead of winter the enclosed skyways can make you forget you are this far north. Nicollet Mall is a focal point in Minneapolis. Its famed Guthrie Theater and Walker Art Center beckon, there's an excellent zoo, and the Grain Exchange offers a look at the operations of a grain market. Across the river in St. Paul you can visit the state capitol, the Science Museum of Minnesota, the opulent Victorian mansion of territorial governor Alexander Ramsey, and if you choose to forsake the comfort of the skyways in late January, the Winter Carnival.

235. *These jagged rocks have long resisted the smoothing action of the St. Louis River.*

3B Valleyfair, Shakopee

9 mi./15 min. Southwest on Rte. 13 and Rte. 101, right on Valley Park Dr. Thrilling rides with such exhilarating names as Looping Starship, High Roller, Corkscrew, and Flying Trapeze entice the adventurous to this 65-acre amusement park. A six-story movie theater with a gigantic screen offers excitement similar to that of the rides, and six theatrical programs throughout the park feature live entertainment. *Open mid-May–Labor Day; weekends only in Sept. Admission charged.*   ⊼

92 Minnesota Zoo, Apple Valley

3 min. South on Cedar Ave.; follow signs. Almost everything about this zoo is exemplary: the grounds are clean and well landscaped, displays are nicely labeled and described, and the animals live in appropriate environments. Five different trails explore a variety of habitats. The Ocean Trail has crabs, clown fish, and sea anemones; the cry of tropical birds echoing from cliffs can be heard on the Tropics Trail; the Minnesota Trail shows animals native to the region; the Northern Trail has hardy outdoor animals; and the Discovery Trail permits close encounters with a number of domestic and exotic animals. *Open daily except Christmas. Admission charged.*   ♿

56 Sakatah Lake State Park

13 mi./20 min. West on Rte. 60. This state park lies on the south shore of Sakatah Lake. The lake, actually a widening of the Cannon River, was created when massive blocks of ice were left behind by retreating glaciers at the end of the Ice Age—some 11,000 years ago. The river is a natural ecological boundary between Minnesota's "big woods" country to the north and the oak barrens to the south. The rolling terrain of the park is wooded with bur oaks, white oaks, walnut trees, and other hardwoods; and it is traversed by a section of the 42-mile Sakatah Singing Hills State Trail. This multiple-use trail, which follows the right-of-way of an abandoned railway line, is suitable for bicycling. *Open year-round. Admission charged.*   ⊼ ⛺ 🚐 🚶 🐟 🎣

92. *Cool cat. A Siberian tiger, obviously comfortable in the snows of Minnesota.*

40 The Village of Yesteryear, Owatonna

3 mi./7 min. East on Rte. 14/218, left on Rte. 6 (Austin Rd.). The centerpiece of this fine historical village in southern Minnesota is Dunnell House, built in 1868–69 and featuring a "widow's walk" cupola modeled after examples in Maine. The house has some unusual antiques, including hand-painted Bavarian china, a decanter once used by President Lincoln, and a variety of antique hats, lace blouses, and dresses. Victorian toys and baby carriages are displayed in the basement. On the grounds are eight other historical buildings, including St. Wenceslaus Church, built in 1876 by Bohemian Catholics in the former town of Saco. *Open P.M. Wed. and weekends mid-May–mid-Sept. Admission charged.*

13 Freeborn County Museum and Village, Albert Lea

5 min. West on I-90 to Exit 158, south on Bridge Ave.; follow signs. Twelve historic buildings are preserved here in southern Minnesota, along with a variety of exhibits that tell the story of this county's early days. The main exhibition hall displays pioneer articles ranging from trunks and baby clothes to a Swedish harp. There's also a well-equipped kitchen, a comfortable parlor, an elegant millinery shop, Indian artifacts, antique bottles, a mammoth

tusk from a local gravel pit, and much more. The Red Barn houses a fully equipped train depot, a barbershop, bank, jail, firehouse, tractors, steam engines, agricultural equipment, and automobiles.

Elsewhere in the village is the first log house in Freeborn County (built in 1853), a rural schoolhouse, a hardware store, a collection of millstones, a genteel parsonage, a cobbler's shop, an 1870's church, and a general store that stocks everything from hatpins to horse collars. *Open P.M. Tues.–Sun. June–Aug.; P.M. Sun. May and Sept.–Oct. Admission charged.*   ♿

11 Helmer Myre State Park

3 min. East on Rte. 46, right on Rte. 38. The sweet smell of tall-grass prairie and the shining expanse of Albert Lea Lake (2,600 acres) are the most immediate attractions of this park in southern Minnesota. The terrain reflects the park's glacial past and varies from prairie to oak savanna, marsh, forest, and esker. The park is well known for its waterfowl and shorebirds, and more than 450 varieties of wildflowers grow here. Hikers will find several well-maintained trails, and canoe rentals are available. An interpretive center on Big Island features an outstanding collection of Indian artifacts. *Open year-round. Admission charged.*   ⊼ ⛺ 🚐 🚶 🎣

27

17C
94

See E–W book, sec. 12.

14   39

3B

92

I-35 West   I-35 East

35   32

56

16

40

27

See E–W book, sec. 5.

13   90

2

11

MN
IA

21

35

35

208

14

194

29

165

54

ROUTE
30

24

I-235 80

See
E–W book,
sec. 21.

15

80 I-235

4

68

12

208 Rice Lake State Park

10 mi./15 min. West on Rte. A38, right on Rte. R74. The park lies on small but attractive Rice Lake, which has an irregular wooded shoreline. A trail for hikers and horseback riders follows the shore; there is also a stone picnic shelter and a place from which to launch canoes. *Open year-round. Admission charged.*

194 Kinney Pioneer Museum

2 min. East on Rte. 18. The museum's comprehensive displays reveal what the old days were like in north-central Iowa. Military collections span the Civil War and World War I, and several period rooms exhibit such local furnishings as the 1878 cradle used for the first child born to settlers in nearby Clear Lake, and a grand piano brought by oxcart from Dubuque. There are good displays of looms, sewing machines, and radios and cameras (including a World War II Japanese gun camera). Antique dolls, music boxes, an apple press, a telephone switchboard, several working models of steam engines, horse-drawn vehicles, vintage automobiles, and a broom maker actually assembling brooms all add to the museum's period atmosphere.

On the grounds you can see a furnished log cabin, a blacksmith's shop, a one-room schoolhouse dating from 1921, and a caboose from the Milwaukee Railroad that's full of related memorabilia: a book of yellowing Iowa Central waybills from 1904, old photographs, telegrams, and overalls. *Open P.M. Wed.–Fri. and Sun., May–Sept. Admission charged.*

165 Beeds Lake State Park

8 mi./11 min. East on Rte. 3; follow signs. A trail winds around the wooded shore of the unusually lovely man-made lake in this park, and a 600-foot dike provides an enticing sandy swimming beach. The dam itself has a high stone spillway, and in the spring a wide pool forms at the bottom of the bubbling waterfall. The park is also an animal and bird refuge. Overall, the gentle and attractive terrain makes an appealing change from the farm country that surrounds the park. *Open year-round. Admission charged.*

ROUTE 30 Ledges State Park

21 mi./30 min. West on Rte. 30, left on Rte. 17; follow signs. This park is a wild area that gets its unusual name from the sand-

208. *This pair of Canada geese created their nest from the available building supplies.*

stone cliffs on Pease Creek, a miniature canyonland in the woods that can be seen from a loop road. (In wet weather the creek may overflow, closing the road.) Several trails wind up and down the park's ravines and ridges, and overlooks (especially the aptly named Inspiration Point) provide some spectacular vistas of the floodplain of the Des Moines River. On the Riverside Floodplain Trail you'll find an observation area in a region of wetlands prairie, and for bird-watchers there's a wildfowl blind on Lost Lake along the Ledges Nature Trail. On the Wildlife Loop Trail you can see exhibits of several native animals in their natural environment. *Open year-round. Admission charged.*

I-235 Des Moines, IA 50309

I-235 *Convention & Visitors Bureau, 309 Court Ave., Suite 300. (800) 451-2625.* Across from the gold-domed capitol, the Iowa State Historical Building provides an introduction to the history and prehistory of the region. The governor's house, Terrace Hill, is a superb example of a mid-19th-century mansion, which is now opulently furnished as it was in the 1870's. Salisbury House is a 42-room replica of King's House in Salisbury, England. The interior spaces contain furnishings in the Tudor style and are highlighted by the rich colors of Oriental rugs and stained-glass windows. Modern tastes in art and architecture are displayed in the Des Moines Art Center. Visitors can ride a train through the grounds of the Blank Park Zoo.

68 Walnut Woods State Park

5 min. East on Rte. 5; follow signs. Here on the bank of the Raccoon River is one of the largest surviving natural stands of black walnut trees in North America. These majestic specimens tower over a stone lodge set on manicured lawns, lending the park an impressive manorial character. Picnickers appreciate the tree-shaded grounds beside the river, while fishermen concentrate mostly on catching catfish. Both walking trails and bridle paths invite further exploration of the park. *Open year-round. Admission charged.*

56. *This is the view of one hot-air balloon in flight as seen from another.*

56 | National Balloon Museum, Indianola

15 mi./17 min. East on Rte. 92, left on Rte. 65/69 (N. Jefferson St.). Indianola is proud of its position as host of a national race of some 200 ballons, usually held for ten days from late July to early August. This museum is an offshoot of that event. Its collection illustrates the colorful history of ballooning as depicted on pewter and china plates, commemorative medals, postage stamps, and enamel lapel badges representing specific balloons as well as in historical photographs, prints, and paintings. Samples of balloon fabrics and gas cylinders and a World War II training basket are also on display. A new building has been designed with an interior spacious enough to accommodate an inflated balloon. *Open Mon.–Fri., by appointment on weekends (515) 961-8415, except holidays.*

56 | Madison County Museum and Historical Complex, Winterset

11 mi./21 min. West on Rte. 92, left on Rte. P71 (1st St.), right on W. Summit St., left on S. 2nd Ave. Set atop a hill in the town of Winterset, this museum commands a view of present-day Madison County, and its large collection illuminates the region's past. Among many other objects you can see dolls, tin toys, musical instruments, local advertising items, clocks, clothing, medical and dental equipment, household utensils, Indian artifacts, portraits, farm equipment, quilts, fossils, and—if you can imagine it—a collection of some 7,500 pencils and ballpoint pens.

Outside the main building are three authentic log structures: a blacksmith's shop, an 1850's schoolhouse, and a log house that later became the Pleasant View Post Office. *Open daily mid-May–mid-Oct. Admission charged.* ♿

4 | Nine Eagles State Park, Davis City

10 mi./12 min. East on Rte. 69, right on Rte. J66. Miles of hiking and equestrian trails wind over the 1,100 acres of ridged and heavily wooded terrain in the park. A sandy swimming beach provides access to the beautifully clear waters of Nine Eagles Lake. The park's notable fauna include white-tailed deer, pheasants, wild turkeys, and a variety of migratory aquatic birds. Anglers can test their mettle against the bass, bluegill, crappie, and channel catfish in the lake. *Open year-round. Admission charged.* 🍽 ⛺ 🚐 🚶 🏊 🎣 ♿

92 | Lake Paho Wildlife Area

23 mi./30 min. East on Rte. 136. The lake comes as a relief to the eye amid the vast green and yellow checkerboard of this rich farm country. Paho (from the Indian word meaning "first") was the first lake constructed by Missouri's Department of Conservation; and it is first and foremost a place for fishermen, who try for catfish, crappie, bluegill, walleye, and largemouth bass. Bow-and-arrow fishing is permitted in season. You can rent boats for fishing. A number of fish-rearing ponds adjoin the lake; the 8- to 10-inch fingerlings are used to stock lakes in all parts of the state. Birdwatchers will delight in the resident flock of huge Canada geese, as well as the migratory birds seen in spring and fall. *Open year-round.* 🍽 ⛺ 🚐 🎣

48 | Wallace State Park

3 min. South on Rte. 69, left on Rte. 121. This is a small park (500 acres), but its terrain is surprisingly wild and heavily wooded. Several hiking trails crisscross the land, allowing visitors to explore the valleys and ridges formed when streams cut through the glacial loess that underlies the rolling landscape of this part of northwestern Missouri. Deer Creek winds through the park, its banks shaded by majestic sycamores. (Some historians claim that a Mormon trail once crossed the creek.)

Six-acre Lake Allaman lies in a natural clearing near the park's center. It has sandy swimming beaches, and it is also popular with anglers, who seek bluegill, largemouth bass, and channel catfish. A trail traces most of its perimeter. Bird-watching is another popular activity here. *Open year-round.* 🍽 ⛺ 🚐 🚶 🏊 🎣

26 | Watkins Woolen Mill State Historic Site, Lawson

7 mi./16 min. East on Rte. 92, left on Rte. RA. These 475 acres, once part of Waltus Watkins's 19th-century plantation, represent an early and very successful example of an enterprise that integrated both farming and industry. The site's main attraction is Watkins Mill—the only 19th-century woolen mill in America that still has all its original machinery, from carding and spinning to weaving and finishing equipment. During the Civil War the mill turned out blankets and cloth that were purchased by both the Union and the Confederacy.

Watkins's brick home, an example of Greek revival architecture, is furnished to reflect the taste of the 1870's. Restored outbuildings include a summer kitchen and the octagonal Franklin School.

The Watkins Mill State Park grounds are mostly wooded, providing a pleasant contrast to the surrounding farmland. A paved biking and hiking trail traces Williams Creek Lake, which fishermen appreciate for its bass, catfish, and sunfish. You can picnic in the historic area near the mill or beside the lake. *Park open year-round; mill open daily except Thanksgiving Day, Christmas, New Year's Day, and Easter. Admission charged.* 🍽 ⛺ 🚐 🚶 🏊 🎣

56

52

4

IA
MO

27

92

44

48

22

26

See N–S book, sec. 15.

29

35

24

I-70 Independence, MO 64050

Truman Home Ticket and Information Center, 223 N. Main St. (816) 254-9929. The man from Independence, our 33rd president, is well remembered here. There is a Harry S Truman Historic District, a walking tour of which begins at the Truman home (the Summer White House) and winds through a neighborhood of brick sidewalks and stately homes. The restored office and courtroom where Truman began his career is in the Independence Square Courthouse. Other historic places include the 19-acre Bingham-Waggoner Estate and the Vaile Mansion, a classic example of Victorian architectural exuberance.

2C Kansas City, MO 64107

Convention & Visitors Bureau, 1100 Main St., Suite 2550. (816) 221-5242; (800) 523-5953 outside MO. It may come as a surprise, but this beautifully planned city has more miles of boulevards than Paris and, like Rome, has many beautiful fountains. Its shopping centers are noted for their appealing ambience. The Country Club Plaza has architectural echoes of Seville, Spain; Crown Center is an 85-acre city within a city; and at Westport Square some

handsome Victorian structures have been converted into shops and restaurants. Among the museums here are the unique Miniature Museum and the Nelson-Atkins Museum of Art, noted for the range of its holdings and an emphasis on works from China and India. Swope Park, with the Kansas City Zoo and other attractions, is one of the nation's largest municipal parks.

I-70 Agricultural Hall of Fame and National Center

18 mi./30 min. West on I-70 to Exit 224, north on Rte. 7; follow signs. An important aspect of Americana is recalled in a national institution dedicated to farmers. In the Hall of Rural Living, displays re-create the parlor, sewing room, and kitchen of the country home of an imaginary grandmother. Her "back-porch yard" overflows with canning equipment. The scenes of rural life in Ye Ol' Town include a general store, a telephone exchange, and a wheelwright's shop. Also noteworthy are the Museum of Farming, a warehouse filled with farm equipment, the National Farmers Memorial, which displays bronze-relief panels, and Farm Town U.S.A., with a 100-year-old railroad station and a restored one-room schoolhouse. *Open daily Apr.–Nov. Admission charged.* ♿

I-70 Wyandotte County Historical Society and Museum

21 mi./30 min. West on I-70 to Exit 224, north on Rte. 7; follow signs. History here in the heart of the Central Plains starts with the Indians, most notably the Wyandots, an educated people who emigrated from Ohio in 1843 and built a town complete with church, school, and council house. These Huron people gave their name to the county that today contains Kansas City, Kansas. The exhibits in this museum trace life in the region from those days until well into this century. Other displays concentrate on local industries. Transportation is a popular theme, with memorabilia from the railroads and riverboats, which caused this strategic crossroads to boom, and from the streetcars that once plied Kansas City's streets. A 1903 steam-driven fire truck is also on display. *Open Tues.–Sun. late Feb.–late Dec. except Thanksgiving Day.*

187 183 Old Depot Museum, Ottawa

5 min. Exit 187: west on Rte. 68, left on Rte. 59 (Main St.), right on Tecumseh St. Exit 183: north on Rte. 59 (Main St.), left on Tecumseh St. The depot-stationhouse that shelters this local historical collection was built in the late 1800's by the Santa Fe Railroad. Spacious rooms—from a typical schoolroom and a Victorian parlor to a general store and a dentist's office—re-create everyday life in 19th-century Kansas. Other displays are devoted to regional military and transportation history. *Open P.M. Sun. May–Sept.*

155 Melvern State Park

11 mi./17 min. North on Rte. 75, left on Rte. 278. Pleasantly located on the northern shore of 6,900-acre Melvern Lake, this well-developed park is popular for camping, fishing, boating, water-skiing, swimming, and horseback riding. One of the park's most attractive features is a 395-acre tract of virgin tallgrass prairie, providing 20th-century vacationers with a glimpse of what the land looked like centuries ago, when vast herds of bison roamed across present-day Kansas. *Open year-round. Admission charged.* ⛽ ⛺ 🚐 🚶 🏊 🎣 ♿

2C. *"The Scout" and his horse overlook a scene that was unimaginable in their time.*

187–183. *This reproduced parlor depicts the engaging clutter of Victorian decor.*

| 130 | **Emporia Gazette Building** |

5 min. South on Rte. 99, left on 12th St., right on Merchant St. This is a working newspaper office, and though formal tours are offered by appointment only, unofficial tours given by well-informed staff members can usually be arranged through the receptionist in the lobby. The *Gazette*, a stronghold of liberal Republicanism, was once the domain of William Allen White, the paper's longtime editor (1895–1944) and the confidant of presidents (including both of the Roosevelts). A display room showcases White's books and other memorabilia, and his small office, used since the turn of the century, can be seen. The newsroom also retains its old-fashioned ambience despite the contemporary computer terminals used by reporters. *Open Mon.–Fri. and A.M. Sat. except holidays.*

| 71 | **Butler County Historical Museum, El Dorado** |

5 min. East on Rte. 54 (Central Ave.). The colorful history of this south-central region of Kansas from the era of the Wichita Indi-

ans, through Old West cattle drives, to the discovery of oil in 1915, is captured in this excellent museum. El Dorado became a boomtown during the era of frenzied oil drilling, and the town remains prosperous to this day. The rambling outdoor exhibit area, which includes a full-size oil derrick, is as engaging as the artifacts and historical exhibits housed inside. A shaded picnic area and playground are near the museum. *Open Tues.–Sat. except holidays.* 🚻 ♿

| 49 | **Wichita, KS 67202** |

Convention & Visitors Bureau, 100 S. Main St. (316) 265-2800. Although it's the largest city in Kansas and a major producer of petroleum and aircraft, the days of the buffalo, cowboys, and cattle drivers are not forgotten in Wichita. The Native American presence is thoughtfully represented in the Indian Center Museum. At Old Cowtown Museum some 30 buildings on 17 acres authentically re-create a frontier town in the days when Wichita was a stopping place on the Chisholm Trail.

A fascinating cross section of life in Victorian times can be seen at the Wichita–Sedgwick County Historical Museum, in a Romanesque revival extravaganza known as the Palace of the Plains, which was built in 1892. Several other interests may be pursued at the Omnisphere and Science Center, the innovative Children's Museum, a beautiful botanic garden, and the city's excellent zoo. For art lovers there's the Wichita Art Museum, and on the Wichita State University campus you can see a superb collection of outdoor sculptures and explore the Ulrich Museum.

| 33 | **Bartlett Arboretum** |
| 19 | |

Exit 33: 10.5 mi./16 min. West on Rte. 53, left on Rte. 81, left on Rte. 55. Exit 19: 16 mi./20 min. West on Rte. 160, right on Rte. 81, right on Rte. 55. This fragrant oasis is a refreshing contrast to the surrounding flat grasslands of south-central Kansas. Its 20 acres of flowers, ornamental trees, and colorful shrubs can be seen from the shaded walkways that follow the edges of the still waters of the lagoon. Some 25,000 tulips bloom in the spring and thou-

sands of chrysanthemums in the fall. But this arboretum is still lovely, and much less crowded, when the flowers have finished blooming. *Open daily Apr.–mid-Nov. Admission charged.*

| 214 | **Pioneer Woman Statue and Museum, Ponca City** |

18 mi./30 min. East on Rte. 60, left on Rte. 60 (business), left on Rte. 77, right on Lake Rd. This memorial to the courage and fortitude of pioneer womanhood stands appropriately on one of the last parcels of land to be homesteaded in Oklahoma. The 17-foot bronze statue depicts a youthful, undaunted pioneer woman striding alongside her young son. Commissioned by oil magnate and onetime Oklahoma governor E. W. Marland, it was dedicated in 1930. The adjacent museum, which was built about 30 years later, has in its collection a variety of appliances, furnishings, clothing, and other pioneer trappings that show what daily life was like for those who settled and tamed the Oklahoma prairie around the turn of the century. *Museum open Wed.–Sat. and P.M. Sun. except Christmas; statue accessible year-round.* 🚻

214. *"Pioneer Woman" and son stride purposefully (and forever) westward.*

59

71

22

49

16

33

14

19

KS

OK

39

214

28

35

See
E–W book,
sec. 39.

186 Cherokee Strip Museum

1 min. East on Rte. 64. On Sept. 16, 1893, more than 100,000 people waited for the gunshot that signaled the start of a race to claim a free piece of this flat cinnamon-colored land. The museum illustrates the hard life of the homesteaders by featuring re-creations of a 19th-century doctor's office, a general store, and a pioneer kitchen. Paintings by local artists, Oto-Missouri beadwork, and other Indian artwork represent the territory's inhabitants before 1893. A one-room schoolhouse, a sorghum mill, a jail, a horse-drawn threshing machine, and an enclosure with two white-tailed deer occupy the tree-shaded grounds of the museum. *Open Tues.–Fri. and P.M.. Sat.–Sun. except holidays.*

157 Oklahoma Territorial Museum, Guthrie

2 mi./6 min. West on Rte. 33, left on Ash St., left on Oklahoma St. This spacious museum incorporates the Carnegie Library, where the first state governor was inaugurated in 1907 during Guthrie's brief reign

157. *The pump organ still evokes the charm of family music-making at home.*

as Oklahoma's capital. The Pfeiffer Memorial Building, also part of the museum, contains displays of pioneer life. New exhibits portray the wild land rush during which the Oklahoma Territory was settled by white pioneers in 1889. Another gallery houses a windmill, and there are stagecoaches, phaetons, and other horse-drawn vehicles. You'll even find examples of pump organs and other musical instruments that somehow found their way to the raw frontier. A large collection of cowboy and Indian portraits also includes a portrait of Lon Chaney, who got his start in show business as a stagehand at a Guthrie music hall. *Open Tues.–Fri. and P.M. Sat.–Sun. except holidays.*

157 State Capital Publishing Museum, Guthrie

2 mi./8 min. West on Rte. 33, left on 2nd St.; follow signs. The fiery editorials of the daily newspaper published in this four-story Victorian building were one reason why officials moved the state capital from Guthrie to Oklahoma City in 1910; a year later the *State Capital* failed. But the building was used for publishing until the 1970's; in 1982 it was converted into a museum. Some aspects of a turn-of-the-century newspaper plant are evoked by a Victorian sales office with a beautifully restored teller's cage and an exhibit of antique typewriters. The pressroom is filled with inky old printshop machinery, including Linotypes and a battery of platen and cylinder presses. *Open Tues.–Sat. and P.M. Sun. except holidays.*

I-40 Oklahoma City, OK 73102

Convention and Tourism Bureau, 4 Santa Fe Plaza. (405) 278-8912. The highlights in this large city, more than 600 square miles in area, are widespread and varied. The National Cowboy Hall of Fame and Western Heritage Center attracts those interested in western lore and artifacts, and the National Softball Hall of Fame appeals to sandlot ballplayers of all ages. The state capitol is unique in that there are producing oil wells on its grounds. Nearby, the State Museum presents the major events in the colorful history of the Indian Territory and Oklahoma. Kirkpatrick Center is a large museum complex featuring African, Oriental, and American Indian art, as well as photography, science, and aerospace displays, a planetarium, and gardens. Oklahoma City's enormous zoo has some 4,000 animals in addition to the Aquaticus, which features dolphin and sea lion shows and varied displays of aquatic life.

108 Little River State Park, Clear Bay Area, Norman

17 mi./20 min. East on Rte. 9; follow signs. Oak-covered hills surround Lake Thunderbird, a popular spot for swimming, sailing, sailboarding, and water-skiing (skis and boats are rented at Calypso Cove). Fishermen try for crappie, bass, and catfish, and a stable in the park offers horseback riding and hayrides. If you hike along the trail, you may see a "rock rose," a reddish-brown rose-shaped cluster of sandy barite crystals sometimes found on sandstone outcroppings. After long weathering, the "roses" become detached and fall down onto the sandy soil. *Open year-round. Admission charged.*

51 Turner Falls Park, Davis

5 min. Exit 51: south on Rte. 77. Exit 47: north on Rte. 77. Where Honey Creek plunges 77 feet over limestone ledges and through holes dissolved in the canyon walls, it forms the largest waterfall in Oklahoma. The creek's two natural pools below the falls, one with a sandy beach, have helped swimmers escape the summertime heat since 1868. Visitors can hike steep trails to caves, a natural limestone arch, and fortresslike rock formations near the falls, or take a 1½-mile trip on a miniature train. The woodlands of oak, sycamore, and eastern red cedar are home to white-tailed deer, raccoons, opossums, and a variety of birds. *Open year-round. Admission charged.*

31A Eliza Cruce Hall Doll Museum, Ardmore

5 min. East on Rte. 199, left on E St. to Ardmore Public Library. This delightful assortment of more than 300 rare and unusual dolls was assembled from many countries by Eliza Cruce Hall of Ardmore. Among the entrancing figures in the display are "court dolls" of carved wood that belonged to Marie Antoinette, an English Queen Anne doll (circa 1728), wood and leather English peddler dolls, dolls made in 1860 to model the latest fashions, and a pair of George and Martha Washington bisque dolls by Emma Clear. Other items include character dolls, miniatures, china dolls, Bye-Lo babies, Kabuki dancers, wax dolls, and toys from around the world. The collection will appeal as much to adults as to children. *Open Mon.–Sat.* ♿

24 Lake Murray State Park

4 min. East on Rte. 77S (scenic). The clear waters of Lake Murray, in Oklahoma's largest park, have made it a favorite site for water sports. Abundant bulrushes, cattails, and other vegetation at the lake provide a habitat for the sizable fish population that draws herons and bald eagles as well as anglers. On land you can play tennis or golf, ride horses or bicycles, or go hiking through forests of oak, ash, elm, red cedar, and hickory. The unique Tucker Tower, a fortresslike museum and nature center set atop a 25-foot rock cliff, features displays of local fossils, minerals, and artifacts. *Park open year-round; tower open Wed.–Mon. mid-May–mid-Sept.; Wed.–Sun. mid-Sept.–mid-May.* ⛢ ⛺ 🚐 🚶 🚤 🎣 ♿

496B Leonard Park–Frank Buck Memorial Zoo, Gainesville

1 min. Southwest on Rte. 51. Aristocratic-looking Chilean flamingos wade through a shallow pool, acrobatic monkeys cavort in their cages, and peacocks fan their multi-colored feathers as they roam freely around the grounds. Named for a Gainesville native who captured and trained wild animals, the Frank Buck Zoo displays animals in ways that permit remarkably close viewing. One of the most popular residents is Gerry, an elephant who survived a Texas flash flood by holding her trunk above the water for 24 hours when her body was pinned between a building and a tree. Verdant Leonard Park features the area's first jail and a Civil War veterans' monument that recounts the grim story of local lynchings. *Open year-round.* ⛢ 🚤 ♿

428D Dallas, TX 75202

Convention & Visitors Bureau, 400 S. Houston St. (lobby of Union Station). (214) 746-6700. Highlights of life in Dallas include the Neiman-Marcus store, the Cotton Bowl, banking, business, glass-walled skyscrapers, and the $50 million Dallas

428D. *A dazzling Dallas skyline brightens the prairie for miles around.*

Museum of Art. At Fair Park the old and the new are combined with a steam train museum, a science museum, and an aquarium. In Old City Park a bit of 19th-century Dallas is preserved. There's a famous zoo and some unusual museums, such as the Biblical Arts Center and the Telephone Pioneer Museum. Although they recall a time of national trauma, the John F. Kennedy Memorial Plaza and the Texas School Book Depository attract many visitors.

54A Fort Worth, TX 76109

54B *Convention and Visitors Bureau, 123 E. Exchange Ave. (817) 624-4741.* Although a large modern city, Fort Worth has not forgotten the Texas of song and story. Activities at the Stockyards Historical District on the north side of the city include cattle trading and shopping for rodeo gear and western wear. The city also boasts three world-famous art museums: the Kimbell, which displays works ranging from pre-Columbian times to the present; the Amon Carter, which has a fine collection of sculpture, photographs, and paintings featuring the American West; and the Modern Art Museum of Fort Worth, noted for its 20th-century art. The Museum of Science and History offers imaginative exhibits of interest to children as well as adults. The city center is enhanced by the terraced Water Gardens.

ROUTE 67 Cleburne State Recreation Area

23 mi./35 min. Southwest on Rte. 67, left on Park Rd. 21. In the midst of rolling and flat grazing land, this tranquil 1,068-acre park provides a beautiful wooded oasis. The deer, quail, and raccoons that made this a favorite Indian hunting ground are still abundant, and many bird varieties can be observed. The park's 110-acre lake, backed up behind an earthen dam, is filled with clear water that comes from underground springs, and it invites swimming, boating, and fishing. *Open year-round. Admission charged.* ⛢ ⛺ 🚐 🚶 🚤 🎣

368A Lake Whitney State Recreation Area

19 mi./30 min. West on Rte. 22, right on Rte. FM933, left on Rte. FM1244. An attractive lake extending for 45 miles along the Brazos River was an added benefit of a dam built to control flooding and produce power. This 1,000-acre park lets the visitor take full advantage of the lake, which has an excellent swimming beach and is a popular spot for fishing. The park's flat grasslands and occasional clumps of hardwoods provide protection for a variety of wildlife, including deer, raccoons, opossums, armadillos, and many kinds of birds. In spring the plains are carpeted with brightly colored wildflowers. *Open year-round. Admission charged.* ⛢ ⛺ 🚐 🚤 🎣

Section ⑲ (356 miles)
See map page IV.

OK
TX
33
496B
I-35 West   I-35 East
61   68
54A
54B   428D
20
See E–W book, sec. 44.
28
ROUTE 67   60
30
I-35 West   I-35 East
368A
33
35

335B
41
294A
35
259
26
233A
18
215
9
206
15
191
16

335B — Texas Ranger Hall of Fame and Museum, Waco

1 min. East from exit. Often outnumbered but rarely outfought, the Texas Rangers have become an American legend. They were established by Stephen Austin in 1823, when Texas was still part of Mexico, to protect American settlers. Fittingly, this museum, dedicated to commemorating the exploits of these colorful lawmen, has one of the finest and largest collections of Old West memorabilia to be seen in Texas. The gun collection is especially notable, including many used by famous people (such as Billy the Kid and Buffalo Bill) or involved at historic incidents (the shoot-out that killed Bonnie and Clyde). Ft. Fisher Park, which surrounds the museum, has more than 100 campsites and fishing piers on the Brazos River. *Park open year-round; museum open daily except Thanksgiving Day, Christmas, and New Year's Day. Admission charged.*

294A — Belton Lake

5 mi./15 min. West on Rte. 190 (business), right on Rte. 317, left on Rte. 439. Backed up behind an earthen dam, this lake, built and run by the U.S. Army Corps of Engineers, extends for some 26 miles along the valleys of the Leon River and Cowhouse Creek. The lake's main purpose is to prevent flooding and to supply water, but the 13 parks along its southern and eastern shorelines also offer more than 225 campsites and access to the water for water-skiing, sailing, and fishing. Although there are no lifeguards and only one developed beach, swimming is permitted at many sites. Check at the headquarters building for maps and information on the parks. *Open year-round.*

259 — Inner Space Cavern

1 min. West from exit. On your way to or from the cavern, which extends under the interstate, you'll pass directly over it. Discovered in 1963, the cavern contains some magnificent examples of stalactites, stalagmites, and flowstone as well as the smaller, much rarer helictites, which grow in all directions and produce beautiful, delicate shapes. Also found here are the remains of a number of Ice Age animals, including the woolly mammoth, saber-toothed tiger, and other extinct species. A guided tour of the cavern takes about an hour, and its natural wonders have been enhanced by sound and light shows. *Open daily Memorial Day–Labor Day; Wed.–Sun. rest of year except 2 weeks during Christmas holidays. Admission charged.*

233A — Austin, TX 78704

Convention & Visitors Bureau, 400BS. 1st St. (512) 478-0098. When Mirabeau Lamar, who later served as president of the Republic of Texas, camped with some buffalo hunters here on the Colorado River in 1838, he reportedly suggested that this would be a good place for the capital of the new republic—which it became. The current state capitol building—in true Texas style—is taller than the U.S. Capitol in Washington. The river, called Town Lake where it runs through the city, is still a major attraction, and Zilker Park, with access to the lake, has canoe rentals. The park is noted for its azaleas, roses, oriental garden, miniature train ride, and the Texas-size spring-fed swimming pool.

In the Texas Memorial Museum you'll see reconstructed dinosaurs, Indian artifacts, dioramas, and a large gun collection.

215 / 206 — Pioneer Town, Wimberley

Exit 215: 21 mi./35 min. West on Rte. 150, left on Rte. 3237, right on Rte. 12; follow signs. Exit 206: 18 mi./25 min. West on Rte. 12; follow signs. With its boardwalks and false-front pawnshop and saloon, this replica of a late 19th-century Texas town looks like a set for a western movie. The buildings include a general store, opera house, livery stable, assay office, log chapel, and—more surprising—a house built from soda bottles. Two museums house an interesting collection of western art, including many bronzes by the noted artist Frederic Remington. A half-scale version of an 1870's steam train offers a 15-minute ride through the surrounding countryside. *Open Thurs.–Tues. Memorial Day–3rd week of Aug.; Sat. and P.M. Sun. Sept.–Nov., Mar.–May.*

206 — Aquarena Springs, San Marcos

5 min. West on Aquarena Springs Dr. In this large, interesting amusement park, the emphasis is on water. Boats with glass bottoms glide over crystalline waters, giving wonderful views of fish and plant life, an archeological site, and even the bubbling springs that feed the lake. A half-hour show features swimmers performing underwater ballet and comedy acts. An especially popular performer is Ralph the Swimming Pig, who dives in and paddles across the water. Other attractions include a trained-bird show, an aerial cable car, a 300-foot tower with observation deck, gardens, and a frontier town. *Open daily except Christmas. Admission charged.*

233A. *The capitol's dome still proudly holds its own on Austin's growing skyline.*

191. *The flotilla of sailboats attests to the size and popularity of Canyon Lake.*

191 Canyon Lake

16 mi./20 min. West on Rte. 306. Several parks border on this 13,000-acre lake, built and maintained by the U.S. Army Corps of Engineers to control the devastating flooding that once plagued this area. Together they offer some 600 campsites and a full range of other facilities with an emphasis on water sports, fishing, and boating. Each park has its own character. On the north shore scuba divers prefer to go to North Park, while Jacobs Creek Park attracts sailboarders and sailors, and Canyon and Potters Creek parks appeal to families. On the south shore fishermen seem most at home at Cranes Mill Park, while younger people gather at Comal Park. *Open year-round.*

175 Natural Bridge Caverns

8 mi./10 min. West on Natural Bridge Caverns Rd. A 60-foot-wide natural limestone bridge provides a fitting entrance to this extraordinary complex of caverns discovered by four college students in 1960. The exceptionally well preserved calcite formations have a striking range of colors. Shapes vary from regular pointed stalactites and rounded stalagmites to those that resemble chandeliers, mushrooms, forests, and almost transparent draperies; and water dripping throughout continues to change the formations. The largest chamber is 350 feet long and 100 feet wide. Guided tours that pass through half a mile of these subterra-

nean wonders are given every half hour and take an hour and a quarter. *Open daily except Thanksgiving Day, Christmas, and New Year's Day. Admission charged.*

158B San Antonio, TX 78205

Visitor Information Center, 317 Alamo Plaza. (512) 299-8155. The Alamo is, of course, the major historical treasure of this city. The second best known attraction is the Paseo del Rio—a below-street-level string of sidewalk cafés, clubs, hotels, and artisans' shops that line the banks of the meandering San Antonio River. A good spot for an overview is the top of the 750-foot-high Tower of the Americas. Be sure to visit the San Antonio Museum of Art and the Witte Museum's displays of anthropology, history, and natural science. The 1749 Spanish Governor's Palace and the Alamo's four sister missions further reveal the city's historic heritage.

158B. *The Alamo: fabled in song and story and a frequently photographed site.*

1A Nuevo Santander Museum Complex, Laredo

2 mi./10 min. West on Washington St. to Laredo Junior College; follow signs. This campus museum is housed in three build-

ings that were once part of Ft. McIntosh. Built around the turn of the century, the main structure was formerly the post's chapel and now displays traveling exhibits that highlight the influence of diverse cultures on local history and art. The 19th-century guardhouse is devoted to military history, while a former warehouse contains implements and vehicles once used on area ranches and farms, as well as displays depicting daily life in these local settings. Guides give tours of the museum and some of the other army post buildings that remain here. *Open Mon.–Thurs., A.M. Fri., and P.M. Sun.*

SU Museum of the Republic of the Rio Grande, Laredo

Santa Ursula Ave. exit: 1 mi./10 min. South on Santa Ursula Ave., right on Zaragoza St. In 1840 three of Mexico's northern states rebelled against the central government and formed the Republic of the Rio Grande. The republic lasted less than a year, but it left behind a legacy that is commemorated in this simple stone and adobe building that was once its capitol. The three original rooms are furnished in period style, while the larger front room, added in 1861, has traveling exhibits of artistic, cultural, historical, and scientific interest. While here, also visit St. Augustine Church and other historic structures around and near the plaza. *Open Tues.–Sun. except holidays and one week in Apr.*

SU El Mercado, Laredo

Santa Ursula Ave. exit: 5 min. South on Santa Ursula Ave., right on Hidalgo St. Laredo's city hall, from its inception in 1883, was intended to house more than the machinery of municipal government. Until 1930 it also accommodated a theater and a market hall. In 1985 the city government moved its offices out and renovators moved in, transforming the space into El Mercado—exclusively a marketplace.

El Mercado is alive with the color and the flavor of this border region, with a range of merchandise that runs the gamut from inexpensive souvenirs and T-shirts to fine hand-wrought jewelry and exquisitely embroidered garments. *Open year-round.*

See E–W book, sec. 52.

175

17

158B

10

157

1A

0

SU TX U.S.A.

End I-35   MEXICO

ROUTE 172

60

48

31

17

17

See E–W book, sec. 13.

1S

94

15 **94**

326

7

333

172. *Beaupre Place (also the Cotton House) reveals a yearning for elegance.*

ROUTE 172 | Heritage Hill State Park, Green Bay

5 mi./6 min. West on Rte. 172, right on Webster Ave.; follow signs. Overlooking the Fox River, this 48-acre park commemorates the settlement and development of northeastern Wisconsin. The pioneer section includes a replica of one of the state's first Catholic churches (a bark-covered chapel built in 1672), a 1762 fur trader's cabin, and a replica of the first courthouse. The small-town area has a village green, a blacksmith's shop, a general store, and two distinguished houses: Tank Cottage, one of Wisconsin's oldest remaining structures (late 1700's), and Beaupre Place, a Greek revival house from the 1840's. Two original buildings from Ft. Howard, the hospital and the company barracks kitchen, form part of the military heritage area. Nearby is the farm heritage area, featuring a Belgian-style farmstead. *Open daily May–mid-Nov. Admission charged.*

ROUTE 172 | The National Railroad Museum, Green Bay

6 mi./9 min. West on Rte. 172, right on Ashland Ave., right on Cormier Ave. A British locomotive, cars that served in General Eisenhower's World War II staff train,

a 1910 engine used to explain how steam locomotives work, and 75 pieces of equipment ranging from one of the smallest engines ever made to the Union Pacific *Big Boy*, America's largest steam locomotive, are among the highlights of this extensive collection. In mid-1989 the museum expects to open a new building, which will feature permanent exhibits on railroading and an audiovisual presentation on the role of the railroad in American history. The admission includes a 20-minute ride on an 1890's Barney and Smith coach. *Open daily May–mid-Oct. Admission charged.*

48 | Kohler-Andrae State Parks, Sheboygan

5 min. East on Rte. V, right on Rte. KK, left on Old Park Rd. Here you'll find two idyllic lakeshore parks with wide sandy beaches, dunes, stands of birches, pines, and aspens, and wild roses that come almost to the water's edge. The Sanderling Nature Center provides an introduction to the ecology of the dunes, and a well-signed trail along the dunes identifies the local flora. *Parks open year-round; nature center open Memorial Day–Labor Day. Admission charged.*

17 | Cedar Creek Settlement, Cedarburg

5 mi./10 min. West on Rte. C, right on Rte. 57 (becomes Washington Ave., Rte. 143). Beside the grassy banks of Cedar Creek stands a pioneer stone building that was once the Wittenberg Woolen Mill. Below the massive tamarack beams of the old mill, a community of craftspeople and others manufacture and sell their wares. The largest establishment is the Stone Mill Winery, located in the old cellars. Tours begin at a small wine museum—which has a collection of spigots, cooper's tools, corks, and wine labels—and end with wine tasting. A blacksmith's shop with a high ceiling, hooded furnace, and a clutter of tools turns out traditional iron products, and on the second floor of the mill you can see a working potter. Other shops sell handmade toys, antiques, clothes, stencils, gourmet goods, candles, grapevine wreaths, and Christmas ornaments. *Open Mon.–Sat. and P.M. Sun. except holidays.*

1S | Milwaukee, WI 53202

Convention & Visitors Bureau, 756 N. Milwaukee St. (414) 273-7222; (800) 291-0903 outside WI. There's still beer in Milwaukee, and three breweries offer tours, but the city has many other attractions. The arts are well represented by the vast Milwaukee Art Museum; Villa Terrace, an Italian Renaissance-style home with displays of antique furniture and decorative arts; and the extensive collection of the Charles Allis Art Museum in a resplendent Tudor-style mansion. No less interesting is the Milwaukee Public Museum, with its environmental dioramas, dinosaur skeletons, and Indian artifacts among other displays. Mitchell Park boasts a noted horticultural conservatory; and the zoo, a few miles west of downtown, is one of the country's best.

1S. *Dolphins at the zoo dance to entertain their audience of other mammals.*

326 | Cliffside County Park, Sturtevant

9 mi./15 min. East on 7 Mile Rd., right on Michna Rd.; follow signs. The park has two distinct areas: one includes the campground, a baseball diamond, and tennis courts; the other, lying behind the children's playground, is an area of woods, rough meadowland, and cliff-top paths. At the first fork in the trail, bear left to cross a meadow leading to the cliffs, or walk through the woods. The loop to the lake is a walk of 30 to 45 minutes; there are good views, but the cliff overlooking the lake is steep and crumbly, and there's no beach access. *Open daily mid-Apr.–mid-Oct.*

333 Racine Zoological Gardens

11 mi./15 min. East on Rte. 20, left on Rte. 32 to Goold St.; follow signs. Situated on the shores of Lake Michigan, this 28-acre zoo has an interesting variety of animals. Wolves and birds of prey make their home in a wooded area near a lake. Nearby, rhesus monkeys and Barbary sheep dwell on a rocky island in a smaller lake, and penguins, pelicans, and other waterbirds have their own watery domains as well. Camels, elephants, kangaroos, deer, and a beautiful white tiger with blue eyes can also be seen here. *Open year-round.*

ROUTE 41 / ROUTE 173 Illinois Beach State Park (Southern Unit), Zion

Rte. 41 exit: 11 mi./15 min. South on Rte. 41, left on Wadsworth Rd. Rte. 173 exit: 8 mi./10 min. East on Rte. 173 (Rosecrans Rd.), right on Rte. 41; proceed as above. This extensive state park on Lake Michigan is divided into northern and southern units. But first-time visitors are encouraged to head for the southern unit. The long beach here is covered with fine sugarlike sand and acres of dunes—the state's only dunes. Beachcombers love to collect the large smooth rocks shaped and polished by the elements. Nature trails wind through a rapidly changing landscape of wetlands, prairie, oak forest, and dunes. *Open year-round.*

41–173. *Echoes of impressionism resound in the reeds and reflections of Dead River.*

OH Chicago, IL 60611

E. Ohio St. exit: Tourism Council, 163 E. Pearson St. (312) 280-5740. This great cosmopolitan metropolis, ideally situated on the southwestern shore of Lake Michigan, boasts a number of world-class attractions. The Art Institute is known for its wide-ranging permanent collection and creative special exhibitions. The Terra Museum, opened in 1987, has a superlative collection of American art; the John G. Shedd Aquarium, the world's largest such indoor facility, with more than 200 tanks, displays some 1,000 wonders of the deep. For an intimate sense of the city, take the El (the elevated railroad) around the Loop; and for a breathtaking overview of the city and lake, try the observation area on the 103rd floor of the Sears Tower, at this writing the tallest building in the world.

250A / 250B Pilcher Park, Joliet

7 mi./10 min. Exit 250A: East on I-80, left on Rte. 30, right on Gougar Rd. Exit 250B: Proceed as above. Situated along the banks of a creek, the wooded park offers upland hikes, ski and bike trails, picnic areas, and an interpretive nature center that has displays of native plants, birds, and mammals. Programs matched to the seasons include maple sugaring, birdwatching, fishing contests, ski races, and

OH. *From the perspective of Sears Tower, other skyscrapers seem rather earthbound.*

pond and woodland study trips. One of the various walks is a quarter-mile self-guiding trail marked with informative story boards. Also featured are an artesian well with mineral water, a greenhouse, and a paved trail for the blind and handicapped. *Open year-round.*

240 Goose Lake Prairie State Natural Area, Morris

7 mi./12 min. West on Pine Bluff Lorenzo Rd., right on Jugtown Rd. More than 1,500 acres of wild prairie, one of the largest remaining tracts in the United States, demonstrate what the Midwest was like before barns, crops, towns, and highways changed the landscape of the Plains forever. The visitor center has displays that explain the prairie, the plants, and wildlife that live there, and the impact of man on its ecology.

From the center the 1½-mile Tallgrass Nature Trail leads through a section of prairie grass amid seasonal wildflowers and past potholes and marshland. Prairies like the one preserved here once covered almost three-quarters of Illinois. A trail-guide pamphlet identifies the native plants and the geology of the area. The park provides the welcome sense of openness and solitude that characterizes this unique environment. *Open daily except Christmas and New Year's Day.*

ROUTE 41
ROUTE 173

18

WI
IL

2

47

See E–W book, sec. 6.

90

OH

90 94

55

46

See E–W book, sec. 23.

250A

80

250B

10

240

4

55

236 Kankakee River State Park

22 mi./25 min. East on Rte. 113, left on Warner Bridge Rd. The many moods of the Kankakee as it changes with the seasons are revealed in the 11 miles of parkland and riverbank and a dramatic canyon watercourse. Whether the river is a springtime torrent or a placid hot-summer stream, the park offers activities that range from angling to ski touring. Hiking and riding trails meander through the wild forest, prairie, sand dunes, and along the riverbanks. Picnic areas and campgrounds are found throughout the park. A favorite feature is Rock Creek Canyon, where a waterfall tumbles through the deep limestone gorge. Canoes and horses are available for rent. *Open daily except Christmas and New Year's Day.*

167 Moraine View State Recreation Area

20 mi./30 min. South on Veterans Pkwy., left on Rte. 9, right on Le Roy-Lexington Rd.; follow signs. In the midst of a rolling prairie landscape, this attractive park surrounds a wooded lake. A scenic drive wanders through varied terrain, going past campsite, picnic, and visitor center facilities. A choice of trails provides opportunities for different activities according to the season. Winter ice fishing and ski touring can become angling and canoeing in July along the more than 5 miles of shoreline. As you stroll along the half-mile Tanglewood Nature Trail, you will find signposts that indicate the glacial ancestry of the various woodland, marsh, prairie, and pond life here. *Open daily except Christmas and New Year's Day.*

157 Miller Park and Zoo, Bloomington

2 mi./10 min. North on Veterans Pkwy., left on Morris Ave. Bird cries of the tropics and the bellow of sea lions are an added aspect of this city park that is set in pleasant tree-studded meadows. There is a lake for swimming and paddleboats, an outdoor theater, tennis courts, miniature golf, and a bandstand. In the small well-managed zoo you'll find snow leopards, Indian lions, and tigers from Sumatra in outside cages, as well as a refreshing pool for the sea lions. A skylit room, with trees and two waterfalls, suggests a tropical rain forest where rare birds fly. The petting zoo has farmyard animals, a llama, and a deer. *Open year-round. Admission charged.*

123 Railsplitter State Park

2 min. East on Rte. 55 (business). This park on the southern outskirts of Lincoln is a quiet and restful place for a picnic, even though it wraps around a state prison. You can glimpse the Lincoln Correctional Center through the trees just after entering the park. Nevertheless, the focus of the 751-acre preserve named for Abraham Lincoln is Salt Creek, with good waters for fishing for bass, bluegill, catfish, carp, and sunfish. There are outdoor stoves beside the creek, and small shelters and running-water outlets throughout the grounds. *Open daily except Christmas and New Year's Day.*

98B 92A Lincoln Home National Historic Site, Springfield

Exit 98B: 3 mi./10 min. West on Clear Lake Ave. and Jefferson St., left on 9th St. Exit 92A: 4 mi./15 min. North on I-55 Loop; continue on S. 6th St., right on Myrtle St., right on 9th St. Abraham Lincoln was 35, recently married, and a partner in a local law firm when he bought this 5-year-old clapboard house in Springfield in 1844. It was his home for 17 years, the only one he ever owned, and three of his four sons were born here. It was in the formal front parlor, where the best furniture was kept—and where the children were not allowed—that he was formally notified of his nomination for the presidency in 1860. Period flavor predominates. There are in all some 65 furnishings that belonged to the family, including Lincoln's lap desk and shaving mirror. The exteriors of other homes along the broad, tree-shaded streets of the 12-acre historic site are being restored. *Open daily except Thanksgiving Day, Christmas, and New Year's Day.*

88 Lincoln Memorial Garden and Nature Center

5 min. East on E. Lake Dr.; follow signs. It was the belief of landscape architect Jens Jensen, who designed this 77-acre woodland garden in the 1930's as a living memorial to Abraham Lincoln, that "art springs from native soil." He proved the concept here, with nature trails that wind for 5 miles among indigenous flowers and trees and beautifully balanced patches of woodland and open spaces. The circular seats of eight "council rings" of local stone encour-

98B–92A. *It is not surprising that Lincoln chose such a simple, straightforward house.*

age discussion and quiet companionship. Perhaps the most striking aspect is that all this, including idyllic Lake Springfield, Shadbush Lane, Witch Hazel Trail, Dogwood Lane, and other walks are man-made but seem to be part of nature's grand design. *Open year-round.* 🚶

60 Beaver Dam State Park

20.5 mi./25 min. West on Rte. 108 to Carlinville; follow signs. Although beavers made the original lake, local fishermen a century ago doubled its depth with dams at both ends. Since then the placid waters and pristine shoreline have endeared the lake to those who come for largemouth bass, sunfish, bluegill, and channel catfish. Most important, it's a quiet place, 737 acres of oak and hickory forests, campgrounds, a shady picnic area, and leafy hiking trails. A small lakeside stand sells bait and tackle and rents boats from April through October; no boats with gasoline engines are allowed. Nothing disturbs the serenity of trees, sky, and water. The only sounds to be heard are those of nature in this domain of raccoons, foxes, songbirds, and wild turkeys. *Open year-round.* 🛆 ⛺ 🚐 🚶 🎣

11 Cahokia Mounds State Historic Site, Collinsville

5 mi./10 min. South on Rte. 157, right on Collinsville Rd. From A.D. 900 to 1250 a mighty society flourished here. Cahokia, a major town built by the people of the Mississippian Indian culture, had 20,000 to 40,000 inhabitants who farmed the surrounding land and traded with peoples as far away as the Atlantic and Gulf coasts. They also labored for centuries to build these impressive earthworks, adding the dirt a basketful at a time. The 100-foot-high Monks Mound, the largest of the 60 surviving mounds here, was the site of a temple that was also the leader's residence. A few of the mounds were burial sites, but most were bases for the homes of the elite or for ceremonial buildings. Woodhenge, a giant circle of cedar posts, was a sun calendar that determined the changing seasons. A museum offers exhibits. *Open daily except Thanksgiving Day, Christmas, and New Year's Day.* 🛆

ARCH St. Louis, MO 63102

Arch/Downtown exit: Convention and Visitors Commission, 10 S. Broadway. (314) 421-1023; (800) 247-9791 outside MO. The three spans across the Mississippi here dramatize the role of St. Louis as a jumping-off place to the West, and the magnificent 630-foot Gateway Arch commemorates the days of the wagon trains, when the only river crossings were by water. From the top of the arch one can contemplate the vast reaches so full of promise and danger in the days of the pioneers, an era graphically interpreted in the Museum of Westward Expansion located beneath the arch.

An excellent zoo has more than 2,500 animals and a miniature railroad to provide an easy introduction. Featured in the 79-acre botanical garden is the domed Climatron greenhouse and the largest Japanese garden in the United States.

ARCH. *The pioneers it celebrates could only be astounded by the Gateway Arch.*

207 196 Six Flags Over Mid-America

Exit 207: 30 mi./35 min. West on I-44. Exit 196: 21 mi./30 min. West on I-270, left on I-44. The grassy, well-tended grounds of this amusement park house attractions with French, Spanish, and English themes. You'll find lots of rides that elicit screams of delighted excitement— shooting the rapids on Thunder River or plunging on the Screamin' Eagle roller coaster. There are gentler rides as well for those who want something less daring. Between the rides you can enjoy a variety of

207–196. *The reality and fantasy of rabbit and friend capture the park's essence.*

musicals, special performances, and changing shows. Guest services include public lockers, a first aid station, wheelchairs, rental strollers, and a free kennel. *Open daily late May–late Aug.; weekends mid-Apr.–mid-May and early Sept.–mid-Oct. Admission charged.* 🛆 ♿

ROUTE M Sandy Creek Covered Bridge

13 mi./20 min. West on Rte. M, left on Rte. 21, left on Goldman Rd., right on Lemay Ferry Rd. To cross this bridge in 1880, it cost 3 cents per foot passenger, 25 cents per carriage drawn by two or more horses, and 37 cents per stage wagon—considerable sums in those days. The 74½-foot span, which is 18 feet wide, still has half its original timbers and is one of only four of its kind remaining in Missouri. Covered to protect the underlying wood structure, the bridge is supported by a Howe truss reinforced by iron rods. Barn-building techniques were used in constructing these bridges; thus their familiar appearance may have made it easier for draft animals to enter. An informative display explains the technology of covered bridges. Shade trees and a sparkling stream make this an ideal spot for a picnic. *Open year-round.* 🛆 🎣

6

92A
4

88

28

60

49

See
E–W book,
sec. 29.

70

11 See E–W
book,
sec. 33.

12

64

IL

70 MO

ARCH
2

207

11

196

11

ROUTE
M

8

55

55

174

24

150

45

105

6

99

3

96

47   See
N–S book,
sec. 25.

57

49

77

105–99. *Covered bridge and water mill reveal the beauty of design for pure function.*

174   Washington State Park

23 mi./35 min. Southwest on Rte. 67, right on Rte. 110, left on Rte. 21, right on Rte. 104. Indians of the Middle-Mississippian culture once carved their ceremonial symbols on limestone outcroppings here. Today informative displays interpret these petroglyphs, now sheltered by lean-tos to protect them from further erosion by the elements. The park's inviting hiking trails, where the rare collared lizard is occasionally spotted, wind through limestone glades and bluffs that tower above the Big River. The park has a fine range of visitor facilities, and swimming, fishing, canoeing, and tubing are permitted on the river. *Open year-round.*

150   Historic Ste. Genevieve

6 mi./15 min. East on Rte. 32 (becomes Center Dr., then 4th St.), right on Merchant St. The 18th-century French heritage of this Missouri town is evident in a number of historic houses built between 1770, when Ste. Genevieve was a part of upper Louisiana, claimed by France, and 1820. The French Creole-style Amoureaux House, with its *poteaux-en-terre* ("posts-in-ground") foundation and long 10-post porch, once belonged to a French noble-

man. On display inside are collections of cast-iron toys and antique dolls. Among other historic houses are the Guibourd-Valle House, with graceful period furnishings and hand-hewn oak beams, and the authentically restored Bolduc House, with 18th-century gardens and frontier kitchen. *Information Center open daily except Easter, Thanksgiving Day, and Dec. 25–Jan. 2. Admission charged to sites.*

105   Trail of Tears State Park

11 mi./15 min. North on Rte. 61, right on Rte. 177. Spectacular cliffs and vistas distinguish this park, which was named for the tragic forced migration of some 13,000 Cherokees from their ancestral lands in the Southeast to western reservations in 1838–39. When about one-third of the Indians died en route of disease, exposure, and starvation, the migration became known as the Trail of Tears. The main hiking trail, some 10 miles long, stretches through some rugged areas, including the 180-foot-high limestone bluffs that overlook the Mississippi River. Hikers, equestrians, and botanists may see the cucumber magnolias, spicebushes, and Indian pinks, as well as deer or the rare bald eagle. A lakeside beach is a pleasant place for a picnic. *Open year-round.*

105   Bollinger Mill State Historic Site, Burfordville
99

Exit 105: 10 mi./20 min. South on Rte. 61, right on Rte. 72, left on Rte. 34; follow signs. Exit 99: 11 mi./22 min. North on Rte. 61, left on Rte. 72; proceed as above. This old mill and a nearby covered bridge, located on the tree-shaded banks of the Whitewater River, make an idyllic scene that is irresistible to both picnickers and photographers. The original mill, constructed of wood about 1800, was partially burned down by Union soldiers during the Civil War and later rebuilt of brick and stone. The mill functioned until 1953, and it can still be made to run. *Open Mon.–Sat. and P.M. Sun. except holidays. Fee charged for guided tour of mill.*

96   Rose Display Garden, Cape Girardeau

3.5 mi./10 min. East on Rte. K (William St.), left on West End Blvd., left on Broadway, right on Perry Ave. Of particular interest to rose growers, this garden set in the northwest corner of Capaha Park boasts more than 200 plantings of outstanding species and varieties. Visitors may admire examples of grandiflora, floribunda, shrub, and hybrid tea roses, among others. Breeders submit roses for various tests for scent, color, hardiness, and disease resistance. The garden is administered by the Council of Garden Clubs. *Open year-round.*

96   The Glenn House, Cape Girardeau

4.5 mi./10 min. East on Rte. K (William St.), right on Spanish St. Local architect Edwin Branch Deane built this Victorian house for his daughter Lulu and her husband in 1883. The interior, much of it still original, includes some intriguing touches: lamps that run on both electricity and kerosene, radiators with plate warmers, and green silk moiré wallpaper. One of the bedrooms evokes life on the river with nautical memorabilia and a model riverboat. The bathroom has a pink marble sink, original lead plumbing, an overhead-tank toilet, and a collection of antique shaving mugs. *Open P.M. Wed.–Sat. Apr.–Dec. except holidays. Admission charged.*

49 44 Hunter-Dawson State Historic Site, New Madrid

Exit 49: 3.5 mi./10 min. South on Rte. 61, left on Rte. U. Exit 44: 5 mi./15 min. North on Rte. 61, right on Rte. U. This gracious home, surrounded by some of the state's oldest trees, was begun by local merchant and sawmill owner William Hunter in the late 1850's and completed by his wife after his death. The building, with its white clapboard siding, green shutters, and long rear porches, is a blend of the Greek revival and Italianate styles typical of the antebellum period in Missouri. The 15 rooms contain furnishings from 1860 to 1880, including portraits of Hunter and his wife. *Open Mon.–Sat. and P.M. Sun. Admission charged.* ☵

44 34 Hampson Museum State Park

Exit 44: 7 mi./10 min. South on Rte. 181, left on Rte. 61; follow signs. Exit 34: 7 mi./10 min. East on Rte. 118, left on Rte. 61; follow signs. The Nodenas were farm-based Indians who lived in this part of Arkansas from about A.D. 1350 to 1700. The museum exhibits weapons, ornaments, and objects they used for hunting and games. The clay they mixed for ceremonial and utilitarian vessels was fortified with shells. One rare "head pot," with incised lines that may represent tattooing, scarification, or skin painting, was used for

ceremonial purposes. The displays, which explain the Nodenas' trade networks, their methods of hunting and agriculture, and other aspects of their lives, are laid out with a clear and concise commentary. *Open Tues.–Sat. Admission charged.* ☵ ♿

12 Memphis, TN 38103

Visitors Information Center, 207 Beale St. (901) 526-4880. King Cotton still plays a major role in the city's economy, Beale Street and W. C. Handy are appropriately memorialized, and a riverboat still plies the mighty Mississippi; but probably the best-known attraction is Graceland, home of Elvis Presley, the King of Rock and Roll. Tours are so popular that reservations are suggested. Call (901) 332-3322; or (800) 238-2000 from out of state.

The river that brought life to Memphis is honored at Mud Island by a scale model of the Mississippi from Cairo, Illinois, to New Orleans and the Gulf of Mexico, as well as by displays on the waterway's history. The Memphis Pink Palace Museum and Planetarium features exhibits on natural history, pioneer life, and the Civil War. The National Ornamental Metal Museum has a working blacksmith on the premises. For nature lovers there is a zoo with an aquarium and a botanic garden. The Victorian Village has some 18 landmarked buildings in styles that include late Gothic revival.

280 Arkabutla Lake

11 mi./16 min. West on Rte. 304, left on Rte. 301 to dam. Well stocked with crappie and catfish, Arkabutla Lake is especially inviting for anglers, but its 34,000 acres of water surface allow plenty of room for water-skiing, swimming, and sailing as well. The lake, named for an Indian chief who allegedly lived here long ago, was created in 1942 by damming the Coldwater River. The area has campgrounds, boat ramps, swimming beaches, nature trails, and a picnic ground shaded by sweet gums and oaks. *Open year-round; field office open Mon.–Fri.* ☵ ⛺ 🚐 🏃 🏊 🎣 ♿

252 John W. Kyle State Park

9 mi./15 min. East on Rte. 315. Chickasaw Indians traded and hunted in this area before settlers began arriving in the 1830's. These days the park is noted for its nature trails and a pine-shaded picnic ground. Sardis Lake is well known for its catfish, crappie, and bass, and boats are available for rent. The campgrounds are supplemented by fully furnished cabins as well as tennis courts and a swimming pool. *Open year-round.* ☵ ⛺ 🚐 🏃 🏊 🎣 ♿

243A Rowan Oak, Oxford

23 mi./28 min. East on Rte. 6, left on Lamar Ave., left on Old Taylor Rd. This columned white frame house, set among cedar and magnolia trees, was built in 1844 by a local planter, Robert Sheegog. It was spared when the town of Oxford was razed by Northern troops in 1864. In 1930 the house was bought and restored by the world-famous southern novelist William Faulkner, who occupied it until his death in 1962. It is now maintained by the University of Mississippi to preserve the memory of Faulkner. The rooms contain such treasures as portraits, paintings, a Japanese doll, and a Chickering piano. In Faulkner's office you can see an outline and notes for *A Fable* that he sketched on the walls. Outside are barns, stables, and other outbuildings. *Open Mon.–Fri., A.M. Sat. and P.M. Sun. except Christmas, New Year's Day, and university staff holidays.*

243A. *Lighted interior at dusk could serve as a reminder of Faulkner's brilliance.*

MO
AR

44

10

34

34

See E–W book, sec. 40.

40

40

AR
TN

12

TN
MS

24

280

28

252

9

243A

16

55

227
206
21
21
185
35
150
17
133
35
98B
20

See
E–W book,
sec. 45.

227 | George Payne Cossar State Park

4 mi./6 min. East on Rte. 32, left on access road. Situated on a peninsula on huge Lake Enid, this state park is a favorite with fishermen and campers. Facilities include playgrounds, boat and bike rentals, a nature trail, picnic areas, a swimming pool, a lodge, and a locally famous restaurant. The park's hardwood forest is especially beautiful in the fall. *Open year-round. Admission charged.*

206 | Historic Old Grenada

4 min. Southeast on Rte. 7. Once Choctaw Indian land, this area in the early 1830's had developed into the two politically rivalrous towns of Pittsburg and Tullahoma, which were divided only by a surveyor's line now known as Line Street. On July 4, 1836, a symbolic marriage ceremony was performed (accompanied by a barbecue), and the two towns were united under the name Grenada. Majestic oaks shade the streets of the historic district, where dozens of lovely old homes built in the early to mid-19th century recall Mississippi's antebellum past. Most of these buildings are located on Margin and Main streets. The Whitaker Manse, whose columns were brought from New Orleans, is one of the most beautifully restored homes in the state, and Townes House, with its elegant columns and balconies, was the headquarters for Jefferson Davis in 1861.

206 | Hugh White State Park

10 mi./15 min. East on Rte. 8; follow signs. Named for a former Mississippi governor, the park is situated around 64,000-acre Grenada Lake, which was created by a dam along the Yalobusha River. The lake offers some of the area's best fishing—for crappie and striped bass—as well as boating, water-skiing, and swimming from a sandy beach. There are tennis courts, a marina, boat-launching facilities, bikes and boats for rent, and overnight accommodations that range from 20 full-service cabins to primitive campsites in a secluded area overlooking the lake. *Open year-round. Admission charged.*

185 | Florewood River Plantation State Park

30 mi./50 min. West on Rte. 82 through Greenwood, left on access road. The invention of the cotton gin in 1793 increased fiftyfold the speed with which cotton bolls could be separated from their seeds. By the mid-1850's King Cotton accounted for more than half of all U.S. exports, and plantations such as Florewood flourished in the fertile Delta region of western Mississippi.

The 28 buildings on this 100-acre site are copies of the 19th-century structures typical in the area. Costumed interpreters (on duty March to December) portray a planter, a mistress of the house, a candlemaker, and other workers. At the Cotton Museum you will see artifacts that explain the history of cotton and its impact in the Old South. In the fall you can pick a few bolls of cotton and try to imagine what it was like to pick cotton from dawn to dusk. *Open Tues.–Sat. and P.M. Sun. except Thanksgiving Day, Christmas, and New Year's Day. Admission charged.*

185. *This humble plant led to vast fortunes—and promoted the evils of slavery.*

150 | Holmes County State Park

2 min. East on access road. Favored by campers, this park has a variety of accommodations that range from tent sites to air-conditioned cabins overlooking a lake. One of the two lakes in the park is for fishing (bass, catfish, and bream), and the other is for paddleboating and swimming (from a sandy beach). Among other facilities, the park provides a skating rink, an archery range, a rustic lodge, and a 4-mile nature trail that winds through groves of white and red oak, dogwood, cedar, and loblolly pine. Its nearness to the interstate highway makes the park a convenient place to stop for a quick and quiet picnic. *Open daily except Christmas. Admission charged.*

133 | Casey Jones Railroad Museum State Park, Vaughan

2 min. East on access road. On April 30, 1900, engineer Jonathan Luther "Casey" Jones, at the throttle of the *Cannonball Express*, was running behind schedule. Racing to make up time, he was unable to stop at a warning signal, rammed into the rear of a freight train near Vaughan, and was killed. A legend was born when a friend of Jones's, engine wiper Wallace Saunders, composed "The Ballad of Casey Jones," and the song was picked up and elaborated on by vaudevillians. The bell from Casey's engine and a rail that Union soldiers heated and twisted into a "Sherman's necktie" are among the artifacts exhibited at this former depot, located a few hundred yards from the site of Casey's wreck. Railroad memorabilia and historical displays chronicle the Illinois Central Railroad's past, and a 1923 locomotive is displayed on the grounds. *Open Tues.–Sat. except Thanksgiving Day, Christmas, and New Year's Day. Admission charged.*

98B | Jackson, MS 39216

Visitor Information Center, 1180 Lakeland Dr. (601) 960-1800. Jackson's importance as a state capital and rail center brought destruction during the Civil War, but it has also helped to make this the state's leading city today; and the sense of local history is still strong. The mansion where 40 state governors have lived, which briefly served as headquarters for Union general Ulysses S. Grant, is furnished with excellent period pieces. The State Historical Museum in the Old State Capitol features dioramas illustrating the history of the state; the Museum of Natural Science also uses dioramas. The homes of two former mayors are of interest: The Oaks, an antebellum wood-

98B. *Great dynasties were built on the simple, ingenious cotton gin.*

frame cottage hand-hewn in 1846, and the Manship House, a charming Gothic revival structure built about 10 years later. The history and culture of blacks in Mississippi is featured in the Smith-Robertson Museum and Cultural Center.

| **98B** | **Mississippi Agriculture and Forestry Museum, Jackson** |

3 min. East on Lakeland Dr. Life-size tableaux, complete with sound effects and voices, show vivid re-creations of loggers in action, workers hauling cotton bales, and life in a sharecropper's cottage. Themes include logging days, the "rail age," and the "era of roads." Exhibits explain cotton processing, the impact of electricity, and the economics of farm life.

Also here is the National Agricultural Aviation Museum, which focuses on the fight against the boll weevil, featuring crop-dusting planes along with strange boll-weevil catchers of pre-spraying days.

At the Fortenberry-Parkman Farm across the street, you can talk to workers about rural life in the South in the early 20th century. *Open Tues.–Sat. and P.M. Sun. except Thanksgiving Day, Christmas, and New Year's Day. Admission charged.* 🛉

| **13** | **Percy Quin State Park** |

5 min. West on Rte. 48. Spread along the shores of Lake Tangipahoa, this beautifully landscaped park features an arboretum of flowering shrubs. During the summertime there's also swimming at a wide sandy beach, pedal boats and canoes for rent, and observation decks overlooking the water shaded by tall loblolly pines. Fishing is also popular. Eight miles of marked trails lead through the park, one of which passes a beaver dam, where these busy builders are occasionally seen. The Liberty White Railroad's red caboose serves as a reminder of another era. *Open year-round. Admission charged.* 🛉 ⛺ 🚐 🚶 🏊 🎣 ♿

| **I-12** | **Fairview-Riverside State Park** |

25 mi./30 min. East on I-12 to Exit 57, south on Rte. 1077, left on Rte. 22. A fine old two-story white house with a handsome galleried veranda greets visitors at the entrance to this 98-acre park. A wood boardwalk on the Tchefuncta River winds among cypresses thickly hung with Spanish moss. Egrets ascend from branches reflected in the murky water, and the surface of the river is rippled by alligators on the prowl. Water-skiing is popular upstream, and fishermen come to the park for the abundance of bluegill, bass, perch, and catfish. *Open year-round. Admission charged.* 🛉 ⛺ 🚐 🚶 🎣

| **I-10** | **New Orleans, LA 70112** |

26 mi./35 min. Tourist & Convention Commission, 1520 Sugar Bowl Dr. (504) 566-5011. The music, food, architecture, history, and ambience have made New Orleans one of America's most celebrated cities. Jackson Square is a good place to start a walking tour of the French Quarter, the city's best-known area. On the square you'll see the beautiful St. Louis Cathedral and the superb wrought-iron balconies of the Pontalba Apartments. At the nearby French Market you'll find outdoor cafés and eye-catching displays of produce. At night the sound of music—blues, ragtime, Cajun zydeco, country, and of course New Orleans jazz—emanates from clubs and bars that line the length of Bourbon Street.

The St. Charles streetcar still clangs and rattles through the Garden District, an area of large live oaks and handsome antebellum houses that also rewards strolling. To experience the majesty of the Mississippi River, which loops dramatically around the city, try the free ferry or one of the cruises.

I-10. *The tried and true sounds of early jazz can still be savored in the French Quarter.*

85

13

MS
LA

49

I-12

30

See
E–W book,
sec. 53.

I-10 10

End I-55

57

94

I-94

See
E–W book,
sec. 13.

80

See
E–W book,
sec. 23.

121

237

34

203

13

190

See
E–W book,
sec. 29.

70

I-94 Chicago, IL 60611

Tourism Council, 163 E. Pearson St. (312) 280-5740. This metropolis, beautifully situated on the southwestern shore of Lake Michigan, boasts a number of world-class attractions. The Art Institute is known for a wide-ranging permanent collection as well as creative special exhibitions. The Terra Museum, opened in 1987, has a superlative collection of American art; the John G. Shedd Aquarium, the world's largest such indoor facility, with more than 200 tanks, displays some 1,000 wonders of the deep. For an intimate sense of the city, take the El (the elevated railroad) around the Loop; and for a breathtaking overview there's the observation area on the 103rd floor of the Sears Tower, at this writing the tallest building in the world.

237 Champaign County Historical Museum

3 mi./10 min. East on I-74 to Champaign, right on Prospect Ave., left on University Ave. This handsomely crafted turn-of-the-century house, on a street with many others of that period, is a museum in itself. The superb detail of the woodwork and cabinetry is done in the arts and crafts style, an American reaction against the over-ornate decor imported from Europe. The rooms, with their furnishings and samples of period dress, portray the lifestyle of the well-to-do in this era and in this neighborhood. *Open daily except Aug. and Jan. Admission charged.*

237 Lake of the Woods County Park

4 min. West on I-74 to Exit 172, right on Rte. 47. The rolling, lightly wooded hills of the park, with nature trails and a 26-acre lake for swimming and boating (rentals available), are an inviting contrast to the surrounding farmland. There's also a golf course, an early American museum, and a botanical garden. The museum features some 3,000 items that illustrate the ingenuity and hard work required to wrest a living from the land in the days of the pioneers. The botanical garden presents plants native to the prairie, dye plants, herbs, roses, and a conservatory with a collection of tropical plants. From the brick bell tower there's an interesting view of the landscape. *Open year-round. Vehicle charge May–Sept.*

203 Rockome Gardens

6 mi./12 min. West on Rte. 133; follow signs. Here in the heart of Illinois Amish country is a commercialized tourist attraction that is nonetheless engagingly eclectic and eccentric. Brightly colored barns and buildings adorned with the obligatory hex signs contrast with the more authentic blacksmith's shop and machine shed. In a class by themselves are the memorable walls, fences, and fanciful forms made of chunks of rock set in concrete and the house built of Fresca bottles. In season craft shows, festivals, and auctions are scheduled every weekend. *Open daily May–Oct. Admission charged.*

190 Fox Ridge State Park

15 mi./30 min. East on Rte. 16 through Charleston, right on Rte. 130. Hills, valleys, and woods come as a welcome surprise here on a plain that seems boundless. This oasis was not made accessible without the obvious labor of building boardwalks, bridges across steep little gorges, and steps up the hillsides for fine views of the forest canopy and the Embarras (pronounced *Am*-braw) River below. Be advised that the trails are on the arduous side, although

203. *On back roads in the Amish country horse-and-buggy days still prevail.*

there is one short trail for the handicapped. Free fishing boats suggest an outing on secluded 18-acre Ridge Lake, perhaps to try for largemouth bass or channel catfish. *Open daily except Christmas and New Year's Day.*

127 Ingram's Pioneer Log Cabin Village, Kinmundy

3 mi./12 min. East to Rte. 37, left on Rte. 37, left on Monroe St.; follow signs. Log cabins are tangible reminders of the dogged resourcefulness of our pioneer forebears. Trees had to be felled, cut to length, squared, and notched with hand tools, and the foundations, fireplaces, and chimneys laid with stones dug and hauled from the fields. The cabins here—several homes, a general store, a cobbler's shop, a preacher's home, an apothecary shop, and an inn—were built between 1818 and 1860 and are furnished with spinning wheels, cradles, rope beds, chests, quilts, and other period pieces. The handwritten family records posted outside confirm their authenticity. The crafts people in period dress demonstrating early-day skills further define the meaning of self-reliance. *Open daily mid-Apr.–mid-Nov. Admission charged.*

116 William Jennings Bryan Museum, Salem

2 mi./10 min. East on Rte. 50 to Rte. 37 (S. Broadway) in Salem, right to museum. Bryan, a former congressman, secretary of state, and three-time presidential nominee, was born in this simple frame house, where he lived for his first seven years. He was a renowned orator, and his style is demonstrated here in a recording of his celebrated cross of gold speech. Here, too, are his baby clothes, his Spanish-American War uniform, and political buttons and ribbons. The modest objects by which he is remembered are in poignant contrast with his accomplishments. *Open Fri.–Wed. except Thanksgiving Day, Christmas, and New Year's Day.*

95 Mitchell Museum, Mount Vernon

2 mi./10 min. East on Rte. 15 (becomes Broadway), left on 27th St., right on Richview Rd. The striking, windowless white

1. *Stands of bald cypress and tupelo gum have established themselves in scenic Horseshoe Lake, where the Mississippi flowed before changing course in its rush to the sea.*

marble museum building, surrounded by an elegantly proportioned colonnade, is on the parklike grounds of Cedarhurst, the 80-acre estate of the late John and Eleanor Mitchell. The structure embodies their dream of providing an art center for this part of Illinois. The exhibits here include shows circulating nationally as well as works by local residents. The judiciously eclectic Mitchell collection of paintings, drawings, and sculpture, displayed in an administration building nearby, has works by Eakins, Sargent, Andrew Wyeth, and other 19th- and 20th-century masters. The attractive wooded grounds contain a lake and two nature trails. *Open P.M. Tues.–Sun. except holidays.*

77   Wayne Fitzgerrell State Park

5 min. West on Rte. 154, across first part of causeway over Rend Lake. As many as 2 million people per year seek recreation here, but the 19,000-acre Rend Lake and 21,000 adjacent acres of public land are sufficient to accommodate them. Stop at the visitor center for orientation and suggestions for your visit. Boating, hiking, swimming, and fishing are popular, and there's a wildlife refuge with a viewing platform. During the tourist season interpretive programs are sponsored. *Park open year-round; visitor center open Apr.–Oct.*

40   Ferne Clyffe State Park

7 mi./15 min. East on road to Goreville, right on Rte. 37. The series of bluffs, rocky gorges, waterfalls, and shelter rocks that flank the varied trails make hiking here a pleasure. Campsites on Deer Ridge catch a welcome cool breeze in summer. The Cherokees hunted here in 1838–39 while traveling west to a new reservation. The lake is stocked with bluegill and bass. *Open year-round except Christmas and New Year's Day.*

1   Horseshoe Lake Conservation Area

12 mi./15 min. North on Rte. 3; follow signs. An enchanting landscape surprisingly reminiscent of swamplands in the Deep South survives here in an oxbow lake formed by a meander of the Mississippi River. Bald cypress, swamp cottonwood, and tupelo gum trees growing in the shallow lake and along its edges are reflected in its dark, still water—except for the places where green algae lie as flat and dense as the baize on a billiard table. Plants and animals typical of a southern swamp flourish here. A spillway stabilized the lake, which is now less susceptible to flooding. Some bald eagles and upwards of 150,000 Canada geese winter at the lake. *Open year-round.*

1   Magnolia Manor, Cairo

3 mi./10 min. Southeast on Rte. 3 to Cairo, right on 28th St. to Washington Ave. Cairo resident Charles Galigher supplied flour to Union troops during the Civil War, profited handsomely, and in 1872 completed this 14-room red brick Victorian house. Great magnolia trees stand in front of the manor, and an ornamental fountain plays in the garden. In 1880 Galigher's friend, President Ulysses S. Grant, attended a glittering reception here and stayed overnight. The Cairo Historical Association, established in 1952, made the restoration of the mansion its first priority. Some furnishings, including Grant's bed, are original, and some antiques have been donated. A cupola atop the fourth story provides a view of the Ohio and Mississippi rivers. *Open year-round. Admission charged.*

1. *Ornamental excess is a surprising element of the stern Victorian era.*

63

127

11

116

21

64

95

64

18   See E–W book, sec. 33.

77

37

40

39

1   IL
    MO

See N–S book, sec. 23.

55

End I-57

65

90

80 84 | 259

See
E–W book,
sec. 6
for I-90;
sec. 23
for I-80;
sec. 13
for I-94.

253

75

178

64

See E–W
book,
sec. 30.

114

70

46

68

6

259 Indiana Dunes National Lakeshore

20 mi./25 min. East on I-94 to Exit 22B, east on Rte. 20, left on Mineral Springs Rd. These 1,800 acres of woodland trails and 3 miles of beach dominated by towering lakefront dunes evince an almost lyrical delicacy in an obviously industrial environment. A number of plants are relics of the colder climates that existed here at the end of the Ice Age, leaving a remarkable diversity of vegetation: arctic bearberry, together with prickly-pear cacti and northern jack pines, shares dune slopes with southern dogwoods. Although the dunes are large (Mt. Tom rises more than 190 feet) and are anchored against the wind by marram grass, sand cherry, cottonwoods, and other native plants, they are susceptible to erosion. *Open year-round.*

253 Wilbur H. Cummings Museum of Electronics, Valparaiso

17 mi./25 min. East on Rte. 30, left on Rte. 2, left on Lincoln Way. Electronic technology changes so quickly that yesterday's marvel soon becomes today's antique. This museum has electronic devices from the period of Edison and Marconi to the present, knowing that its latest state-of-the-art exhibits will soon be obsolescent. Among the highlights are a 1950's Seeburg jukebox that plays 78-r.p.m. records, Admiral Byrd's transmitter from a South Pole expedition, one of the first pinball machines, and radios by Atwater-Kent, Crosley, Philco, and other noted manufacturers. The museum is on the campus of Valparaiso Technical Institute. *Open year-round.*

178 Tippecanoe Battlefield

5 mi./17 min. North on Rte. 43, right on Rte. 225; follow signs. In 1811, Gen. William Henry Harrison, who was to become the ninth president of the United States some 30 years later, led his troops to victory over the Indian Confederacy at Tippecanoe Creek in what is now north Indiana. Fortunately, Harrison faced The Prophet rather than his brother, the formidable Tecumseh. The Prophet had convinced his followers that the white man's musket balls would pass through them harmlessly. This led to ill-advised bravado and defeat for the Indians, with relatively few losses for the whites. Indians had inhabited this area for a period of more than 2,000 years. But this battle put the region firmly in the hands of the other side; and in the War of 1812, Harrison finally ended the Indian threat to the old Northwest Territory by defeating Tecumseh himself at the Battle of the Thames. *Open daily except Thanksgiving Day, Christmas, and New Year's Day. Admission charged.*

178. *The size of the battlefield monument almost overwhelms the victorious general.*

114 Indianapolis, IN 46225

Convention & Visitors Association, 1 Hoosier Dome, Suite 100. (317) 639-4282. Nearly everyone knows that in May, Indianapolis boasts one of the world's largest sports events, the Indy 500. But there are also other attractions worthy of note. Consider, for example, the Indianapolis Museum of Art, the Indiana State Museum, and the Children's Museum, one of the largest and most varied of its kind. You can visit the home of James Whitcomb Riley and the 16-room Victorian mansion of Benjamin Harrison. There's a new zoo and three large parks. Festival Market Place in old Union Station has shops and restaurants, while City Market offers fresh produce and restaurants. And even if it isn't May, the Speedway is worth a visit. The Hall of Fame Museum displays antique and classic cars and more than 32 speedsters that have won the race since it began in 1911; and you can get the feel of the "Brickyard" on a minibus ride around the circuit.

68 Brown County State Park

14 mi./25 min. West on Rte. 46. This park's 15,543 hilly acres of pine, spruce, locust, and walnut trees, most of them planted by the Civilian Conservation Corps in the 1930's, are a change of scene from the miles of surrounding farmland. Impressive vistas in the park, Indiana's largest, can be seen from the 26 miles of bridle paths and 11 miles of hiking trails; a self-guiding nature trail is available, and there is fishing as well as a variety of other recreational activities at the lodge. The nature center in the park is equipped with a bird-watching station and a snake exhibit. *Open year-round.*

33 Hardy Lake State Recreation Area

9 mi./15 min. East on Rte. 256; follow signs. Hardy Lake was created in 1970, when Quick Creek was dammed as a water conservation project. Today anglers gravitate to the lake's southern section, which is well stocked with largemouth bass, crappie, and channel catfish. Launching ramps scattered around the lake and a marina with boats for rent (May–October) attract water-skiers and boat-racers. The beach is equipped with a bathhouse, rest rooms, and food concessions. A hookup campground with rest rooms, showers, and drinking fountains is a short walk through the woods from the lake. Primitive camping is available at water's edge. *Open year-round. Admission charged Apr.–mid-Sept.*

114. *Engineers and ironworkers cooperated to create the classic City Market in 1886.*

ROUTE 62 | Howard Steamboat Museum, Jeffersonville

5 min. East on Rte. 62, right on Spring St., left on Market St. Overlooking the Ohio River, this 22-room mansion was built in 1894 by Edmunds Howard, whose family-owned shipyard produced some of the world's most elegant steamboats. The same superb craftsmanship of the Howard vessels was also lavished on this luxurious Victorian home. The hand-carved wooden archways, 36 chandeliers, and a grand stair-

62. *The steamboat models are as carefully crafted as were the originals.*

case are all modeled on ones originally designed for steamboats. Also on display are scale models of famous boats, the neo-Louis XV–style furniture, a $35,000 brass bed, a 9-foot-wide pilot's wheel, and related memorabilia. *Open Tues.–Sun. except holidays. Admission charged.*

JEF | Louisville, KY 40202

MAB *Jefferson St. exit; Muhammad Ali Blvd. exit. Visitors Information Center, 400 S. 1st St. (502) 584-2121.* Since Churchill Downs is a primary attraction here, the grounds are open out of racing season; and at the Kentucky Derby Museum at the Downs, various media are employed to give the feel of Derby Week. For those with a little time to spend, the *Belle of Louisville*, an honest-to-goodness stern-wheeler, cruises the Ohio River in a style that travelers were once accustomed to. The J. B. Speed Art Museum, next to the University of Louisville, has contemporary and traditional art in a handsome neoclassical building; and the Museum of History and Science features natural history, aerospace exhibits, and hands-on learning. Old Louisville (Victorian houses), Butchertown (a German neighborhood), and Portland (French and Irish) are among the lovingly restored city districts.

94 | Schmidt's Coca-Cola Museum, Elizabethtown

6 mi./12 min. West on Rte. 62, right on Ring Rd., left on Rte. 31W. Located in a bottling plant run by the Schmidt family since the turn of the century, this museum celebrates some 100 years of Coca-Cola with countless examples of advertising and memorabilia. After passing by a pool of Japanese carp in the lobby and a gallery demonstrating the latest high-speed bottling techniques, the visitor enters an area with an astonishingly large collection of trademark-emblazoned items: glasses, toys, clocks, fans, trays, cards, ashtrays, and dispensers. An especially nostalgic touch is the 1893 soda fountain with a marble and onyx counter, elaborate mirrors, and Tiffany lamps. *Open Mon.–Fri. except holidays. Admission charged.*

91 | Abraham Lincoln Birthplace National Historic Site

81 *Exit 91: 13 mi./18 min. South on Rte. 61. Exit 81: 12 mi./20 min. East on Rte. 84, right on Rte. 61.* The first two years of Lincoln's life were spent at the Sinking Spring farm, where the legendary one-room log cabin with dirt floor is now preserved within a dignified memorial building reached by a flight of 56 steps (one for each year of Lincoln's life). The visitor center displays the Lincoln family Bible, and the nearby limestone spring for which the farm was named is speckled with shiny coins, like a wishing well. *Open daily except Christmas.*

53 | Kentucky Action Park, Cave City

5 min. West on Rte. 70. Don't worry—on the Alpine Slide you can control your own speed as you ride down the steep quarter-mile chute from the hilltop to a meadow below. Other attractions include go-carts and bumper boats; and on the chair lift ride up to the Alpine Slide, you'll enjoy some beautiful views of the valley. In the glassware store, artisans can be seen shaping glass into animals, stagecoaches, galleons, and other designs. *Open daily Memorial Day–Labor Day; weekends only Easter–Memorial Day and Labor Day–Oct. Admission charged.*

35

33

33

ROUTE 62   IN

2   KY
64

JEF   See E–W book, sec. 33.

0

MAB

42

94

3

91

10

81

28

53

31

65

22 The Hobson House, Bowling Green

4 mi./14 min. West on Scottsville Rd. (becomes Broadway, then 12th St.), right on State St., left on Main St.; follow signs. This handsome Italianate mansion overlooking the Barren River owes its survival to the fraternal sentiments of two officers on opposite sides of the Civil War. Union colonel Atwood Hobson built the three-story brick mansion; his friend, Confederate general Simon Bolivar Buckner, spared the partially built house when his forces occupied Bowling Green from September 1861 to February 1862. Now fully restored as a living museum, the house contains many choice period pieces from Kentucky and environs, including a charming rococo Louis XV–style bed from Louisiana. An elegant central hall leads to double parlors with frescoed ceilings. *Open Tues.–Sun. Admission charged.*

92 The Hermitage

I-40 *Exit 92: 8 mi./20 min. East on Old Hickory Blvd.; follow signs. Exit I-40: 16 mi./25 min. East on I-40 to Exit 221, north on Rte. 45; follow signs.* Andrew Jackson—war hero, Tennessee gentleman, and the seventh president of the United States—is fittingly remembered at this 625-acre historic site, where two of his homes have been faithfully restored. The "early Hermitage" is a simple log cabin in which Jackson lived happily with his wife, Rachel, from 1804 to 1819. The Hermitage, their second home, is a gracious mansion with wide verandas and Doric columns. Most of the furnishings belonged to the Jackson family, including the crystal, the fine banquet table, mirrors, and a number of impressive family portraits. *Open daily except Thanksgiving Day and Christmas. Admission charged.*

90 Opryland U.S.A., Nashville

80

Exit 90: 5.5 mi./8 min. South on Rte. 155 (Briley Pkwy.); follow signs. Exit 80: 12 mi./20 min. East on I-440 to Exit 53, left on Rte. 24, right on I-40 to Exit 215, north on Rte. 155 (Briley Pkwy.); follow signs. This 120-acre stage show and park complex combines the Grand Ole Opry, the legendary country music showcase, with numerous other attractions. The amusement park rides, some with names based upon musical themes—from "The Old Mill Scream" to the "Rock n' Roller Coaster"—appeal to both adults and children. Also part of Opryland are the Roy Acuff Museum, which has a fine collection of memorabilia from country music's early days, and the *General Jackson*, a paddlewheel showboat that offers both day and night cruises. *Open daily Memorial Day–Labor Day; weekends Mar.–May and Sept.–Oct. Admission charged.*

85 Nashville, TN 37213

Tourist Information Center, James Robertson Pkwy. (615) 242-5606. The city's renown as the headquarters of country music tends to obscure the many other rewarding aspects of this gracious state capital. Tribute is paid to antiquity in the splendid Greek revival capitol and in the Parthenon, an exact-size replica of the ancient temple containing a museum and a gallery. Exhibits in the Tennessee State Museum depict life from prehistoric times through the Civil War, and at Fort Nashborough cabins, stockaded walls, and artifacts recall pioneer days. The Country Music Hall of Fame and other museums celebrate Nashville's musical heritage.

65 Carnton Mansion, Franklin

4 mi./10 min. West on Rte. 96, left on Mack Hatcher Memorial Bypass, right on Rte. 431, left on Carnton Lane. Randal McGavock, at one time mayor of Nashville, built this imposing three-story brick house in 1826 and probably planned it to take advantage of the prevailing breeze—it can sweep past the columns of the south-facing front porch, through the central hall, and up the grand staircase to freshen the upper rooms. The mansion's sparse but elegant furnishings include family portraits and parlor and dining room settings. *Open Mon.–Sat. and P.M. Sun. Apr.–Dec.; Mon.–Fri. Jan.–Mar. Admission charged.*

65 The Carter House, Franklin

4 mi./10 min. West on Rte. 96; follow signs. The pockmarks and bullet holes on the house and smokehouse here recall the Bat-

340. *The latest developments in rocketry soon become historic artifacts of engineering.*

tle of Franklin, one of the bloodiest engagements of the Civil War. On November 30, 1864, Confederate general John B. Hood launched a desperate attack against the Union forces that were entrenched around the house and its outbuildings. Among the more than 1,700 Confederate fatalities was Capt. Theodrick "Tod" Carter, whose father and sisters found him mortally wounded less than 200 yards from the family home. The visitor center has a small museum and auditorium. The modest but handsome house, with hand-poured glass windows and Doric columns, is furnished with original family and period pieces. *Open Mon.–Sat. and P.M. Sun. except holidays. Admission charged.* 🌲♿

46 | President James K. Polk Ancestral Home, Columbia

10 mi./20 min. West on Rte. 99, left on Rte. 315 (becomes N. Garden St.), right on W. 7th St. This unpretentious two-story brick house, built by President James K. Polk's father in 1816, was the Tennessee home of the 11th president of the United States for only 6 years, between his college days and his marriage. The contents of the building, however, represent Polk's entire career. Among the paintings is a series showing Polk as a young lawyer and at both the beginning and end of his presidency. Several pieces of White House china, silver, and crystal are on display, and an Inauguration ball gown worn by Sarah Polk, along with the ornate fan given to her for that occasion, are also exhibited. *Open daily Mon.–Thurs. and P.M. Sun. except Thanksgiving Day, Christmas Eve, Christmas, and New Year's Day. Admission charged.*

340 | Mooresville Historic Town

1 min. East on Rte. 20/Alt. 72. Like Rip Van Winkle, this charming and well-preserved hamlet seems to have slumbered for many years. And since it has not been featured as a tourist attraction, it retains a good measure of grace and dignity. Incorporated in 1818, Mooresville is one year older than the state of Alabama itself. The streets, lined by venerable shade trees and virtually free of cars, retain their 19th-century serenity. It takes 15 or 20 minutes to stroll

through the village and admire the fine old federal-style houses, all inhabited and immaculately maintained. You might start at the circa-1840 post office, which is constructed of poplar and still has its original post office boxes; and you can also pay a visit to the Mooresville Brick Church, built in 1839 for Robert Donnel, one of the founding fathers of the Cumberland Presbyterian Church. 🚶

340 | Point Mallard Park, Decatur

10 mi./20 min. West on Rte. 20/Alt. 72, left on Rte. 31, left on 8th St. SE. Pleasantly situated on a wooded peninsula across the Tennessee River from a national wildlife refuge, this 750-acre park is a swimmer's paradise. As bathers bob on floats in the churning waters of the turbine-driven wave pool (America's first), they look like strangely contented survivors of a shipwreck. Three serpentine water slides, a sandy river beach, and a huge swimming pool round out the aquatic fun. You can also sample an 18-hole golf course, minigolf, tennis, a hiking trail, playing fields, and in winter, an outdoor ice-skating rink. *Open year-round.* 🌲⛺🚐🚶🏊🎣

340 | The Space and Rocket Center, Huntsville

15 mi./20 min. East on Rte. 20/Alt. 72; follow signs. You can ride in a simulated space shuttle, spin in a centrifuge, or amble through a space station; or you can explore the Lunar Lander, walk alongside a *Saturn V* rocket displayed in stages, and watch Space Camp trainees practice their zero-gravity skills. In any case you'll be impressed at the courage it takes to sit on top of a rocket filled with thousands of gallons of volatile fuel and about to be launched for the moon. *Open daily except Christmas. Admission charged.*

318 / 310 | Hurricane Creek Park

Exit 318: 4 min. South on Rte. 31. Exit 310: 5 min. East on Rte. 157, left on Rte. 31. This deep Appalachian gorge surrounded by trails and tunnels is an intriguing place to explore. William Rodgers, an air force major, spotted it from

a jet plane in 1958, and upon his retirement he bought the land, developed it, and opened the rugged canyon to the public in 1963. Steep trails of varying degrees of difficulty descend through narrow rock fissures to a creek spanned by a rope bridge. The most challenging route leads to Twilite Tunnel, a dark and winding 600-foot passage up through the mountain. The gorge is laced with hickory, pine, and mountain laurel. *Open year-round.* 🌲🚶

308 | Ave Maria Grotto

5 mi./12 min. East on Rte. 278; follow signs. This unique garden of architectural miniatures is the result of one man's loving labor. During the almost 70 years that Brother Joseph Zoettl lived in the Benedictine Abbey of St. Bernard, he created more than 125 scaled-down reproductions of shrines and famous buildings. You'll see the city of Jerusalem, the Lourdes Basilica, the Hanging Gardens of Babylon, a fanciful Temple of the Fairies, and the elaborate 27-foot-high Ave Maria Grotto. Amazing for both sheer quantity and accuracy (Brother Joseph saw only two of the originals, basing most of his constructions on research and photos), these highly detailed works were made with a variety of ordinary found and donated materials, such as floats from Irish fishing nets, cold cream jars, marbles, and for the dome of St. Peter's Basilica in Rome, an old birdcage. *Open year-round. Admission charged.*

308. *St. Peter's Basilica is the centerpiece in the grotto's Roman group.*

308

284

24

24

See
E–W book,
sec. 46.

20

260

1

259B

13

246

34

212

7

205

24

181

8

173

1

172

308 — Clarkson Covered Bridge, Cullman

8 mi./15 min. West on Rte. 278; follow signs. Doves like to roost in the rafters beneath this circa-1904 covered truss bridge, supported by four massive stone piers. With a span of 275 feet, it is one of the largest structures of its kind in Alabama. Retired, restored, and inscribed in *The National Register of Historic Places*, the bridge provides a charming focal point for the adjacent small park. As you stroll across, notice the shadows that are cast by the latticelike construction. A short nature trail and picnic area are idyllically set amid tall trees beside the creek. *Open daily Memorial Day–Labor Day.*

284 — Rickwood Caverns State Park

4 mi./10 min. West on Rte. 160, right on access road. Your descent into this cool, eerie labyrinth takes you back some 260 million years. The shells and marine fossils embedded in the walls verify that this was once below the ocean. At the lowest level lies an underground lake, where blind fish swim through dark waters. The 102 steps leading out of the caverns may be difficult for some. In addition to the usual camping facilities, the park has an Olympic-size swimming pool, and a narrow-gauge train circles it. *Open daily June–Labor Day; weekends March–May and Sept.–Oct. Admission charged.*

260 / 259B — Birmingham, AL 35203

Convention & Visitors Bureau, 2027 1st Ave. N. (205) 252-9825. The character of the city as viewed from the base of Vulcan's statue on Red Mountain is dramatically different from the smokestack industry image that originally inspired the 55-foot cast-iron monument. Alabama's largest city now boasts an excellent museum of fine arts, the Southern Museum of Flight, a children's museum, and the unique Red Mountain Museum, where a deep cut into the mountain for a highway provides close-up observation that reveals some 150 million years of layers of sedimentation and fossils from ancient seas. At the Birmingham Botanical Gardens there's a conservatory of rare plants and a charming Japanese garden; the excellent zoo is nearby. Arlington Antebellum Home, a handsome Greek revival house, has extensive gardens and interesting collections of furniture and decorative art. The early days of the iron industry are recalled in the reconstructed Sloss Furnaces, which are now a walk-through museum.

246 — Oak Mountain State Park

5 min. Follow signs. Opportunities for recreation here in Alabama's largest state park—nearly 10,000 acres set in a deep, wooded Appalachian valley—range from canoeing, fishing, swimming, and tennis to BMX bike riding and rugged mountain hiking. Those interested in waterside pursuits have three lakes to choose from, and there are some 30 miles of hiking trails. For the adventurous, a twisting and unimproved mountain road leads to a parking lot and the half-mile walk to scenic Peavine Falls. *Open year-round. Admission charged.*

212 — Lay Dam Generating Plant Tour

10 mi./15 min. North on Rte. 145, right on Rte. 55; follow signs. Here is a rare opportunity to descend into the heart of a mammoth hydroelectric dam and to see how running water is transformed into megavolts of electricity. The tour begins 40 feet below the top of the dam in the central generating area, where 85-foot-high turbines are situated in each of the 26 gates of the dam. In the control room, walls of gauges and meters monitor every function of the plant's machinery. The observation deck looks across Lay Lake to a wooded valley where a receding line of towers transmits the boon of light and power to distant places. *Open year-round. For tour call (205) 755-4520.*

205 — Confederate Memorial Park

9 mi./15 min. South on Rtes. 31 and 143. This park was established to commemorate the Confederate veterans who, long after the fighting had ceased, were left destitute and without federal pensions. To help these victims of circumstance, Jefferson Manley Falkner Soldiers Home opened its doors in 1902. Civil War memorabilia and photos and accounts of the home's occupants are displayed in the visitor center–museum. On two hillsides overlooking the park, cemeteries contain the graves of more than 200 veterans, 15 Confederate wives, and the tomb of an unknown soldier. Most of the headstones date from 1912 to 1936. *Open year-round. Admission free but donations encouraged.*

181 / 173 — Jasmine Hill Gardens, Montgomery

Exit 181: 17 mi./23 min. East on Rte. 14, right on Rte. 231, left on Jasmine Hill Rd. Exit 173: 18 mi./22 min. East on North Blvd., left on Rte. 231, right on Jasmine Hill Rd. Added to the seasonal color of the lovely trees, shrubs, and flowers in this 17-acre garden is the constant refreshing sense of fun and fantasy provided by more than 30 originals and reproductions of classic Greek sculpture. The Greek gods, nymphs, animals, athletes, and heroes are charmingly displayed throughout the grounds. A replica of the ruins of Hera's Temple surrounds a reflecting pool, where water lilies bloom and goldfish glide under Hera's steady gaze. Terra-cotta dogs guard stone pathways lined with roses and honeysuckle, and ivy-shaded arbors lead to romantic pavilions and some secluded stone benches. *Open Tues.–Sun. and Mon. holidays except Thanksgiving Day, Christmas, and New Year's Day. Admission charged.*

172 — Montgomery, AL 36104

Chamber of Commerce, 41 Commerce St. (205) 834-5200. Montgomery bears witness to two of the South's most momentous events. Near the state capitol is the official residence used by Jefferson Davis as president of the Confederacy. It is now a Confederate museum. Nearby is the Dexter Avenue King Memorial Baptist Church, where the Reverend Dr. Martin Luther King, Jr., advocated nonviolent protests as a way of ending racial segregation. The Old South lives again in the 27 homes and buildings of the Old North Hull Street His-

172. *Cozy bedroom in the Jefferson Davis house. Note the flip side of the quilt.*

toric District, and at the Teague House and the Rice-Semple-Haardt House. For a restful interlude there's an excursion cruise on the *General Richard Montgomery,* an Alabama River paddle wheeler.

130 Sherling Lake Park

4 mi./7 min. North on Rte. 185, left on Rte. 263. When William Bartram, the well-known naturalist, passed through this site in 1775 on his exploration of the Southeast, he probably admired the many giant umbrella magnolias that still grace this tranquil place. A wide boulevard leads to a jade-green lakeshore where manicured lawns separate Sherling Lake from the surrounding dense woodland. You can circle the lake on a 2-mile-long boardwalk with handsome bridges and observe the many bird species attracted to the shore by strategically placed feeders. *Open year-round.*

57 Claude D. Kelley State Park

9 mi./12 min. North on Rte. 21; follow signs. A paved road leads through secluded pine woods to the Little River, where a dam has created a small lake. The knee-deep water near the dam is favored by children for wading. More adventurous swimmers will find the reddish waters of the river refreshing on summer days. Anglers will enjoy casting off from atop the dam. A short distance from the lake area, shaded picnic tables, barbecues, and a playground enhance this pleasant park, whose tranquillity is protected by the Little River State Forest across the road. *Open year-round.*

31 Historic Blakeley State Park

16 mi./20 min. South on Rte. 225. This wooded 3,800-acre park memorializes the last great battle of the Civil War, where fighting continued for hours on April 9, 1865, after General Lee had surrendered in Virginia. Self-guiding maps of the Blakeley park and battleground are available from the park ranger. One trail traverses woodland atop some well-preserved Confederate breastworks; near the beaver pond, a bucolic picnic and cane-pole fishing spot, you can see the incongruously peaceful remains of a gun emplacement. The park sponsors an annual reenactment of the South's heroic last stand in early April.

Another trail leads to the 1,000-year-old Jury Oak, which early 19th-century settlers reportedly used as a courthouse. The judge sat in a fork among the lower branches while the defendant stood below. And if the verdict was guilty, the Hanging Tree was just a few steps away. *Open daily except Christmas. Admission charged.*

1 Mobile, AL 36602

Chamber of Commerce, 451 Government St. (205) 433-6951. In this charming city one feels the essence of the Old South: the magnolias, live oaks, crape myrtles, camellias, and azaleas in abundance and scores of gracious antebellum houses. The five historic districts and the neighborhoods adjoining them constitute a veritable museum of architectural styles—from federal to Victorian—including Oakleigh, a classic of southern design, and the Richards–D.A.R. House, adorned with ornate lace ironwork. Other highlights include the City Museum and a reconstructed French fort. In Battleship U.S.S. *Alabama* Memorial Park, you can board the World War II battleship as well as a submarine and see a B-52 bomber and other aircraft of the era.

I-10 Bellingrath Gardens and Home, Theodore

15 mi./20 min. West on I-10, left on Rte. 90, left on Bellingrath Rd. Floral exuberance and abundance characterize these 65 acres of gardens, created in the midst of a semi-tropical jungle along a river. One of the first delights along the walking tour is the Oriental-American garden. Here a wooden teahouse sits between a carp stream and a placid lake, where swans glide against a backdrop of weeping Yoshima cherry trees. Near the imposing brick house are brilliant beds of perennials. The wheel-shaped rose garden—where roses bloom in every shade from lemon-yellow to deep scarlet—is an inviting source of color and fragrance for 9 months of the year. In the fall one of the world's largest outdoor displays of chrysanthemums—some 80,000 plants—brightens the landscape. A conservatory houses orchids and other exotic plants.

Antique furnishings and objets d'art are displayed in the former Walter D. Bellingrath home, and the nearby Boehm Gallery houses more than 230 of the famed porcelain sculptures created by Edward Marshall Boehm. *Open year-round. Admission charged for garden and home.*

I-10. *Azaleas add a splash of color to the subtle palette of the Japanese garden.*

42

130

73

57

26

31

34

1   See E–W book, sec. 54.

2

I-10

10

End I-65

69

CANADA
U.S.A.
MI

94 | I-94

See
E–W book,
sec. 14.

61

137

75

See
N–S book,
sec. 30.

47

90

15

ROUTE
27B

44

See
E–W book,
sec. 14.

94 | 38

2

36

39
MI
IN

80 | 90

154

See E-W book,
sec. 23 for I-80;
sec. 7 for I-90.

90–27B. *One property of static electricity is the creation of instant hairdos.*

I-94 Lakeport State Park

8 mi./11 min. East on I-94, north on Pine Grove Ave. (becomes Rte. 25). The south (FDR) unit of this lakeside park has pleasant picnic grounds shaded by tall oaks, maples, and pines, as well as a fine swimming beach that looks out on ships making their way to or from Port Huron, Detroit, or Windsor. The north unit, located a mile farther along Route 25, is a spacious campground set in open and wooded terrain. The north unit also has access to a beach on Lake Huron. *Open year-round. Admission charged.*

137 Crossroads Village and Huckleberry Railroad, Flint

8 mi./11 min. North on I-475 to Exit 11, east on Carpenter Rd., left on Bray Rd.; follow signs. The village re-creates a Genesee County community of the 1870's, with costumed interpreters playing the parts of local characters. Old-style mills grind corn and turn logs into lumber, and an old Baldwin steam locomotive takes visitors on a 45-minute scenic tour of the village. *Open daily Memorial Day–Labor Day, P.M. Fri.–Sun. in Dec. Admission charged.*

90 Impression 5, Lansing

ROUTE 27B

Exit 90: 7 mi./12 min. South on Rte. 127 to Grand River Ave. exit; continue on Howard St., right on Michigan Ave., left on Museum Dr. Rte. 27 (business) exit: 7 mi./15 min. Northeast on Rte. 27 (business; becomes I-496), north on Larch St., left on Michigan Ave., left on Museum Dr. This imaginative science museum offers excellent hands-on demonstrations that make it fun to learn about the sciences of physics, chemistry, electronics, biology, and computing. Visitors of all ages can take a sensitivity test, play with molecules and fiber optics, experiment with integrated circuits, look through stereoscopic microscopes, or produce computer artwork on a "flatbed plotter-digitizer." *Open Mon.–Sat. and P.M. Sun. except Memorial Day, Thanksgiving Day, Christmas Eve, Christmas, New Year's Day, and Easter. Admission charged.*

38 Binder Park Zoo

11.5 mi./14 min. West on I-94 to Exit 100, south on Beadle Lake Rd.; follow signs. Set in the woodland of Binder Park, the zoo provides naturalistic environments for many of its animals. A boardwalk through a pinewoods overlooks the exhibit areas, where Formosan sika deer reside; bison, peacocks, and prairie dogs can also be seen; and llamas, Sicilian donkeys, ponies, and a yak can be fed and petted at the petting zoo. A variety of waterbirds inhabit the zoo's pond, and around its edge are enclosures for gibbons, eagles, emus, and wallabies. *Open daily late Apr.–late Oct. Admission charged.*

36 Honolulu House, Marshall

5 min. East on I-94 (business loop); follow signs. This curious home, modeled on the executive mansion in Honolulu, was built in 1860 by Judge Abner Pratt, a former U.S. consul in the Sandwich (Hawaiian) Islands, who strove to create the exotic atmosphere of the Pacific islands in Michigan. The two-story house has a broad veranda and an observation tower that is reached from the central hall by a spiral staircase; the rooms have 15-foot ceilings, and the murals—wreaths of tropical plants mixed with lilies, cattails, and classic cupids—have been restored to their appearance in 1885, when a new owner remodeled the house and had the original murals embellished. The furnishings are from the mid- to the late 19th century. *Open P.M. daily late May–Oct. Admission charged.*

154 Pokagon State Park

2 min. West on Rte. 727. This park, named for Potawatomi chief Pokagon, has year-round appeal. In winter the thrill seekers head for the 1,780-foot refrigerated toboggan slide, where they can streak down and over hills at 45 miles per hour. The slide is open from Thanksgiving to March, and the toboggans, rented by the hour, can hold up to four passengers. Other attractions in this

36. *Over 4,000 miles from the original, but the architectural mix retains its charm.*

vast area include trails for hikers and cross-country skiers (rentals available), ice fishing, ice skating, sledding, and year-round camping. In summer, visitors come to fish, boat, and swim from Lake James's wide and sandy beaches. *Open year-round. Admission charged.* 🌲 ⛺ 🚐 🚶 🏊 🎣 ♿

129 | Auburn Cord Duesenberg Museum

2 mi./6 min. East on Rte. 8; follow signs. This exceptionally fine collection of classic cars enshrined in the art deco Auburn Automobile Company showroom elegantly illustrates the golden age of automotive design. The display includes a silver and black 265-h.p. Duesenberg, a scarlet and chrome Cord, a 1937 black and chrome Cord Sportsman, a Stutz Bearcat, early Auburn sedans, a racing Bugatti, a Ferrari, and an Aston Martin. *Open daily except Thanksgiving Day, Christmas, and New Year's Day. Admission charged.*

111A | Historic Fort Wayne

102 | *Exit 111A: 3 mi./15 min. South on Rte. 27, left on Superior St., then left on Barr St. Exit 102: 10 mi./30 min. East on Jefferson Blvd., left on Rte. 27, left on Superior St., right on Barr St.* A reconstructed fort of stout log and mud-chinked walls with formidable blockhouses recalls Ft. Wayne's role as an important frontier outpost in the early 19th century. The fort's colorful history is illustrated with weaponry, tools, and documents from the warring Indians, English, French, and the newly established Americans. *Open daily mid-Apr.–Labor Day; Tues.–Sun. early Sept.–late Oct. Admission charged.* 🌲 ♿

86 | Huntington Lake

78 | *8 mi./15 min. Exit 86: west on Rte. 224, left on Rte. 5. Exit 78: north on Rte. 5.* The 8,322-acre Huntington Reservoir property, which once belonged to the Miami Indians, offers a variety of recreational opportunities, from model-airplane flying to camping in a mature forest of oak and shagbark hickory on a steep bluff over the water. A beach, a boat ramp, and attractive picnic areas and shelters are located

129. *Auburns still rank high among the all-time classics of automobile design.*

along the shore. The narrow lake is stocked with channel catfish, walleye, bass, bluegill, and crappie, and there is small game and waterfowl hunting in season. *Open year-round. Admission charged Memorial Day–Labor Day.* 🌲 ⛺ 🚐 🚶 🏊 🎣

41 | Ball Corporation Museum, Muncie

11 mi./20 min. East on Rte. 332, right on Wheeling Ave. (becomes High St.). The Ball brothers' ventures in containers of every kind, from wooden egg barrels in the late 1800's to Pepsi-Cola cans, are chronicled in an exhibit in the reception area of the Ball Corporation headquarters. Glass preserving jars of all shapes, sizes, and hues are displayed, including one filled with elderberry syrup put up in 1888. *Open Mon.–Fri. except holidays.*

34 | Mounds State Park

26 | *Exit 34: 3 mi./10 min. West on Rte. 32; follow signs. Exit 26: 5 mi./15 min. North on Rte. 9, right on Rte. 232.* The fate of the ancient Adena and Hopewell Indians who built these burial and ceremonial mounds and earthworks is unknown. At one time there were 11 mounds

here, but today only three are recognizable. Replicas of the tools these Indians used are displayed in the mid-19th-century Bronnenberg House. Trails for horseback riding, hiking, and cross-country skiing pass the mounds and earthworks. *Open year-round. Admission charged.*
🌲 ⛺ 🚐 🚶 🏊 🎣

5 | Conner Prairie, Noblesville

4 mi./8 min. West on 116th St., right on Allisonville Rd.; follow signs. Visitors are encouraged to take part in the activities of this convincingly reconstructed early-19th-century village. Interpreters dressed in period clothing play the parts of people from the era. Townspeople exchange gossip at the inn, the teacher gives an Old World history lesson in the schoolhouse, and costumed weavers, potters, carpenters, a blacksmith, and a physician discuss and demonstrate their work in houses and shops. The most noteworthy of the 39 buildings here are the Museum Center, which features an audiovisual presentation, and the Conner Mansion, built in 1823. *Open Tues.–Sat. and P.M. Sun. May–Oct.; Wed.–Sat. and P.M. Sun. Apr. and Nov. except Thanksgiving Day and Easter. Admission charged.* 🌲 ♿

I-465 | Indianapolis, IN 46225

Convention & Visitors Association, 1 Hoosier Dome, Suite 100. (317) 639-4282. Nearly everyone knows that in May, Indianapolis boasts one of the world's largest sports events, the Indy 500. But there are also other attractions worthy of note. Consider, for example, the Indianapolis Museum of Art, the Indiana State Museum, and the Children's Museum, one of the largest and most varied of its kind. There's a new zoo and three large parks. In Union Station in the heart of downtown, Festival Market Place, with its many shops and restaurants, attracts crowds. And even if it isn't May, the Speedway is worth a visit. The Hall of Fame Museum displays antique and classic cars and more than 32 speedsters that have won the race since it began in 1911; and you can get the feel of the "Brickyard" on a minibus ride around the circuit.

Section 29 (412 miles)

See map page V.

25

129

18

111A

9

102

16

86

8

78

87

41

7

34

8

26

21

5

5

I-465

65 70

End I-69

See E–W book, sec. 30 for I-70; N–S book, sec. 26 for I-65.

To reach I-70 or I-65 go south on I-465.

75

CANADA

U.S.A.
MI

394

8

386

47

339

57

282

23

259

20

339. *The palisaded fort is an accurate reconstruction of a British outpost.*

394 Soo Locks, Sault Sainte Marie

2 mi./7 min. East on Easterday Ave., left on Rte. 75 (business), left on Portage Ave. More than 20 vessels per day pass through the Soo Locks —from small pleasure boats to 1,000-foot-long giant freighters carrying more than 70,000 tons of cargo. The oldest of the four locks dates back to 1914, while the newest and biggest was completed in 1968. A hydroelectric power plant at nearby St. Marys Rapids provides power for the locks, and the surplus is sold by a private company for homes and businesses in Sault Sainte Marie. Comprehensive displays at the information center describe the history of the locks and their importance. *Open daily mid-May—mid-Nov.* ♿

386 Brimley State Park

11 mi./14 min. West on Rte. 28, right on Rte. 221, right at T-junction; follow signs. This attractive little park looks out across Brimley Bay to Lake Superior. The lake narrows here as it approaches the St. Marys River (which connects it with Lake Huron), and from the park you can see 1,000-foot-long freighters on their way to and from the Soo Locks. *Open year-round. Admission charged.*

339 Colonial Michilimackinac State Historic Park

2 min. Headed south: north on Louvingny St., right on Huron St. Headed north: north on Nicolet St. Ft. Michilimackinac, built here about 1715 by the French and occupied by the British from 1761 to 1781, has been reconstructed on its original site, re-creating with great authenticity the spirit and character of the settlement's early days. Within the fort's walls are a powder magazine, the commanding officer's house, and merchants' quarters stocked with pelts, barrels, and trade goods. The adjacent Mackinac Maritime Park displays maritime artifacts from ships and boats that once plied these waters, including the hull of an 1891 steam yacht. At the old Mackinac Point lighthouse a museum features exhibits on the maritime history of the Straits of Mackinac. *Open daily mid-May—mid-Oct. Admission charged.*

282 Call of the Wild, Gaylord

4 min. East on Rte. 75 (business), right on S. Wisconsin Ave. This wildlife museum has numerous bird and animal specimens, ranging from a polar bear to cougars, realistically mounted in dioramas representing their natural habitats. Most are shown in some characteristic pose or activity (the beavers, for example, are gnawing on aspens beside their dam), and often birds and animals that share an environment are grouped together. In many cases, recordings of the creatures' voices can be heard. An ingenious system of mirrors allows you to see some scenes and animals in different seasons. *Open daily except Thanksgiving Day, Christmas, and New Year's Day. Admission charged.*

259 Hartwick Pines State Park

4 min. North on Rte. 93. The glory of the park is a 49-acre forest of majestic virgin pines more than 140 feet tall, a remnant of the days when vast tracts of Michigan were densely covered by primeval forests. A visitor center and museum recall the lumberjacks, lumber barons, and pulp mills of Michigan's so-called White Pine Era from 1840 to 1910. Those roistering days are brought vividly to life by the authentic lumber camp, with a bunkhouse, a store, a blacksmith's and a carpenter's shop, and the foreman's cabin. Logging equipment and a steam-operated sawmill are also on display. The 2-mile Mertz Grade Nature Trail follows the track of a railroad that once carried lumber to mills in Grayling, and the AuSable River Foot Trail cuts through forest and clearing to skirt the East Branch of the AuSable River. *Park open year-round; exhibit buildings open Apr.—Oct. Admission charged.*

239 South Higgins Lake State Park

7 mi./9 min. West on Rte. 103, left on Rte. 100. More than 1,000 acres of woods and lake here include some well-developed facilities for camping and picnicking, a boat basin, a long sandy beach, and a nature trail animated by gulls and black squirrels. Fringed with birch and evergreen trees, the crystalline lake has distant views of woods and hills on its far shores. Just across the road from the park is the 700-acre Marl Lake area, a smaller lake with a much wilder environment (no camping permitted), with trails through the woods along the lake's perimeter. *Open year-round. Admission charged.*

190 Gladwin City Park

23 mi./26 min. West on Rte. 61, left on City Park St. Set in the midst of central Michigan country, which is known for its abundant lakes and rivers, Gladwin is a pleasant little town in which to stop and relax—and it is made all the more pleasant by this lovely city park along the Cedar River. The recreational facilities here are unusually complete: camping and picnic grounds are supplemented by tennis courts, a ballfield, and a playground for children; river swimmers enjoy a sandy beach; and a riverside path makes for scenic strolling. *Park open year-round; camping permitted Apr.–Nov.*

168 Tobico Marsh

5.5 mi./7 min. East on Beaver Rd., left on N. Euclid Rd. The varied habitat provided by woods, the wetlands of Tobico Lagoon, and dry uplands make this 1,700-acre refuge, about half a mile from Bay City State Park's entrance, a bird-watcher's paradise. Trails wind among rare flowers and shrubs to the water's edge, and two 30-foot-high observation towers afford treetop views of the lagoon and the more than 60 species of water birds that come by the thousands during spring and fall migrations. To enter the refuge, get the gate key from the park manager or the nearby Jennison Nature Center. *Open year-round.*

162A Historical Museum of Bay County, Bay City

3 mi./6 min. East on Rte. 25, right on Washington Ave. The museum occupies the old Michigan National Guard Armory building, a severe but handsome structure that dates from 1909—just 10 years before the museum itself was founded. Today, the collections contain some 60,000 artifacts, representing all aspects of life in Bay County. A chronological history of Bay County is depicted in a planned history maze, with displays portraying Indian life and early industries, such as mining and shipping. *For hours call (517) 893-5733.*

149B Saginaw-Tokushima Friendship Gardens

4 mi./9 min. West on Rte. 46, right on Rte. 13 (Washington Ave.). In 1970 the sister cities of Saginaw, Michigan, and Tokushima, Japan, marked their friendship by creating these traditional Japanese gardens. Greeted by a beautiful antique stone lantern, visitors proceed along a garden path to a charming bridge of ancient design that crosses a stream beside a tranquil lake. The Japanese Cultural Center and Tea House, one of the few fully authentic Japanese tea houses in America, is a true international joint effort. Americans built the foundation, external walls, and roof while Japanese craftsmen finished the interior, with its ceiling of handwoven cedar strips, walls made of a light brown mud-plaster, and

cedar-frame shoji screens with rice paper. Visitors may participate in a traditional Japanese tea ceremony. *Gardens open Tues.–Sun. Memorial Day–Labor Day; tea house open P.M. Tues.–Sun. Memorial Day–Labor Day; gardens and tea house open P.M. Wed.–Sun. Labor Day–Memorial Day. Admission charged.*

149B Shiawasee National Wildlife Refuge, Saginaw

12 mi./20 min. West on Rte. 46, left on Rte. 13, right on Curtis Rd. From September to November, as many as 25,000 Canada geese and 50,000 ducks visit this refuge on their fall migration, lured here by thousands of acres of wetlands and 1,500 acres that are sharecropped for the birds' benefit. There are some 5 miles of hiking trails that cross farmland, shallow pools of water, and green-tree impoundments (areas annually flooded by a system of dikes to provide the birds with access to new sources of food). Another 5 miles of trails in the northern section of the park (west on Route 46, south on Center Road, left on Stroebel Road) explores mostly hardwood forests and bottomland. Bald eagles have begun to nest here, and white-tailed deer are common. *Open year-round.*

125 / 111 Crossroads Village and Huckleberry Railroad, Flint

Exit 125: 6 mi./10 min. East on I-475 to Exit 11, east on Carpenter Rd., left on Bray Rd.; follow signs. Exit 111: 13 mi./15 min. North on I-475 to Exit 11, east on Carpenter Rd.; proceed as above. The village re-creates a Genesee County community of the 1870's, with costumed interpreters playing the parts of the miller, doctor, apothecary, printer, sawyer, and other local characters. Old-style mills grind corn and turn logs into lumber, and an old Baldwin steam locomotive takes visitors on a 45-minute scenic tour through the village and along Mott Lake on the Huckleberry Railroad. Special events take place in summer, ranging from antique auto and hot-air balloon shows to festivals. During December the village becomes a wonderland of colored lights. *Open daily Memorial Day–Labor Day, P.M. Fri.–Sun. in Dec. Admission charged.*

168. *A Canada goose escorts goslings on the algae-tinted waters of Tobico Lagoon.*

239

49

190

22

168

6

162A

13

149B

24

125

14

69

111

See N–S book, sec. 29.

10

75

101 Seven Lakes State Park, Fenton

4 mi./8 min. West on Grange Hall Rd., right on Fish Lake Rd. This unusually lovely park has varied landscapes, scenic views, and six lakes of different sizes. The largest has a gravel beach, and its irregular shoreline embraces numerous small bays and inlets. Foot trails wind along the shores of three lakes and through meadows dotted with wildflowers. The rich avian life includes ring-necked pheasants and downy woodpeckers. *Open year-round. Admission charged.*

81 Bald Mountain Recreation Area, Lake Orion

6 mi./8 min. North on Rte. 24, right on Greenshield Rd. The wild scenery here is crisscrossed by several hiking trails; and there are three lakes, one of which (Upper Trout Lake) has a broad, sandy swimming beach. The park is known for the abundance of its wildflowers, which flourish in habitats ranging from young woodlands to rough meadows and bottomlands. The less developed north unit of the park can be reached by continuing north on Route 24 and following signs. *Open year-round. Admission charged.*

50 Detroit, MI 48226

Convention and Visitors Bureau, 2 E. Jefferson Ave. (313) 567-1170. Although best known for its automobiles, Detroit still keeps an antique electric trolley system in service, along with an ultramodern elevated people mover, which provides an interesting perspective of the city. To take a tour of the auto plants always requires some advance planning. But the industry is powerfully represented in Diego Rivera's great frescoes of the city in the Detroit Institute of Arts, which in addition has exceptionally well-rounded collections from every major period.

The city also offers such varied attractions as the bustling open-air Eastern Market, with its vast displays of flowers and vegetables, two zoos, a children's museum, a family amusement park, and a freshwater aquarium. You can also take a tour of a Motown recording studio.

41 Henry Ford Museum and Greenfield Village, Dearborn

8 mi./12 min. North on Rte. 39 (Southfield Hwy.), left on Oakwood Blvd. The scope, variety, and quality of one of the nation's largest museum complexes are extraordinary. The exhibits represent most of the aspects of America's cultural and technological history. In the extensive Henry Ford Museum you will see George Washington's campaign chest and the rocking chair Abraham Lincoln was sitting in when he was assassinated; the 600-ton Allegheny locomotive, one of the largest coal-burning engines ever built; and steam engines as big as houses. The adjoining Greenfield Village, spread over 81 acres, has most of the amenities, and all of the charm, of a small 19th-century town. You'll find tree-lined streets and historic buildings brought here from their original sites—the Wright brothers' cycle shop, Henry Ford's birthplace, and Thomas Edison's laboratory complex from Menlo Park, New Jersey, among others. *Museum open daily except Thanksgiving Day and Christmas; village interiors open daily except early Jan.–mid-Mar. Admission charged for each.*

156. *Prices—and styles—have changed but the barber pole remains the same.*

I-280 / 201B Toledo, OH 43604

Office of Tourism & Conventions, 218 Huron St. (419) 243-8191. This major Great Lakes port is a city of iron and coal, where bicycle and wagon shops gave way to auto parts makers and a thriving glass industry. The Toledo Museum of Art has magnificent glass displays, as well as extensive collections in many periods of painting and sculpture. The Portside Festival Marketplace, on the waterfront, is a lively and likely focus for a visit.

193 Fort Meigs State Memorial

4 mi./10 min. South on Rte. 20, right on Rte. 65; follow signs. Built on a bluff above the rapids of the Maumee River, Ft. Meigs played a key role in America's victory in the War of 1812. It was built in February 1813, and in May survived a siege and bombardment by the British Army; in July the British were repulsed again, and this failure paved the way for their defeat in the Battle of Lake Erie. The present fort is a reconstruction of the original; three of the seven blockhouses contain exhibits about the war and about the construction of forts. *Open Wed.–Sat., P.M. Sun and holidays late May–early Sept.; Sat. and P.M. Sun. early Sept.–late Oct. Admission charged.*

156 Ghost Town

6 mi./15 min. South on Rte. 15/68; continue on Rte. 68; follow signs. The quaint houses, stores, and other buildings here, some original and some faithfully reproduced, are so full of authentic memorabilia from pioneer days that they almost give visitors the impression that their occupants might return at any moment. A row of businesses in this homey town includes the Noah's Ark Emporium, a Chinese laundry, a barbershop, an undertaker, and other establishments, all fully equipped with 19th-century goods and utensils and peopled by mannequins. In the middle of town a replica of an original Drake oil derrick stands next to a 25-foot covered bridge, one of the shortest in Ohio. *Open Tues.–Sun. Memorial Day–Labor Day; weekends only in Sept. Admission charged.*

75
101
20
81
31
See E–W book, sec. 14.
94
50
9
41
47
MI
OH
I-280
7
201B
8
80 90
See E–W book, sec. 24. for I-80; sec. 7 for I-90.
193
37
156

58–54C. *The Valkyrie is an experimental bomber with dramatic implications of speed.*

125 Railroad Exhibit, Lima

5 min. West on Rte. 309/117 (Bellefontaine Ave.), right on Shawnee St.; follow signs. A massive steam locomotive built in 1949 was the last one constructed at the Lima Locomotive Works (originally called the Lima Machine Company), which had been manufacturing steam engines since 1878. Painted black with white-rimmed wheels, *Nickel Plate No. 779* is a marvel of brute power intricately harnessed by a network of pipes, cylinders, and valves. The cab of the engine, several coaches—including a luxurious private Pullman car—a red caboose, an outfitted depot–ticket office, and an old signal standard add to this nostalgic memorial to the days of steam power. *Open year-round.* ⅋

111 Neil Armstrong Air and Space Museum, Wapakoneta

2 min. West on Wapak-Fisher Rd.; follow signs. This futuristic winged structure set on a hillside is dedicated to Ohioan Neil Armstrong, the first man to walk on the moon. The Infinity Room illustrates the vastness of space with endlessly receding perpectives in a mirrored cubicle and an Astro-Theater dealing with space life. Another area chronicles the history of flight and the part played by other Ohioans, most notably the Wright brothers. From their embryonic flight at Kitty Hawk, it is indeed a giant leap to the *Gemini 8* spacecraft, which has been cut away to show the cramped interior conditions and the complicated array of dials and switches that the pilot had to master. *Open daily Mar.–Nov. Admission charged.* ♿

58 / 54C United States Air Force Museum, Dayton

Exit 58: 6 mi./15 min. East on Needmore Rd. (becomes Harshman Rd.), right on Springfield St. Exit 54C: 5 mi./10 min. East on Rte. 4, right on Harshman Rd.; proceed as above. "Where eagles rest" is the motto of this museum with an impressive array of military aircraft and related displays. Fighter biplanes from World War I still look sleek and deadly. Messerschmitts, Spitfires, and Mustangs from World War II nestle under the wings of Flying Fortresses and Liberators. In the museum's main hangar and nearby annex you will see almost 200 planes and missiles on display. They span the history of aviation from the Wright brothers' kitelike 1909 Military Flyer to a charred and battered Apollo capsule that circled the moon. *Open daily except Christmas.* ⅋ ♿

53A Dayton, OH 45402

Convention & Visitors Bureau, Chamber Plaza, 5th and Main Sts. (513) 226-8248 or (800) 221-8234; (800) 221-8235 outside OH. This river city, settled in 1796, seems to have invention in the air. The cash register, the electric starter, and the pull-tab tin-can top all were devised by Daytonians. But the best-known local wizards were Orville and Wilbur Wright. One of their first planes is among the attractions in Carillon Park. Also to be seen there are relics of canals, railroads, and airways.

Dayton is also the home of the last Wright bicycle shop, as well as the printshop where the brothers published the work of the black poet Paul Laurence Dunbar, whose home is now a museum. Other highlights: the National Aviation Hall of Fame and the baroque collections in the Dayton Art Institute.

1F / 1E Cincinnati, OH 45202

Convention and Visitors Bureau, 300 W. 6th St. (513) 621-2142. In the downtown section of this city, which was a starting place for settlers heading west on the Ohio River, a modern 16-block skywalk now connects department stores, specialty shops, and restaurants. The Cincinnati Art Museum's galleries—numbering more than a hundred—offer works from all major cultures and periods. The Taft Museum, in a federal-style house, displays porcelains, enamels, and paintings by European masters.

The Museum of Natural History features a large, realistic cave and exhibits related to prehistoric Indians and primitive cultures. The outstanding zoo has more than 1,200 species and is especially noted for its gorillas and white tigers.

Across the river, in Covington, Kentucky, the Riverside Historic District recalls the early days in the area.

31

125

14

111

53

See E–W book, sec. 30.

70

58

4

54C

1

53A

52

1F

0

1E

OH

KY

19

75

175
Big Bone Lick State Park

8 mi./15 min. West on Rte. 338; follow signs. The coming of the Ice Age drove huge herds of prehistoric mammals southward. Drawn to this marsh for the mineral deposits of its sulfur springs, many woolly mammoths, mastodons, enormous ground sloths, peccaries, and polar bears were fatally mired in the soft ground. Their bones, once so plentiful that early explorers used them to pitch tents, are now gone—but not forgotten. Two life-size models of the extinct mammals are on display side by side along the 1-mile self-guiding trail. A small museum, tennis courts, and a pool are additional enticements to visit this scenic spot. *Open year-round.*

115
Lexington, KY 40507

104
Convention & Visitors Bureau, 430 W. Vine St. (606) 233-1221. For all the publicity about horses here in the bluegrass country, it's not necessary to be an equestrian to enjoy a visit. There are historic houses of note, two inviting university campuses, and some interesting renovated shopping areas. In the Georgian-style Mary Todd Lincoln House, you can see furnishings similar to the ones that were here when the future First Lady lived in the structure as a girl. While the Todd House has an engaging charm, the Hunt-Morgan House, with its 19th-century furnishings and woodwork, is a study in restrained elegance of the federal style. Ashland, the handsome estate of the famous statesman Henry Clay, lies on the outskirts of town. The Italianate house, surrounded by lawns and woodlands, also has an attractive formal garden. The University of Kentucky campus offers an art museum and a mile-long "Tree Trail" through the area.

95
Fort Boonesborough State Park

6 mi./10 min. Northeast on Rte. 627, right on Rte. 388. In 1775 Daniel Boone had just established this vital frontier post on the banks of the Kentucky River when his daughter was captured by Indians. With a few companions Boone set off after the marauders and, against all odds, recovered

the girl. On a hill close to its original site, Boone's fort has been lovingly reconstructed, from its log walls and blockhouses to the pioneer lifestyle itself. You'll see blacksmiths, toymakers, weavers, and spinners at work. You can also swim in the river or fish for perch, catfish, and bass. *Park open year-round; fort open daily Apr.–Sept.; Wed.–Sun. Sept.–Oct. Admission charged to fort.*

76
Churchill Weavers, Berea

2.5 mi./7 min. Northeast on Rte. 25, right on Rte. 1016; follow signs. The ancient art of handweaving is practiced to perfection by the skilled Churchill Weavers. The founder, Carroll Churchill, designed a fly shuttle loom—which is used here—when he and his wife were missionaries in India. In 1922 the Churchills started a local cottage industry to provide employment in impoverished Appalachia. A self-guiding tour of this now-thriving business begins with the finished blankets and accessories in the gift shop, then goes through tagging, inspection, and mending areas to the actual loom room, where weavers produce original designs. *Loomhouse open Mon.–Fri.; gift shop open Mon.–Sat. and P.M. Sun. except Christmas and New Year's Day.*

38
Levi Jackson Wilderness Road State Park

4 mi./10 min. East on Rte. 192, right on Rte. 25, left on Rte. 1006. During the late 18th century an estimated 200,000 pioneers surged westward across the Appalachians along the Wilderness Road, part of which was originally known as Boone's Trace, which passes through this fascinating park. The hardships of the journey are memorialized by a profusion of roadside graves and a small cemetery in which some 20 members of the McNitt Party, who were massacred by Indians in 1786, lie buried. The Mountain Life Museum consists of seven original relocated log cabins, including a two-room schoolhouse, a blacksmith's shop, and an 1880's Methodist church. Period furnishings, a collection of Indian artifacts, and examples of pioneer utensils bring a bygone era vividly to life. *Open year-round.*

25. *A carpet of moss and subtle rainbows puts this falls in a class by itself.*

25
Cumberland Falls State Resort Park

15 mi./30 min. Southwest on Rte. 25W; continue west on Rte. 90. In 1780 Zachariah Green led a party of hunters down the uncharted waters of the Cumberland River in what is now Kentucky. His poplar boat meandered gently between wooded bluffs until it rounded a curve and suddenly came upon a 68-foot drop in the river. Scrambling for safety, the hunters abandoned their craft. Cumberland Falls is now a popular resort favored by honeymooners for its wonderfully romantic cascade and frequent rainbows, or on a moonlit night, lovely "moonbows" in the falls' mist. *Open year-round.*

122
Museum of Appalachia

3 min. Northeast on Rte. 61. The atmosphere of an Appalachian mountain village-museum stems from the authenticity of each detail. A lifetime's labor of love by owner and operator John Rice Irwin, this living museum began as one log cabin and grew to a 65-acre village of more than 30 buildings. Some 250,000 period artifacts illustrate every aspect of the lives led by the resourceful mountain folk, who either made what they needed or did without. The 10,000-square-foot barn-museum is home

See E–W book, sec. 34.

to cooper's, carpenter's, and leather shops and displays of folk art, musical instruments, early agricultural tools, Appalachian basketry, textiles, and rifle making. You'll also see a log church, a loomhouse, a gristmill, an iron jail, an underground dairy, and a dirt-floor cabin. *Open daily except Christmas. Admission charged.* 🪑♿

122 81 American Museum of Science and Energy, Oak Ridge

Exit 122: 15 mi./ 25 min. Southwest on Rte. 61; follow signs. Exit 81: 20 mi./25 min. Northwest on Rte. 321, right on Rte. 95. The secret life of Oak Ridge, Tennessee, helped to change the course of world history. An important part of the Manhattan Project in World War II, it produced the uranium required for the first atom bomb. Oak Ridge has remained in the forefront of nuclear research and production ever since that time. The museum's purpose is to inform the visitor of contemporary energy requirements and the methods of energy generation as well as the history of energy use in the United States and alternatives for the future. The exhibits are dynamic, inviting participation wherever possible. Models demonstrate the basic principles of science. *Open daily except Thanksgiving Day, Christmas, and New Year's Day.* 🪑♿

I-275 I-40 Knoxville, TN 37902

Convention and Visitors Bureau, 500 Henley St. (615) 523-2316. The colorful time of year in Knoxville is mid-April, when the dogwoods are in bloom; but the city's historic houses, the museums, and the excellent zoo are reasons enough for a visit any time of year.

Early colonial days are recalled at the Gen. James White Fort with its stockade. The territorial era (1790–96) is represented by the handsome home of the then governor, William Blount. The Armstrong-Lockett House, built in 1834, has notable collections of old silver and furniture, and the Civil War era is recalled at Confederate Memorial Hall. The Knoxville Museum of Art, which is located on the 1982 World's Fair site, features a popular display of period rooms re-created in miniature.

49 McMinn County Living Heritage Museum, Athens

5 mi./10 min. East on Rte. 30, right on Jackson St., left on Robeson St. A visit to this charming museum is akin to rummaging through the attic of an entire community. The large collection is housed in the Old College Building, a porticoed mid-19th-century red brick edifice that is now part of the Tennessee Wesleyan College campus. Displays cover the region's heritage from the era of the Cherokee nation to the 1930's. Quaint surprises among the exhibits include a once-elegant single-seater phaeton, a handmade doll with chicken feathers for hair, and 17th-century African trade beads. The quilt collection is a highlight. *Open Tues.–Fri. and P.M. weekends except holidays. Admission charged.*

I-24 Chattanooga, TN 37402

Convention and Visitors Bureau, 1001 Market St. (800) 338-3999; (800) 322-3344 outside TN. Towering majestically over the city, Lookout Mountain offers an interesting variety of attractions in itself. A steep-incline railway runs to the summit, where on a clear day the rocky lookout that gave Chattanooga its Cherokee name provides a view of several states. Rock City Gardens, also at the top, features intriguing rock formations and trails that lead to spectacular vistas. If you take an elevator deep within the mountain, you can see 145-foot-high Ruby Falls and some spectacular caverns. Significant Civil War battles are commemorated at Cravens House and at Confederama, both located at Lookout Mountain.

In the city proper, a railroad museum and the Chattanooga Choo-Choo center celebrate a bygone era and offer rides in vintage-style cars. The Hunter Museum of Art, overlooking the Tennessee River, has a fine collection of American paintings, and the Houston Museum presents American and European antiques and decorative arts.

141 Chickamauga–Chattanooga National Military Park

7.5 mi./15 min. West on Rte. 2, left on Rte. 27. Dedicated in 1895, this was the first national military park in the U.S. It was established not only to commemorate the 34,000 men who were casualties at Chickamauga—either killed, missing in action, or wounded—during the Civil War, but as a place to study what occurred from a historical and military perspective. The grounds look much as they did in the autumn of 1863, when more than 120,000 troops were engaged in a widespread bloody conflict, the objective of which was to control Chattanooga (the North proved victorious). A row of Civil War–era cannons greets you at the visitor center. Inside, there are displays illustrating the battles as well as a fine collection of firearms dating from 1690 to 1917. *Open daily except Christmas.* 🪑🚶♿

I-24. *The cannon is a reminder that it was not always peaceful on Lookout Mountain.*

64

122

15

I-275

4

I-40

See E–W book, sec. 41.

20

40

81

32

49

59

I-24

TN

GA

141

33

75

75

131

29

124

13

116

21

PT

INT

20

See E-W
book,
sec. 46.

92

42

67

26

58

10

53

131 New Echota State Historic Site

3 min. Northeast on Rte. 225; follow signs. In 1825 the Cherokee nation established its capital, New Echota. The tribe adopted a republican form of government, developed a written form of their language, and adapted in other ways to the white man's world. But in 1838–39 they were forced by the government to leave their land and move to Oklahoma, traveling on what became known as the Trail of Tears. New Echota fell into disuse and all but vanished, but it was partially restored in the 1950's. Today five structures represent the onetime capital of the Cherokees: the Supreme Court Building, a tavern, a typical Cherokee cabin, the house of Samuel Worcester (a missionary who devoted his life to the Cherokees), and the tiny printing office where the bilingual *Cherokee Phoenix* was published. *Open Tues.–Sat. and P.M. Sun. except Thanksgiving Day and Christmas. Admission charged.*

124 Etowah Mounds State Historic Site, Cartersville

5 mi./15 min. West on Rte. 113 to Cartersville, left on Etowah Dr.; continue on Indian Mounds Rd. These ceremonial earthen mounds are located on a 54-acre site along the banks of the Etowah River, which between about A.D. 1000 and 1500 provided

124. *Marble mortuary figures of striking sculptural power found at Etowah.*

water, nourishment, protection, and transportation for a thriving community of Indians. The mounds served as temples and tombs, and also provided the foundation for the priest-chief's home. Three flat-topped mounds remain, along with the vestiges of a moat that encircled the town in a protective arc from the riverbank. The largest mound, at 63 feet, may have served as an observatory. This site has been partially excavated, and some of the most outstanding archeological finds are displayed in a museum at the visitor center. *Open Tues.–Sat. and P.M. Sun. except Thanksgiving Day and Christmas.*

116 Kennesaw Mountain National Battlefield Park

5 mi./12 min. Southwest on Barrett Pkwy., right on Rte. 41 (Cobb Pkwy.), left on Old Rte. 41; follow signs. The Battle of Kennesaw Mountain in June 1864, part of Sherman's campaign against Atlanta, was one of a series of bloody engagements in which the Confederate forces fought to save the vital railroad and manufacturing center. The Southerners managed to repel Union attacks and hold their position for about 2 weeks, but ultimately had to retreat.

The road to the top of the mountain leads to a line of gun emplacements complete with cannons. The site affords a view for miles in all directions, including the skyline of Atlanta. It is easy to understand why the Confederates thought their position was exceptionally strong. A self-guiding auto tour and miles of hiking trails lead to key battle positions and interpretive exhibits. *Open daily except Christmas and New Year's Day.*

PT / INT Atlanta, GA 30303

Peachtree Street exit. International Blvd. exit. Convention & Visitors Bureau, 233 Peachtree St., Suite 2000. (404) 521-6600. As this bustling modern metropolis continues to grow, the essence of the Old South becomes more difficult to find. One place to look is the Tullie Smith House Restoration, an 1840's farmhouse with outbuildings, herb gardens, and craft demonstrations. On the same site is the Swan House, a 20th-century Palladian-style structure with a formal garden. The Civil War Battle of Atlanta, depicted in the circular painted cyclorama at Grant Park, has sound and light effects and is viewed from a revolving platform. The High Museum of Art, a handsome modern building on Peachtree Street, has an excellent collection of European and American art.

The birthplace and the tomb of Nobel Prize winner Martin Luther King, Jr., are honored in a two-block national historic site. Other famous Georgians are commemorated in the Capitol's Hall of Fame.

92 Six Flags Over Georgia

13.5 mi./20 min. West on I-20 to Exit 13; follow signs. At this attractive and well-landscaped theme park just west of Atlanta, the first thing you are likely to hear is the screams of anguished delight coming from riders on such aptly named attractions as Mindbender (a loop-the-loop), Free Fall (a 10-story drop), and Great Gasp (a parachute drop). Water rides take visitors over rapids and falls and down log chutes, but there are plenty of gentler rides as well, including an 1820's-style train that circles the entire park. Other attractions to be enjoyed are performances by divers, acrobats, and musicians. *Open daily June–Aug.; weekends only mid-Mar.–May and Sept.–Oct. Admission charged.*

67 Indian Springs State Park

14 mi./20 min. East on Rte. 16, right on Rte. 23, right on Rte. 42. Creek Indians told white traders of this mineral spring, with alleged healing properties, and by the 1820's it was being enjoyed by all. But in 1825, William McIntosh, a Creek chief (with a Scottish father), signed a treaty exchanging land in southwestern Georgia for acreage west of the Mississippi—plus a cash bonus for himself. Fellow tribesmen, angered by the unauthorized treaty and the apparent bribe, murdered McIntosh. A later treaty gave whites the land, and resorts were soon developed. The spring is still here, and there's a historical museum, a miniature golf course, and a 105-acre lake for swimming, fishing, and pedal boats. *Open year-round.*

92. *Passengers on the Thunder River rapids ride can expect a dousing of white water.*

58 52 Museum of Arts and Sciences, Macon

Exit 58: 10 mi./15 min. South on I-475 to Exit 4, left on Rte. 41 (becomes Forsyth Rd.). Exit 52: West on Rte. 41 (Forsyth Rd.). The galleries in this museum feature changing exhibits of work by established international, national, and local artists. The impressive permanent collection has items ranging from sculpture to abstract drawings, minerals, handwoven rugs, and African handiwork. In the science wing the main attraction is the 40-million-year-old whale fossil. The Science Hall features changing science displays, with hands-on exhibits. The petting zoo includes goats, sheep, and other animals. Also located here is the Mark Smith Planetarium, which offers educational programs along with a variety of popular entertainment. *Open daily except holidays. Admission charged.*

53 Ocmulgee National Monument, Macon

5 min. East on I-16 to Exit 4, north on Martin Luther King Blvd., right on Rte. 80, right on Emery Hwy. Archeological excavations begun in 1933 have revealed that an ancient people lived in this area for more than 10,000 years. Huge earthen mounds, some up to 60 feet tall, were built between A.D. 900 and 1100 by people of the Mississippian culture. Known today as the People of the Naked Plateau, they were

skilled farmers with a sophisticated social hierarchy and some knowledge of astronomy. The mounds were used for burials and other purposes not fully understood. An earth lodge has been reconstructed. *Open daily except Christmas and New Year's Day. Admission charged.*

44 John Cranshaw's One-Horse Farm and Gardens, Kathleen

14 mi./20 min. East on Rte. 96, right on Rte. 41, left on Sandefur Rd. What began in 1950 with a gift of a dozen daylilies has grown into a 5-acre garden of more than 700 varieties. This is now a commercial nursery, and Cranshaw's lilies, many of which are varieties John Cranshaw himself developed, are in demand from as far away as New Zealand. The lilies are at their best in May and June. Peacocks roam the property. *Open year-round.*

33 Georgia Veterans Memorial State Park

10 mi./13 min. West on Rte. 280. This 1,327-acre park pays tribute to veterans of every U.S. conflict from the French and Indian War to the Vietnam War. Among the many varied relics on display in the visitor center are U.S. cavalry saddlebags, a Civil War cannon, a German spiked helmet, and an M-6 survival weapon (a combination rifle and shotgun). Outdoors you'll see a collection of armored vehicles and artillery pieces, including a 155-mm howitzer, the

B-29 bomber used for photographic work during the first atomic bomb mission, and a heavy Patton tank used in the Korean War. Nearby, Lake Blackshear provides a peaceful contrast, as well as some of the state's best largemouth bass fishing. Model-airplane flying is a very popular activity. *Open year-round.*

20 Georgia Agrirama, Tifton

2 min. West on 8th St. As you tour the 95 acres and see the buildings that make up the state of Georgia's official museum of agriculture, you'll get a firsthand impression of what life was like on various farms and rural towns in the post–Civil War South. Survival hinged on self-sufficiency, and reminders of that fact are provided by the log farmhouse with rope-sprung beds, the water-driven gristmill, and the wood-burning turpentine distillery, believed to be the last of its kind still operating in the South. Basic skills, such as quilting and soap making, are explained and demonstrated by guides in period costumes. You'll see a sugarcane mill, a smokehouse, a blacksmith's shop, and a restored railroad depot. *Open daily except Thanksgiving Day, Christmas, and three days prior to Christmas. Admission charged.*

4 The Barber-Pittman House, Valdosta

4 mi./10 min. East on Rte. 84, left on Ashley St. An eye for detail will find much to admire in this carefully restored neoclassical home, built in 1915 for E. R. Barber, one of the founders of Valdosta's Coca-Cola Bottling Works. The building's handsome exterior provides a hint of the intricate treasures that you'll find inside. Beyond the marble steps, tiled porch, and six Ionic columns that support the front porch lie such ornate surprises as a handsome fanlight over the door, brass light fixtures, a uniquely designed sheet music cabinet, a dining room illuminated by 60 bulbs set in concentric rectangular ceiling beams, and one of the earliest central vacuum-cleaning systems. Although it now houses the county's chamber of commerce, it also contains 52 pieces of original family furniture. *Open Mon.–Fri. except holidays.*

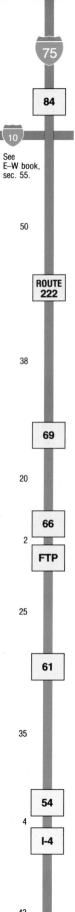

See
E–W book,
sec. 55.

84 Stephen Foster State Folk Culture Center

5 mi./10 min. East on Rte. 136, left on Rte. 41. The familiar strains of "Old Folks at Home," "Oh, Susanna," and other Stephen Foster melodies ring out from the carillon tower. While listening, the visitor can peruse the composer's scores and manuscripts, see a piano he composed on, and admire the instruments and costumes of the minstrel bands that played such an important role in popularizing his music.

In the visitor center ingeniously mechanized dioramas depict the themes of his famous songs: horses run in the "Camptown Races," steamboats ply the Suwannee River, and cowboys gather around to hear "Oh, Susanna." Traditional crafts are represented by Seminole baskets, Cuban cigars, and artifacts from local turpentine camps. Headphones bring you the music of the region, played on banjos, by steel bands, and by a Latin dance band. *Open year-round. Admission charged.*

ROUTE 222 Devil's Millhopper State Geological Site

5 mi./7 min. East on Rte. 222, left on 43rd Ave., left on Rte. 232. The cool interior of this vast sinkhole, 120 feet deep and 500 feet in diameter, contains plant and animal species not normally found this far south. Formed when the roof of a cavern collapsed millennia ago, the sinkhole has yielded fossils of sharks' teeth and bones of extinct land animals. Interpretive plaques along a staircase to the bottom of the giant depression explain various aspects of this phenomenon. To early settlers who named it, the sinkhole must have conjured up visions of a satanic grain grinder. *Open year-round. Admission charged.*

69 Florida's Silver Springs

9 mi./17 min. East on Rte. 40. From glass-bottomed boats on the crystal-clear water of 17 artesian springs, you can see fish, alligators, snakes, and the bottom of the river some 80 feet below. Shows at the Reptile Institute feature rattlesnakes, boa constrictors, and a performer who wrestles with an alligator. For children the petting zoo presents deer and other approachable animals. The automobiles in the antique and classic car collection include a 1914 Overland Speedster and a model of the never-produced 1955 Gaylord. *Open year-round. Admission charged.*

66 Lake Griffin State Recreation Area

17 mi./24 min. East on Rte. 44, left on Rte. 27. The live-oak hammock here on typical central Florida sandhills adjoins a marsh filled with water lilies, water lettuce, and water hyacinths. The length of Dead River, connecting the marsh with Lake Griffin, can be paddled in a canoe in about an hour. Denizens of this watery realm include alligators, egrets, anhingas, ospreys, and the gallinule. Nature trails wind through the hammocks, and a moss-draped live oak that grows here is said to be the second oldest in the state of Florida. *Open year-round. Admission charged.*

40. *The Ringling eye for dramatic splendor is clearly revealed in the garden.*

61 Florida's Weeki Wachee

22 mi./32 min. North on Rte. 98, left on Rte. 50, left on Rte. 19. An underwater mermaid show at this theme park presents aqua dancing, magic tricks, and a closed-circuit televised view of a 3-minute dive to a depth of 117 feet on lung power alone. Other attractions found here include a walk through an animal forest, a birds of prey show starring hawks, owls, and eagles, and a bird show featuring parrots and macaws on bikes and roller skates. The half-hour Weeki Wachee River cruise on a silent electric boat passes an orphanage where injured pelicans are cared for. A colony of raccoons frequently shows up for a handout. *Open year-round. Admission charged.*

54 Busch Gardens, The Dark Continent, Tampa

5 mi./10 min. West on Rte. 582, left on N. McKinley Dr. Three thousand exotic animals, from Asian elephants to Bengal tigers, performing dolphins, stage shows, and rides such as the Congo River Rapids and the 360°-loop Scorpion roller coaster are featured at this theme park and zoo. A Moroccan street bazaar has snake charmers, while in Nairobi elephants bathe in a swimming hole. Through the viewing windows of the nursery you can observe some of the 1,200 animals that are born here every year. The animals in the Serengeti Plain, including zebras, camels, ostriches, crocodiles, orangutans, tigers, and giraffes, can be seen via a steam-powered train, a monorail, or an overhead skyride. *Open year-round. Admission charged.*

40 The John and Mable Ringling Museum of Art, Sarasota

7 mi./11 min. West on University Pkwy., left on Rte. 301, right on DeSoto Rd. The treasures of this museum on the estate of the circus magnate comprise more than 10,000 objects, both ancient and modern. Its collection of baroque art is one of the finest in America. There are also works by Cranach, Van Dyck, Hals, El Greco, Reynolds, and Gainsborough. Rubens is represented by five massive canvases of "The Triumph of the Eucharist." The Circus Galleries display posters, costumes, bandwagons, and other memorabilia, and have tributes to such greats as Emmett Kelly and the Wallendas. The mansion of the Ringlings, Ca' d' Zan ("house of John" in Venetian dialect), is a whimsical interpretation of a Venetian palazzo, with touches copied from the facade of the famous Doge's Palace in Venice and the tower of the noted 1890 Madison Square Garden in New York City. *Open daily except Thanksgiving Day, Christmas, and New Year's Day.*

If You Have Some Extra Time: Walt Disney World Resort

FTP
I-4

Florida Tpk. exit: 68 mi./90 min. I-4 exit: 65 mi./90 min. To walk through the turnstile is to enter a world as you would like it to be—immaculately clean, beautifully landscaped, perfectly maintained, safe, orderly, and filled with happy people. In the Magic Kingdom, you'll find an enchanting Cinderella Castle surrounded by Frontierland, Tomorrowland, Adventureland, Fantasyland, and more. Fifteen minutes away by car or monorail is Epcot Center, which is in two parts: Future World includes pavilions, exhibits, and rides with an educational or futuristic accent; and World Showcase, set around a beautiful wide lagoon, has buildings, reconstructed street scenes, shops, and restaurants representing a dozen different countries. Unlike traditional park rides, the rides at Disney World transport you into new worlds of imagination.

For a representative sample try the Magic Kingdom's Space Mountain, Pirates of the Caribbean, or The Haunted Mansion—all three can be seen in half a day. At Epcot Center you can walk into a replica of Beijing's famed Temple of Heaven, take a ride through the greenhouses of The Land pavilion, and see remarkable agricultural innovations. The Magic Eye Theater has incredible 3-D images.

Disney World can be crowded, and some attractions have long lines, but for the most part its 20,000 employees make it work like a well-oiled machine. It takes 4 full days for a visitor to feel reasonably satisfied, but even if you have only a day it will be unforgettable. *How to get there: Florida Tpk. exit, east on turnpike to Orlando; follow signs. I-4 exit, east on I-4 to Orlando; follow signs. Open year-round. Admission charged.*

---

37 | Myakka River State Park

9 mi./12 min. East on Rte. 72. In this 28,875-acre park (including a 7,500-acre wilderness preserve) the scenic views of Lake Myakka and the Myakka River are rivaled only by the vast expanse of prairies, hammocks, and marshes. Birding is excellent, and careful observers may be rewarded with a glimpse of a bobcat at dusk or deer grazing in the pinelands or otters by the river. The park offers some 40 miles of hiking trails and informative tours by tram or airboat. You can rent bikes, boats, and canoes, but you must bring your own horses to enjoy the 12 miles of riding trails. An interpretive center features wildlife exhibits and a movie about the park. *Open year-round. Admission charged.* ♿ ▲ 🚐 🚶

16. *Are relationships being pondered?*

22 | Thomas Edison Winter Home, Fort Myers

7 mi./12 min. West on Rte. 884, right on Rte. 867. In 1885, when Thomas Edison's doctors advised a Florida vacation to restore his health, the 38-year-old inventor headed south, where he not only regained his vigor (he lived to be 84) but found a second home. Today Seminole Lodge and its gardens and laboratory evoke images of the tireless American genius performing his many experiments or puttering among his flowers. Edison bulbs light the house (they burn 10 hours a day and have yet to burn out). The museum here includes examples of early motorcars as well as a large number of Edison phonographs and light bulbs. The laboratory, devoted to extracting rubber from a hybrid strain of goldenrod, remains as it was when Edison was working here. *Open Mon.–Sat. and P.M. Sun. except Thanksgiving Day and Christmas. Admission charged.* ♿ ♿

16 | Jungle Larry's Zoological Park at Caribbean Gardens, Naples

6.5 mi./10 min. West on Pine Ridge Rd., left on Rte. 851. This 52-acre park is a colorful mixture of circus and safari. Leopards and lions leap through blazing hoops, and enchanting macaws play basketball and ride tiny bicycles. Walk—or take the tram— along a trail through a junglelike environ-

ment where you will see tiglons (a rare cross between tiger and lion), Bengal tigers, alligators, chimpanzees, elephants, and exotic birds. A well-shaded petting zoo gives youngsters a chance to hold rabbits and other tame animals. For an insight into how wild creatures are actually tamed and taught to do tricks, stop at the Animal Training Center. *Open daily. Admission charged.* ♿ ♿

5 | Topeekeegee Yugnee Park, Hollywood

25 mi./15 min. East on Rte. 820, left on I-95 to Exit 24, left on Sheridan St., right on N. Park Rd. The name means "gathering place" in the Seminole Indian language, and this quiet park surrounded by a busy urban area still serves that purpose. People come here to relax and enjoy the wide shaded lawns, the picnic tables and grills, or to take advantage of the park's 40-acre lake and athletic facilities. There's a filtered and chlorinated swimming lagoon boasting a wide sand beach, and a nearby 50-foot-high water slide provides excitement with 700 feet of turns, drop sections, and occasional tunnels. You'll also find a volleyball net, a basketball court, and playing fields, and paddleboats, sailboats, sailboards, and canoes are available for rent. *Open year-round. Admission charged.*

♿ ▲ 🚐 🏊 🎣 ♿

40

9

37

67

22

29

16

5

89

End I-75

77
90
See E–W book, sec. 7.
E9TH
2
23
See E–W book, sec. 23.
80

E9TH Cleveland, OH 44114

E. 9th St. exit: Convention & Visitors Bureau, 1301 E. 6th St. (216) 621-4110. The observation deck in the Terminal Tower gives the best bird's-eye introduction to the city. You can get a more intimate look on a trolley tour; and to see where some of America's great fortunes were founded, take a boat trip down the Cuyahoga River near the steel mills. You can also view the Flats entertainment district, with its waterfront restaurants and boutiques, or stroll through one of Cleveland's many parks and visit the city's renowned zoo.

Cultural attractions in the city include the Cleveland Museum of Art, the Western Reserve Historical Society, and the Cleveland Museum of Natural History, where dinosaurs, fossils, and a variety of artifacts are on display. An exhibit at the Health Education Museum imaginatively depicts the workings of the human body.

Not to be missed is the downtown Arcade, where shops and restaurants are housed in a marvelous five-level skylit cast-iron fantasy—one of the largest such structures in the world.

WH Hale Farm and Village, Bath

Wheatley Rd. exit: 5 mi./12 min. West on Wheatley Rd., left on Cleveland-Massillon Rd., left on Ira Rd., left on Oak Hill Rd. Rural life in the mid-19th century is faithfully re-created in this engaging cluster of buildings, located on what was once the Western Reserve—the land "reserved" for settlers from Connecticut. Many of the buildings were moved to this site from other areas of Ohio. The federal-style 1826 brick farmhouse of Jonathan Hale is surprisingly elegant for an owner who had to hew his farm out of a wilderness. The village comprises a saltbox house, a meetinghouse, a log schoolhouse, a law office, a smithy, and a barn. Demonstrations of spinning and weaving, smithing, glassblowing, and candlemaking evoke the life of earlier times. The farm and village lie within the 32,000-acre Cuyahoga Valley National Recreation Area. *Open Tues.–Sat. and P.M. Sun. and holidays mid-May–Oct. and Dec. Admission charged.* ⛩

118. *The quiet charm of this secluded cove is enhanced by the morning mist.*

118 Portage Lakes State Park

7 mi./15 min. West on Rte. 619, left on Rte. 93. This meandering series of pleasant lakes and ponds extends for miles through a residential section, making it difficult to find public access. Stop first at the main park office for guidance (directions above). The park's Nimisila Reservoir, ideal for boating and fishing, is known for its walleyed pike, muskellunge, and bass. Launching ramps are available, and some areas are set aside for speedboats and water-skiing. *Open year-round.* ⛩ ▲ 🚐 🚶 🏊 🎣

WH. *Broom making is one of the old-time crafts demonstrated in the village.*

107A Pro Football Hall of Fame

2 min. East on Fulton Rd.; follow signs. In a domed rotunda with colored glass windows, 140 stars of pro football are honored, each commemorated by a life-size bronze head, a photograph of the star in action, and a rundown of his playing history. Other sections of this four-building complex contain mementos, photographs, descriptions, and videos that relate the history of the game from its 1892 beginnings to the present. There is a comprehensive display of old and new uniforms and gear and a complete set of helmets from all the major league teams. A football action movie is shown hourly. *Open daily except Christmas. Admission charged.*

105B Canton Classic Car Museum
105A

3 mi./10 min. Exit 105B: east on W. Tuscarawas St., right on S. Market Ave. Exit 105A: east on 6th St. Some 30 carefully restored cars from the golden age of automobiling are on display here. They stand in two rows separated by a red carpet, as though they were high-ranking dignitaries—which in a way they are. Mostly pre-World War II models, they include Franklins, a McFarlan, a Holmes, a Benham, and a Kissel among such handsome familiars as Rolls-Royces, Cadillacs, Lincolns, Pierce-Arrows, Packards, and a Model T Ford with as much brightwork as a royal yacht. Early auto advertising signs, gowns, and hats can also be seen here. *Open Tues.–Sun. May–Oct.; weekends only Nov.–Apr. Admission charged.*

93 Zoar Village State Memorial

3 mi./6 min. East on Rte. 212. Taking biblical Zoar, Lot's sanctuary from destruction, as an example, a group of German separatists, searching for religious freedom, built this communal village early in the 19th century. The buildings, ranging from simple log cabins to handsome brick structures, surround the rectangular Garden of Peace. This is still a thriving community, a living memorial to a dream fulfilled. Craftsmen demonstrate the way of life and work in that earlier era, while seven museums display original artifacts and furniture. *Open Wed.–Sun. Memorial Day–Labor Day. Admission charged.* 🚶

81 Schoenbrunn Village State Memorial

4 mi./5 min. East on Rte. 39, right on Rte. 259. This village has been re-created on the site of a mission established by David Zeisberger, one of the Moravian Brethren who had come to America seeking religious freedom. The Delaware Indians invited the Moravians to settle here in 1722. Today you'll find neat rows of log cabins, a school, and a church. God's Acre, a plot of land with rough gravestones, bears witness to the relatively high rate of infant mortality in frontier days. Costumed interpreters may demonstrate early crafts. The museum, through films, audiotapes, and exhibits, depicts the lives of the missionaries and the Christian Indians. *Open Wed.–Sun. Memorial Day–Labor Day; weekends only Labor Day–Oct.* 🏕

47 Salt Fork State Park

6 mi./12 min. East on Rte. 22. In this 21,000-acre park the extensive lake is the centerpiece, with its many arms that provide areas for boats with unlimited power, no-wave zones for sailboats and other quiet

craft, and sandy beaches for swimmers. There's also an 18-hole golf course, two marinas, boat rentals, and some 26 miles of bridle paths that meander through the wooded rolling hills in the park. *Open year-round.* 🏕 ⛺ 🚐 🚶 🏊 🎣 ♿

47 Degenhart Paperweight and Glass Museum, Cambridge

1 min. West on Rte. 22. Examples of fine glassmaking are on display here in a collection established by Elizabeth Degenhart, whose husband, John, founded the Crystal Art Glass Company. This impressive assortment of hand-cut glass lamps, glass puppies and owls, midwestern patterned glass, and paperweights (some used as doorstops and grave markers) provides a broad survey of the progression of taste and styles in glassmaking from the 1840's to 1900. A reproduction of Mrs. Degenhart's dining room, with its well-stocked china cabinets, reveals the quality and extent of her personal collection. *Open Mon.–Sat. and P.M. Sun. Mar.–Dec. except holidays. Admission charged.*

47. *Not for sale but a great place for shoppers to sharpen an eye for quality.*

28 Wolf Run State Park

5 min. South on Rte. 821, left on Rte. 215. This quiet park with its 220-acre lake, its attractive beach for swimming, its boat ramp, and its good reputation for bass, catfish, crappie, bluegill, and trout fishing, is also sought out by campers. A 2½-mile hiking path along the lake's western shore follows a stretch of the old Buckeye Trail.

In winter, visitors come for cross-country skiing, sledding, and ice fishing. And for those who like to arrive by air, 20 primitive campsites are located within walking distance of Nobles County Airport. *Open year-round.* 🏕 ⛺ 🚐 🚶 🏊 🎣

1 Campus Martius Museum, Marietta

3 mi./10 min. West on Rte. 7 (3rd St.), left on Washington St. Named for an ancient Roman military training camp, Campus Martius (Latin for "field of Mars") was a fortress built in the late 1700's by Revolutionary War veterans who established the first organized American settlement in the Northwest Territory at Marietta, Ohio. The museum includes the restored five-room apartment of Rufus Putnam, a leader of the settlers and a U.S. surveyor-general, as well as Hepplewhite furniture, frontier rifles, and 18th-century women's clothing. Surveying implements and a model of a flat-bottomed riverboat complement a wealth of written and pictorial materials about pioneer life in the Marietta area. A large model of the town at the time shows the extensive prehistoric earthworks left by the Adena and Hopewell peoples. *Open daily May–Sept.; Wed.–Sun. Mar.–Apr. and Oct.–Nov. except Thanksgiving Day. Admission charged.* ♿

176 Blennerhassett Island Historical Park

5 mi./15 min. West on Rte. 50, left on Rte. 68S; follow signs. A half-hour trip on a stern-wheeler ferries visitors from Point Park to this 4-mile-long island in the Ohio River near Parkersburg, West Virginia. It was settled in 1798 by Harman Blennerhassett, a wealthy Irish immigrant who built an imposing mansion here. In 1806 he joined Aaron Burr's conspiracy to form an empire in the Southwest. Both were arrested, and Virginia seized Blennerhassett's property. In 1811 the mansion burned to the ground, and the estate fell into neglect. The island, with its ancient sycamores, walnuts, and poplars, has remained undeveloped. The mansion, its three sections harmoniously joined by a curving colonnade, has been rebuilt. *Open daily May–Oct. Admission charged.* 🏕 🚶

81

34

47

See
E–W book,
sec. 31.

19

28

27

1   OH

  WV

10

176

76

77

See E–W book, sec. 34, for I-64; N–S book, sec. 38, for I-79.

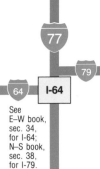

I-64 Sunrise Museums, Charleston

3 mi./6 min. West on I-64 to Exit 58A, east on Oakwood Rd., right on MacCorkle Ave. (Rte. 61); bear right and go up C & O ramp, right on Bridge Rd., right on Myrtle Rd. The Children's Museum, housed in a former governor's stone mansion, captivates young visitors with "open us" discovery boxes of seashells and fossils, an exhibit that explains myths and legends about natural phenomena in various cultures, a dollhouse, a ray table that bends and bounces light, a 60-seat planetarium, and models of coaches and a circus wagon. The Art Museum has a outstanding collection of 17th- to 20th-century American art, together with etchings by Rembrandt and Picasso and engravings by Matisse and Dürer. *Open Tues.–Sat. and P.M. Sun. except holidays. Admission charged.* ♿

I-64 Kanawha State Forest

9 mi./19 min. West on I-64 to Exit 58A, south on Rte. 119, left on Oakwood Rd.; follow signs. Amid these 9,250 acres of West Virginia forest, there are 17 trails ranging from a steep climb on Overlook Rock Trail to a gentle stroll along Spotted Salamander Trail (designed for the handicapped). Joggers and bikers enjoy the paved road through this wilderness of hemlock, pine, dogwood, and sycamore trees. Beside the quiet lake there are wooden seats from which to view the scenic mountain backdrop; fishermen can try for bass, catfish, and bluegill. Deer, black bears, and raccoons populate the forest. *Open year-round. Admission charged for swimmers.* ⛩ ⛺ 🚐 🚶 🏊 🐟 ♿

44 The Beckley Exhibition Coal Mine

4 mi./9 min. East on Rte. 3, left on Rte. 16; follow signs. The procedures, problems, and perils encountered in this turn-of-the-century hillside mine are explained by retired miners, who ride with visitors in a "man trip" car along 1,500 feet of underground rails. At the workstations, the guides demonstrate with hand tools and machinery how coal was cut, dynamited, and loaded onto carts. They explain the

44. *On the underground tour you'll get a sense of the mine worker's hard life.*

crude safety precautions of 1900, such as the use of live flame lamps to eliminate deadly methane gas. At the museum, old-time photos, early union banners, and company scrip are graphic reminders of the union's battle for better pay and safety. *Open daily May–Oct. Admission charged.* ⛩ ⛺ 🚐 🚶 🐟 ♿

40 Grandview State Park

13 mi./15 min. East on I-64 to Exit 129; follow signs. Impressive views of the New River are a prime attraction of this park. At North Overlook you'll see the horseshoe bend in the river where hawks nest in a rocky gorge; and from Main Overlook the river and the trains that run beside it are some 1,500 feet below. The steep hillsides, covered with mountain laurel, hemlock, dogwood, pink lady's slipper, and rhododendrons, come alive with color in the spring and summer. There is a self-guiding nature trail, and other trails lead to beautiful rock formations and tunnels in a high cliff. Hikers may see some of the turkey vultures, grouse, wild turkeys, and deer that inhabit the park. *Open year-round.* ⛩ 🚶 🐟 ♿

20 Camp Creek State Forest

5 min. South on Rte. 19; follow signs. Set in the mountains of southern West Virginia, this recreation area takes its name from the well-stocked stream that offers anglers excellent trout fishing from February through May. Hunting is also permitted, the most favored quarry being wild turkeys; permits for fishing and hunting are available in the forest office. Several scenic hiking trails meander through the woods, and the picnic areas have tables and fireplaces. *Forest open year-round; picnic and camping facilities open last weekend of Apr.–last weekend of Oct.* ⛩ ⛺ 🚶 🐟

40. *The New River and the railroad found an easy way through the hilly terrain.*

1   Pinnacle Rock State Park

13 mi./23 min. North on Rte. 52. Hiking trails in this 245-acre park pass through stands of rhododendron, mountain laurel, dogwood, ash, and maple trees. The park's name comes from a towerlike formation of stony gap sandstone that remained standing after eons of erosion had cut away the softer surrounding material. A steep path with stone steps leads to the top of Pinnacle Rock. There, 2,700 feet above sea level, the views of several surrounding counties are spectacular, especially during the fall foliage season. The picnic tables at the base of the rock are pleasantly shaded. The nearby town of Bramwell has many historic houses. *Open year-round.*   🏕 🚶

5   Shot Tower Historical State Park

3 min. East on Rte. 69, left on Rte. 52. Thomas Jackson, an immigrant from England, built this park's fortresslike tower, with its thick limestone walls, in about 1807; it was used to make lead shot for guns. Molten lead was poured through sieves at the top and allowed to fall some 150 feet into buckets of cooling water in an underground shaft (it was believed that the fall molded the shot into its round shape).

The park has lovely shaded picnic areas. About 100 feet from the Shot Tower is the midpoint of the New River Trail, with attractions such as an access point for fishing, a historic ferry site, and beautiful views of the New River. *Open daily late May–early Sept.; weekends late Apr.–late May and early Sept.–late Oct. Admission charged for tower.*   🏕 🚶 🐟

85   Stone Mountain State Park

18 mi./23 min. West on CC Camp Rd., right on Bypass 21 (becomes Rte. 21), left on Rte. 1002, right on John P. Frank Pkwy. Native rhododendron, mountain laurel, dogwood, and southern hemlock trees provide cover for the ruffed grouse, gray and red foxes, deer, mink, and bobcats that inhabit this beautiful, remote area. In dry weather the bare, rocky dome for which the park is named draws experienced climbers. A river and several streams are stocked with

1. *Even when viewed from the air, Pinnacle Rock is an impressive phenomenon.*

trout, attracting fishermen (who must use fly rods only) as well as beavers and otters. Pileated woodpeckers and scarlet tanagers can be seen flashing by overhead. *Open year-round.*   🏕 ⛺ 🚐 🚶 🐟

6A   The Charlotte Nature Museum

4 mi./10 min. East on Rte. 4, left on Park Rd., right on Princeton Rd., left on Sterling Rd. Children will be fascinated by this well-organized museum, where exhibits are designed to stimulate curious minds. The Live Animal Center houses owls, chipmunks, alligators, and small reptiles; and in an adjacent room visitors can pluck clams and other shellfish from a man-made tidal pool. Elsewhere the mysteries of volcanoes are explored through hands-on exhibits, and rudimentary physics is taught through play with lenses, mirrors, and lights. A self-guiding half-mile nature trail winds through mature oaks and hickories, massive sycamores, and 100-foot-high tulip trees. *Open Mon.–Sat. and P.M. Sun. except Thanksgiving Day and Christmas. Admission charged.*   🚶 ♿

6A   Mint Museum, Charlotte

7 mi./16 min. East on Rte. 4, left on Randolph Rd. The outbreak of the Civil War put an end to the minting of locally mined gold in this building, designed by the influential 19th-century architect William Strickland. The building's name survived its subsequent use by various agencies and organizations, and today the Mint is a major regional museum. The eclectic collection includes decorative art such as European porcelain and pottery, Japanese prints, African objects, and outstanding examples of pre-Columbian art. Among the painters represented here are Robert Henri, Everett Shinn, and fellow members of the Ashcan school of American painting. There are also classic works by Benjamin West, John Singer Sargent, Gilbert Stuart, John Constable, Winslow Homer, Amedeo Modigliani, René Magritte, and many others. *Open Tues.–Sat. and P.M. Sun.*   ♿

6A   Hezekiah Alexander Homesite 1774, Charlotte

10.5 mi./25 min. East on Rte. 4, right on Shamrock Dr. Influential planter, justice of the peace, and patriot Hezekiah Alexander completed handsome Rock House in 1774. The cozy parlor is furnished with several fine pieces, including a Jacobean chair, a Queen Anne tilt-top table, and a Chippendale secretary. In the keeping room, where the table is set with pewter, wood, and clay dishes, you'll see a small window that enabled hot food to be passed from the kitchen. The upstairs bedrooms contain a fine blanket chest, a sampler, quilts, toys, and rope-sprung beds. A special wrench was used to tighten the ropes on the beds when they began to sag; the popular expression "Sleep tight" is believed to have come from this practice.

On the grounds is an herb garden, a reconstructed two-story springhouse, and a small museum with rotating displays from a collection reflecting the history of the Piedmont region of North Carolina and of the city of Charlotte and the local county of Mecklenburg. *Open Tues.–Fri. and P.M. Sat. and Sun. except Thanksgiving Day, Christmas, and New Year's Day. Admission charged.*   ♿

VA
NC
45

85

79

6A

NC
SC
28

See
E–W book,
sec. 47.

82B Glencairn Garden, Rock Hill

3 mi./8 min. South on Cherry Rd., left on Charlotte Ave., left on Edgemont St. Here we have the ideal conditions for a municipal park: a convenient, accessible, intimate enclave of beauty, repose, and privacy located in the hubbub of a modern city. This tranquil garden was bequeathed to Rock Hill's citizens by the widow of a wealthy doctor who built it in 1928 and named it after his ancestral Scottish home. Follow the wide brick steps down the slope to the water lily pond, which is fed by a decorative fountain. Tall pines and oaks soar above the plantings of azaleas and dogwood. Gravel paths, with attractive views at every turn, lead through shady hollows, and the wooden seats are in all the right spots. Truly a medicine for melancholy. *Open year-round.* ♿

77 Landsford Canal State Park

12 mi./17 min. South on Rte. 21. In the early 1800's, railroads began to compete with canals for transporting heavy freight. Because of delays in development, the Landsford Canal did not start operating until 1837, and by 1839 the more efficient steam trains put it out of business. The Catawba River, however, still flows, and visitors can still walk the 2-mile towpath along its banks and let imagination picture the cargo barges as they were pulled around the rapids on their way to and from the port of Charleston.

In spring, spider lilies anchored to rock fissures and gravel along the river create a blaze of color against the white and blue of the water. A stone building once used as a lockkeeper's house is now the Canal Museum, where local memorabilia are shown, including a marker stone dated 1823, the year construction began, and bearing the names of the designer and building supervisor of the canal. *Open Thurs.–Mon.*

41 Lake Wateree State Park, Winnsboro

10 mi./13 min. East on Rte. 41, left on Rte. 21, right on River Rd. Angling is a favorite subject at Lake Wateree, one of six major lakes in the area that sponsor popular fishing tournaments. At any time of day in the combination park store and tackle shop you'll find experts ready and willing to offer advice on how to hook bass, bream, catfish, or crappie, to argue the comparative virtues of lure, spinners, and live bait, and to compare lines and poles. Nature lovers immune to the appeal of fishing take their pleasure spotting great blue herons, egrets, and ospreys along a pleasant 1½-mile nature trail. *Open year-round.*

17 Sesquicentennial State Park, Columbia

5 min. East on Two Notch Rd. Three fine trails here—a challenging 3½-mile exercise course, an easy 2-mile hiking loop, and a quarter-mile nature trail—and the pedal boats on the 30-acre lake make this a good place to stretch your legs. The nature trail, for which there's an interpretive folder, can also be informative.

This area, the Carolina Sandhills, once covered by a primeval sea, now supports a cedar bog and a forest of scrub oak and pine. Evidence of an early-day turpentine plantation can be seen in the slash marks on several of the old longleaf pines. A restored two-story log cabin, built in 1756, was moved to the park and is now an artist's studio. The name of the park is derived from the 150th anniversary of the city of Columbia, when souvenir coins were sold and the proceeds used to purchase the 1,455 acres here. *Open year-round.*

108 Riverbanks Zoo, Columbia

2 mi. South on I-126, right on Greystone Blvd. More than 700 animals inhabit this remarkable 50-acre zoo, where specimens and spectators are separated not by bars and fences, but by light, water, and other subtle barriers—conditions ideal for snapshots. Along with the expected familiar faces, you'll find such rarities as ruffed lemurs, lion-tailed macaques, Siberian tigers, golden-lion tamarins, and South American sakis. The ecosystem birdhouse, containing one of the world's finest displays of exotic birds, provides such an authentic

108. *Polar bear finds a comfortable place to nap, far from its native land.*

habitat that several species have bred in captivity for the first time. Don't miss the man-made thunderstorms that drench the tropical rain forest exhibit several times a day. *Open daily except Christmas. Admission charged.*

111 Lexington County Museum

8 mi./15 min. West on Rte. 1. This 18-building complex is rightly called a gateway to yesterday. History comes alive here—in the Oak Grove Schoolhouse; in the 1772 Corley Log House, whose single open hearth once served for cooking, light, and heat; and in the eight-room Hazelius House, where an 1891 revival meeting inspired evangelist Charlie Tillman to write the spiritual, "Give Me That Old-Time Religion." Lovers of antiques will savor the federal-style Fox House, with its locally made furniture in the style of Sheraton and Hepplewhite and a large collection of quilts. On the grounds are dairy sheds, smokehouses, ovens, rabbit hutches, beehives, herb gardens, and a horse-operated cotton gin. *Open Tues.–Sun. except July 4, Thanksgiving Day, Christmas, and New Year's Day. Admission charged.*

149 Edisto Memorial Gardens, Orangeburg

6 mi./12 min. West on Rte. 33, right on Riverside Dr. There's an affecting contrast here between the bustle of the city and the quiet beauty of this 110-acre memorial to those who died in the four American wars of the 20th century. The gardens' most colorful plants are the roses—some 10,000 in all—which are in bloom from mid-April until the frosts of November. In springtime the azaleas, dogwood, and crab apples stand out in a setting of ancient cypress and oak trees. There are also some huge pines with wisteria climbing the trunks. Winding paths, shaded lawns, and picnic shelters combine to invite strolling, reflection, and repose. *Open year-round.*

154 / 169 Santee State Park

Exit 154: 23 mi./30 min. North on Rte. 301 to Santee; follow signs. Exit 169: 18 mi./25 min. North on I-95 to Exit 98, west on Rte. 6; follow signs. Lake Marion, which is fed by the Santee River, is world-renowned: state records were set here with a 55-pound striped bass and a 73-pound blue catfish. Bream, crappie, and rockfish also provide good sport, and you can rent a boat and buy bait and tackle in the park. Enticements for non-fishermen include tennis, swimming, and boating. Pedal boats and bicycles are for rent, and there's a 4-mile bike path. Three nature trails invite walkers into the wooded realm of rabbits, squirrels, and birds of many kinds. The nature center provides daily summertime activities. *Park open year-round; day-use area open mid-Mar.–mid-Oct. Admission charged in summer only.*

199A Middleton Place

13 mi./21 min. West on Rte. 17A, left on Rte. 165, left on Rte. 61. A signer of the secession document that helped touch off the Civil War, Williams Middleton came home at war's end to find that except for the south flank, his handsome three-section house was a smoldering ruin. The remaining building, repaired in 1870, stands today as a memorial to an illustrious family that includes a president of the first Continental Congress, a signer of the Declaration of Independence, and a governor of South Carolina. Portraits by Thomas Sully and Benjamin West adorn the walls, and there are many superb pieces of furniture. Among the rare first editions in the library are bird prints by Audubon and Catesby. On the grounds are the nation's oldest formal landscaped gardens, circa 1741, which have the first camellias planted outdoors in America. *Open daily except holidays and 2 weeks in Jan. Admission charged.*

216A Drayton Hall

10 mi./15 min. South on Rte. 7, right on Rte. 61. When Union troops swept through Charleston in early 1865, they burned almost every plantation home on the west bank of the Ashley River. This one was spared because the owner said (inaccurately) that it was in use as a smallpox hospital. Drayton Hall stands today as a splendid tribute to the architectural design and craftsmanship of the antebellum South. Built in 1742 for John Drayton, scion of a prominent local family, it exemplifies the best in Georgian-Palladian architecture. The absence of furnishings accentuates the symmetrical proportions of the structure and the exquisite detail of its hand-carved doorways, pilasters, overmantels, and ornamental plaster. Fortunately, temptations to deface the building by installing electricity, running water, and central heating were resisted. Some of the original 18th-century interior paint still remains, although most of the rooms were repainted in the late 19th century. *Open daily except Thanksgiving Day, Christmas, and New Year's Day. Admission charged.*

221 Charleston, SC 29403

Visitor Information Center, 85 Calhoun St. (803) 722-8338. Few American cities have quite the degree of grace, charm, and civility as historic Charleston. Among the stately old homes that one can visit are the Heyward-Washington House, a federal-style mansion built in 1772 and once visited by the first president; the Nathaniel Russell and Joseph Manigault houses, fine examples of post-colonial architecture; and the Calhoun Mansion, a Victorian home noted for its furnishings and woodwork. At the Charles Towne Landing, a 664-acre state park, there is a reconstructed settlement of 1670 and a replica of a merchant ship from the period, as well as a zoo, gardens, and nature trails. From White Point Gardens there are views of the city, the harbor, and historic Ft. Sumter. A life-size replica of a Civil War submarine is featured in the Charleston Museum, the nation's oldest.

221. *Carpenters' and wood turners' skills are well displayed here at White Point Gardens.*

38

149

5

154

15

See
N–S book,
sec. 50.

169 95

30

199A

17

216A

5

221

End I-26

79

12TH

See
E–W book,
sec. 7.

90

51

34

See
E–W book,
sec. 24.

80

30

29

34

19

8

I-279

21

8

8E

0

70

See
E–W book,
sec. 31.

12TH Presque Isle State Park, Erie

12th St. W. exit: 5 min. West on W. 12th St., right on Rte. 832. Excellent exhibits at the nature center will enhance one's appreciation of this unique Pennsylvania park. The 7-mile-long sandy peninsula serves not only as a recreational area but also as a laboratory where all stages of a 600-year ecological succession exist, from fragile sandspit to a climax forest of hemlocks, oaks, and sugar maples. To the north is the expanse of Lake Erie, to the south Presque Isle Bay, in whose sheltered waters Commodore Perry's fleet was constructed for the War of 1812. Park amenities include lake and bay fishing, a marina, sandy beaches, and miles of trails. In winter, ice fishing and cross-country skiing are popular. *Park open year-round; beach open Memorial Day–Labor Day.*

12TH Erie, PA 16501

12th St. E. exit. Chamber of Commerce, 1006 State St. (814) 454-7191. Echoes of the War of 1812 still reverberate here. In September 1813, Commodore Oliver Hazard Perry won a stunning victory over the British on Lake Erie. Six of the nine ships in Perry's fleet were built in Erie, and one of them, the reconstructed flagship *Niagara*, is proudly berthed here. The strategy and details of the historic battle are depicted in the Erie Historical Museum.

The past is further recalled in the Old Custom House, built in 1839, now an art museum open to visitors. The Cashiers House, built the same year, features some fine antique furnishings. In the Dickson Tavern, the oldest surviving building in Erie, one can savor the 19th-century equivalent of a cocktail bar.

34 Maurice K. Goddard State Park

4 mi./8 min. West on Rte. 358; make first right turn; follow signs. Lake Wilhelm, an 1,860-acre reservoir created in 1972 to control flooding, is the centerpiece of this 2,658-acre Pennsylvania park. Recreational facilities include a 200-slip marina, where rowboats, pontoon boats, canoes, and fishing tackle can be rented. Fishermen try for perch, bass, walleye, and northern pike, and because of the relatively shallow waters, enjoy excellent ice fishing in winter. Hunting is permitted in designated areas of the park, where deer and waterfowl are the usual game. Several hiking trails wind around the lake, and there's a scenic drive along the southern shore. *Open daily Memorial Day–Labor Day; Mon.–Fri. Labor Day–Memorial Day.*

29 McConnell's Mill State Park

5 min. West on Rte. 422. After driving through miles of flat farmland, you will find the sudden, violent beauty of this 400-foot-deep glacial gorge, which is studded with gigantic sandstone boulders, a dramatic surprise. From the top of the gorge, where there's a park office and a picnic area, a graded trail descends to the turbulent waters of Slippery Rock Creek and the well-restored gristmill on its bank. You can walk or drive across the nearby covered bridge (circa 1874) that spans the creek and follow any number of trails through the park's challenging but rewarding terrain. Rappeling, white-water canoeing, fishing, and hunting are popular (bring your own equipment), but swimming is forbidden. *Park open year-round; gristmill open Memorial Day–Labor Day.*

19 Old Economy Village

9 mi./12 min. North on Rte. 65; follow signs. The German-born pietists known as Harmonists came to America seeking religious freedom. They founded a communal society in 1805 at Harmony, Pennsylvania, and established Economy in 1825. The community existed until the society, which believed in Christian piety, celibacy, and hard work, was dissolved in 1905. More than a dozen structures have been restored, including homes, craft shops, and an enormous Feast Hall, which now contains a small museum featuring the Harmonists' simple, straightforward furniture, a silk exhibit, and changing displays of decorative arts. The George Rapp House, the residence of the group's founder, has also been restored. Its formal garden, where walks edged with boxwood lead through several flower beds, symbolizes the group's sense of neatness and order. *Open Tues.–Sat. and P.M. Sun. except holidays.*

I-279 Pittsburgh, PA 15222

Convention & Visitors Information Center, 4 Gateway Center Plaza. (800) 255-0855; (800) 821-1888 outside PA. Like the phoenix rising from its ashes, this clean, handsome, and eminently livable city has

I-279. *Passengers in the balloons enjoy Pittsburgh's dramatic setting from on high.*

laid to rest its former image as a place of smoke and soot. For spectacular views of the Pittsburgh area, you can take a ride on either of two inclines to the top of Mt. Washington. The Allegheny and Monongahela rivers merge to form the Ohio at Point State Park, where a museum and a 1764 blockhouse impart a sense of history. Bird lovers will find the Pittsburgh Aviary filled with exotic birds in free flight. Flower lovers can stroll through acres of tropical plants in the Phipps Conservatory. Each of 21 "nationality classrooms" reflects a different ethnic group at the University of Pittsburgh's Cathedral of Learning, and the nearby Heinz Chapel has lovely stained-glass windows. Pittsburgh has many museums: you can see European art at the Frick Art Museum, sky shows at the Buhl Science Center, and art and natural history at the complex known as The Carnegie.

8 | 8E | Arden Trolley Museum, Washington

Exit 8: 4 mi./7 min. West on Race Track Rd.; follow signs. Exit 8E: 3.5 mi./6 min. East on Pike St.; follow signs. In this indoor-outdoor museum trolley buffs and children of all ages can savor the pleasure of a 1-mile ride on a 1920's trolley car, fitted with polished woodwork, chrome, and brass. Twenty-five or more trolley cars, some in working order, others undergoing restoration, are exhibited in a large carbarn. The cars come from several towns in Pennsylvania and from Boston, with one veteran of New Orleans's famous Desire car line. *Open daily P.M. July 4–Labor Day; P.M. weekends only May–June and Sept.*

148 | Coopers Rock State Forest

15 mi./25 min. East on Rte. 48. Great rocks extending from the edge of lofty bluffs provide a platform for spectacular views of the Cheat River and the West Virginia valley below. There are railings for safety and telescopes to use. The park was named for an escaped prisoner, a cooper by trade, who made the area his hideout. Rock climbers come here to challenge the crags, and hikers can enjoy the miles of trails that crisscross the forest, where mountain lau-

rel and rhododendron abound. For anglers there are two trout streams and a lake. The Henry Clay Iron Furnace, once a major source of pig iron, looms unattended in the woods, its overgrown stones the last reminder of this flourishing 19th-century industry and the village that grew up around it, of which there is no trace today. *Main park road open daily May–Nov.; trails open year-round.*

139 | Pricketts Fort State Park

4 min. West from exit; follow signs. Built in 1774 on the banks of the Monongahela River for protection against Indian attack, the fort, with its stockade, blockhouses, and log cabins, has been completely reconstructed. Costumed staff members demonstrate pioneer tasks, including weaving and open-fire cooking as well as fiddling. In midsummer an outdoor drama, *Pricketts Fort: An American Frontier Musical*, is presented. The nearby Job Prickett House, built in 1859, represents the more comfortable lifestyle that evolved here. *Open daily mid-Apr.–Oct. Admission charged to fort. Additional charge for drama.*

110 | Watters Smith Memorial State Park

7 mi./15 min. West from exit; follow signs. A replica of the log cabin built in 1796 by pioneer Watters Smith stands here, along with the original barn, blacksmith's shop, other outbuildings, and the well. Nearby, the blue and white clapboard house built in 1876 by a later member of the Smith family contains period furnishings, including a 1912 typewriter. An elegant antique wicker two-horse open sleigh is displayed in the visitor center. Hiking trails lead through the hilly landscape. *Open daily Memorial Day–Labor Day. Admission free but donations encouraged.*

79 | Cedar Creek State Park

15 mi./30 min. West on Rte. 5, left on Rte. 33/119, left on Rte. 17 (Cedar Creek Rd.). A winding road leads to this secluded valley that follows the course of a creek in the steeply wooded Allegheny foothills of West Virginia. Seven hiking trails range in

79. *A rainy scene worthy of a Japanese woodcut or an impressionist painting.*

difficulty from a rugged climb up a ridge that offers impressive views of the area to a pleasant stroll between the swimming and picnic areas. Unusually tame deer can often be seen nibbling on oaks and poplars. The park has three fish ponds, stocked with different fish at different times of year. *Park open year-round; camping Apr.–mid-Oct.; recreational facilities open Memorial Day–Labor Day.*

I-77 | Sunrise Museums, Charleston

22 mi./30 min. South on I-77; continue west on I-64 to Exit 58A, east on Oakwood Rd., right on MacCorkle Ave. (Rte. 61); bear right and go up C & O ramp; right on Bridge Rd., right on Myrtle Rd. Two museums make up this complex, which occupies neighboring stone mansions. The Children's Museum, housed in a former governor's home, captivates young visitors with "open us" discovery boxes of seashells and fossils, a dollhouse, a ray table that bends and bounces light, models of coaches and a circus wagon, and a 60-seat planetarium. The Art Museum, situated next door in the mansion of the governor's son, has a fine collection of 17th- to 20th-century American art. *Open Tues.–Sat. and P.M. Sun. except holidays. Admission charged.*

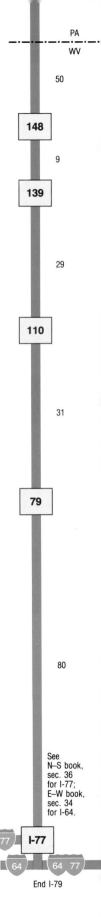

PA
WV
50
148
9
139
29
110
31
79
80
See
N–S book,
sec. 36
for I-77;
E–W book,
sec. 34
for I-64.
77 I-77
64   64 77
End I-79

50 Grass Point State Park

3 min. South on Rte. 12. This cool, breezy expanse overlooking the St. Lawrence River offers a tempting change of scene after a day at the wheel. Especially appealing are the campsites along a small bluff above the river's ship channel. At the narrow part of this very busy waterway you can see an unending stream of pleasure craft, as well as merchant ships, from around the world. Enhancing this interesting view are the many islands—both large and small—in the Thousand Islands chain.

There are picnic tables on well-tended lawns, a sandy beach at the bottom of a gentle slope, and several boat slips. A short fishing pier provides a vantage point for outwitting perch, pike, and at times, smallmouth bass. *Open mid-Apr.–mid-Sept. Admission charged.*

49 47 Agricultural Museum at Stone Mills

Exit 49: 10 mi./20 min. West on Rte. 411, left on Rte. 180. Exit 47: 11 mi./14 min. Northwest on Rte. 12, right on Rte. 180. Sponsored by the Northern New York Agricultural Historical Society, this fascinating museum is a complex of seven buildings. Exhibits of 19th-century farm equipment here include a Mehring Milker, which milked cows with a foot-operated mechanism similar to that of some early vacuum cleaners; a rare 15-foot-high horse-operated hay baler; and a seed drill with a 15-foot-long wooden box. Wall displays explain maple sugaring in the days when every farm had its "sugar bush." Across the road from the main complex, a cheese factory, built in 1897, contains old steam-powered machinery and other equipment for handling milk and making cheddar cheese, along with a display that explains the process of cheese making in this part of New York. *Open daily mid-May–Sept. Admission charged.*

45 Sackets Harbor Battlefield State Historic Site

10 mi./20 min. West on Rte. 3, right on Sulphur Springs Rd. (later called Main St.), left on Hill St. Situated on a bluff high above Black River Bay, this was the scene of two battles during the War of 1812. Today several of the buildings, including the restored Commandant's House, are open to the public. On the third weekend in July some 30,000 people come here for the annual Canadian-American 1812 Days festival, complete with parades, fireworks, and military demonstrations. The Union Hotel, built in 1817, is now a visitor center and features an exhibit that shows the way of life on the military base from 1812 to 1815. *Open Wed.–Sun. late May–mid-Oct., including holidays.*

36 Selkirk Shores State Park

Exit 36, headed south: 6 mi./15 min. Left on Rte. 2, right on Rte. 2A, right on Rte. 13, left on Rte. 3. Exit 36, headed north: 5 mi./10 min. Left on Rte. 13, left on Rte. 3. Set among sand dunes at the mouth of the Salmon River, the park is a favorite with fishermen, who try for the specimens here that often weigh more than 30 pounds. Other diversions include 6 miles of easy hiking trails, a bathing beach, a picnic grove, camping areas, sand-sculpting classes and softball games for children, and occasional afternoon concerts. Woodlands of pine, oak, birch, and larch have a rich undergrowth of ferns and wildflowers. *Open year-round.*

31 Oliver Stevens Blockhouse Museum, Brewerton

4 min. West on Bartell Rd., right on Rte. 11. Oliver Stevens, an early settler in the region, built a two-story blockhouse of logs and bricks in 1794 for protection from attack by the Onondaga Indians. Although the current blockhouse is a reconstruction, it is a faithful copy and highly evocative of bygone days on the frontier. An excellent collection of arrowheads traces local Indian craftsmanship from 8100 B.C. to A.D. 1100. An Owasco campsite dating back 900 years is represented by a rare clay pipe and a large stone mortar and pestle used for grinding maize. In the museum the fort's history is told with photographs, a Civil War Medal of Honor, and models of ships that once plied the local waterways. *Open June–Sept. Admission free but donations encouraged.*

18 Syracuse, NY 13202

Convention and Visitors Bureau, 100 E. Onondaga St. (315) 470-1343. In New York's fourth largest city you can visit the Everson Museum of Art, which is noted for its collections of ceramics, Oriental art, and American paintings. The Landmark Theatre, a fantasy palace built in 1928, has a richly ornate interior and is a center for plays, movies, and concerts. Other attractions in the city include the Erie Canal Museum, the Erie Canal Center, the modernized Burnet Park Zoo, and the Discovery Center of Science and Technology. A stroll on the Syracuse University campus might include stops at the Lowe Art Gallery or the huge Carrier Dome stadium. In early June some 50 huge, colorful balloons ascend to the heavens at the Hot Air Balloon Festival. And for 11 days ending on Labor Day, the Great New York State Fair offers an appealing variety of exhibits as well as many types of entertainment.

15 Lorenzo State Historic Site, Cazenovia

16 mi./22 min. South on Rte. 11, left on Rte. 20, right on Rte. 13. The beautifully proportioned federal-style mansion, built overlooking the shores of Lake Cazenovia in 1807–08 by John Lincklaen, a Dutch land developer, remained in the family for 160 years, until in 1968 it was presented to New York State. It is thought that the estate may have been named for the Florentine Medici prince. The mansion, with many original furnishings, including a copy of the desk of George Washington, an 1820's carved mahogany "plantation bed," family portraits, and fine old silver, radiates elegance and comfort. A small museum traces the history of both the family and the area and displays 19th-century vehicles. A self-guiding walking tour winds through the grounds. *Open Wed.–Sun. and Mon. holidays May–mid-Oct. Admission free but donations encouraged.*

11 The 1890 House Museum, Cortland

4 min. South on Rte. 13 (becomes Tompkins St.). Chester Franklin Wickwire, who made a fortune in copper-wire window

11. *Such opulent 19th-century luxuries as this conservatory are hardly affordable today.*

screening, fencing, and other copper products, was so impressed with the New York City mansion of James Bailey of the Barnum & Bailey Circus that he had an exact replica in reverse of that châteauesque mansion built. When completed in 1890, it featured the latest conveniences, such as central heating, indoor plumbing, and soon a few electric lights; and with its stained glass windows, cherry and oak woodwork, intricately patterned inlaid parquet floors, and handsome period furnishings, it stands today as a symbol of the height of 19th-century elegance and fashion.

The magnificent stained glass domed ceiling of the conservatory, the huge parlor fireplace, and the cozy nook beneath the stairs are classics of their kind; and the hinges, doorknobs, and latches are embossed with a woven wire design—a humble reminder of the source of the fortune that created the great house. *Open Tues.– Sun. except holidays.* ♿

4 | Binghamton, NY 13902

Chamber of Commerce, 80 Exchange St. (607) 772-8860. At the Ross Park Zoo, one of the nation's oldest, you'll see beavers, otters, geese, and even a pack of wolves move about in re-created natural habitats. Children can pet the animals (not the wolves) and take a ride on a vintage carou-

sel. The Roberson Center for the Arts and Sciences has a planetarium and diverting exhibits as well as permanent art, historical, and scientific collections. Downtown Binghamton offers specialty and antique stores that both shoppers and casual strollers will find inviting. Anyone interested in architecture will be intrigued by the onion dome churches that reflect the area's Eastern European heritage.

60 | Lackawanna State Park

3 mi./6 min. West on Rte. 524. The pleasant surroundings of this well-designed park entice visitors who come to sail, fish, and canoe on the 215-acre lake, and to swim in the 160-foot pool. A bathhouse is provided. The campsites and picnic area along the lake's western shore are shaded by oak, beech, and hemlock trees. Hiking trails wind through the park, which is home to ruffed grouse, pheasants, and other bird species, as well as deer. During the summer there are frequent hot-air balloon launchings. *Open year-round.*

⛺ ⛺ 🚐 🚶 🐾 🎣 ♿

47 | Swetland Homestead, Wyoming

7 mi./16 min. North on Rte. 115, left on Rte. 315, right on Rte. 309, right on Rte. 11 (Wyoming Ave.). Built in 1797, this white

clapboard house with fluted columns at the entrance sheltered the same family for 161 years. The structure was donated to the Wyoming Historical and Geological Society in the early 1960's by the great-great-great-granddaughter of the original owner. *Open P.M. Thurs.–Sun. Memorial Day– Aug. Admission charged.*

I-80 | Eckley Miners' Village

13 mi./20 min. East on I-80 to Exit 39, right on Rte. 309, left on Freeland-Drums Hwy. to Freeland, right on Rte. 940; follow signs. Eckley is a living-history museum and hopes to maintain this status. Established in 1854 as a planned company "patch," it became home to generations of immigrant coal miners and their families. Early Victorian cottages, churches, mine buildings, and the company store stand today much as they were when shovels dug into the hillsides and daily life followed the tune of the steam whistle. More than 50 people remain, and the 58 buildings on this 100-acre site reveal the disciplined quality of life in a company town. The preserved cottages and visitor center have informative displays that tell the story of the mine patches in this anthracite region. *Visitor center open daily May–Sept., daily except holidays Oct.–Apr.; village buildings open Memorial Day–Labor Day and weekends Sept.–Oct. Admission charged.* ⛺

I-80. *For workers' houses in a company town, one plan is sufficient for all.*

11

40

4

NY
PA

49

60

30

47

22

See
E–W book,
sec. 25.

I-80   80

19

81

37 | Tuscarora State Park

5 mi./10 min. East on Rte. 54; follow signs. Against a backdrop of Locust Mountain, a 96-acre lake offers swimming, fishing, and winter ice skating. Three unmarked hiking trails penetrate a virtual wilderness, where in their season deer, pheasants, ospreys, hawks, and bald eagles are likely to be sighted. The shaded picnic area offers a view of the lake through the trees. The park is for day use only, but fishermen are exempt from the rule as they pursue crappie, trout, channel cats, and walleye bass. *Open year-round.*

30 | Coleman Memorial Park

9 mi./13 min. South on Rte. 72. At the turn of the century these 90 acres contained five summer mansions of the Coleman family, a successful mining and railroading clan. The land is now open to the public for daytime fun and relaxation. Six macadam tennis courts, four baseball diamonds, and a huge pool with diving boards and changing rooms offer a choice of recreation. Picnic tables are shaded by oaks, maples, pines, and sycamores, and there's stacked cordwood for the cooking fireplaces. Deer, rabbits, and many birds may be seen along an easy 2-mile trail. *Open year-round.*

28 | Hershey Park, Gardens, and Chocolate World

8 mi./12 min. South on Rte. 743 to Hershey Park Dr. It started with chocolate in 1903, but today there's a theme park and zoo, 23 acres of gardens, a "Chocolate World," and a town—all named for Milton S. Hershey, the man who worked wonders with the exotic cocoa bean. When chocolate plant tours became so popular that they overwhelmed the facility, Chocolate World was set up to explain all aspects of the growing and making of Hershey's famous product. The gardens started as a rose garden but now include several other types of gardens. The theme park has 45 rides (the most popular: shooting rapids), along with live entertainment, restaurants, and shops. Although part of the park, the zoo can be visited separately. *Chocolate World open daily except winter holidays; theme park open daily Memorial Day–Labor Day, two weekends in May and Sept; zoo open daily except winter holidays; gardens open daily Apr.–Oct. Admission charged for theme park, zoo, and gardens.*

25 | Harrisburg, PA 17108

Chamber of Commerce, 114 Walnut St. P.O. Box 969. (717) 232-4121. This state capital boasts an impressive Renaissance-style statehouse with a dome based on St. Peter's Basilica in Rome and a grand interior staircase copied from the Paris opera house. The nearby State Museum contains a wealth of regional artifacts from every era. The Museum of Scientific Discovery, in the business district, delivers successfully on the promise of its name. The beauty of the Susquehanna River can be enjoyed at Riverfront Park, a 5-mile stretch with a paved riverside esplanade. Some handsome 18th- and 19th-century mansions are other attractions in the Riverfront District.

17 | Carlisle Barracks

3 mi./6 min. South on Rte. 11. Said to have been built by Hessian prisoners in 1777, the powder magazine now houses the Hessian Powder Magazine Museum, devoted to the history of Carlisle Barracks from the 18th to the 20th century. Exhibits include military artifacts and displays depicting life at the now defunct Carlisle Indian School, once famous for its outstanding athletes (among them the football star and Olympic decathlon and pentathlon gold medalist, Jim Thorpe). Uniforms, military awards, and photographs in the nearby Omar N. Bradley Museum present a visual biography of the distinguished high-ranking officer. In World War II he commanded more than 1.3 million men and later became a five-star general and chairman of the Joint Chiefs of Staff. *Hessian Museum open P.M. weekends May–Sept; Bradley Museum open A.M. Mon. and P.M. Wed. and Fri.*

11 | Pine Grove Furnace State Park

8 mi./9 min. South on Rte. 233. This state park is named for the Pine Grove ironworkers' community that flourished here in the 1700's and 1800's. Activities include bicycling, summer and winter sports, a self-guiding walking tour of the remaining structures of the ironworkers' village, and a number of hiking trails. Deer are sometimes sighted, and birds abound. Once a stop for slaves heading north on the Underground Railroad, the ironmaster's mansion now serves as a youth hostel offering overnight shelter. In the summertime don't be surprised to see someone at the camp store

1. *The setting's quiet beauty makes it hard to imagine the carnage wrought here.*

consuming a whole half-gallon of ice cream within an hour—it's a traditional celebration for hikers who reach this, the midpoint of the 2,000-mile Appalachian Trail, which runs from Georgia to Maine. *Park open year-round; camp store open Memorial Day–Labor Day.*

6 | Caledonia State Park

9 mi./12 min. East on Rte. 30, left on Rte. 233. Fine mountain country, rich in hemlocks, white pines, oaks, and rhododendrons, awaits visitors to this 1,130-acre park. The famed Appalachian Trail, running through the grounds, is just one of several hiking trails. There is an attractive 18-hole golf course, a summer stock playhouse, campfire programs, and a restaurant made of old railroad cars—complete with a Pullman dining car and caboose kitchen. A reconstructed blacksmith's shop marks the site of the ironworks that were established here by Thaddeus Stevens in 1837. His outspoken abolitionist views prompted Confederate troops to burn his plant to the ground in 1863. What are now children's playing fields once served as dressing stations for wounded soldiers brought from Gettysburg. *Park open year-round; campgrounds open mid-Apr.–mid-Dec.*

6A | The Hager House, Hagerstown

5 min. East on Rte. 40, right on Prospect St. to City Park, right on Key St. German immigrant Jonathan Hager, for whom Hagerstown was named, completed this restored fieldstone house in 1740 on what was then the western frontier. So that his family could survive a possible Indian attack, he built the house over twin springs for a water supply and constructed walls 22 inches thick. In the basement the stone-lined pools are still filled with water, and in an adjacent fortified room narrow musket ports attest to the perils of that time and place. The interior is authentically furnished and reflects Hager's status as a fur trader and political leader. Pelts are laid across a table in the fur trading room, which also includes a mid-18th-century painted armoire and a 1777 chest painted

with German designs. A separate museum building displays Hager family possessions, along with period artifacts unearthed here. *Open Tues.–Sat. and P.M. Sun. Apr.–Dec. Admission charged.*

1 | Antietam National Battlefield

12 mi./15 min. East on Rte. 68, right on Rte. 65. It is remembered in history as the bloodiest single day's conflict of the Civil War. For one dreadful day in September 1862, a battle raged here through woods and cornfields that today appear much as they did then. Outnumbered more than two to one by Union forces, the Confederates inflicted more than 12,000 casualties, themselves sustaining almost 11,000—a loss they could ill afford. Although it was far from a clear-cut victory for the North, President Lincoln judged it sufficiently successful to warrant issuing his preliminary Emancipation Proclamation, which announced the abolition of slavery within the Confederacy. An excellent self-guiding auto tour provides insight into each phase of the battle. Highlights include the rebuilt Dunker Church (used as a hospital) and the 1836 Burnside Bridge, where 400 Georgia sharpshooters delayed hordes of attacking Federal troops. *Open daily except Thanksgiving Day, Christmas, and New Year's Day. Admission charged.*

80 | George Washington's Office Museum, Winchester

2 mi./8 min. West on Rte. 50, right on Pleasant Valley Rd., left on Cork St. In 1755–56, during the French and Indian War, Col. George Washington is believed to have used one of the rooms in this 1748 log building as his office. Still in his early 20's, he was responsible for the construction of some 30 forts along Virginia's western frontier. This museum houses several interesting displays—including a model of Ft. Loudoun built from Washington's original plans, a photocopy of a list in his handwriting of all tools and materials used in the construction of the fort, a Brown Bess musket with bayonet, late 18th-century surveying instruments, and a large Danner compass similar to Washington's. *Open daily Apr.–Oct. Admission charged.*

If You Have Some Extra Time:

Harpers Ferry National Historical Park

12 | *23 mi./30 min.* The turbulent history of this small town, at the junction of three states and two rivers, has been dictated by the strategic importance and scenic beauty of its location. People heading into the Shenandoah Valley crossed the rivers on Robert Harper's ferry. George Washington, with the eye of a strategist, saw the potential for a federal armory, and one was established in 1796. In 1859 John Brown and his abolitionist followers staged a futile attempt to capture the armory and ignite a slave revolt. Brown was captured and hanged, but the incident helped to precipitate the Civil War. During the war, the town changed hands many times and sustained damage with every battle.

The remaining 18th- and 19th-century buildings, along with the spectacular scenic beauty of the site, inspired the gradual renovation of the town and its designation as a national historical park. The visitor center in Stagecoach Inn offers exhibits and a self-guiding walking tour. Among the highlights are the quaint fire engine house where John Brown took refuge; Robert Harper's original house; the Master Armorer's House Museum; and the high rock outcrop from which Thomas Jefferson proclaimed the view to be "worth a voyage across the Atlantic." *How to get there: Exit 12, southeast on Rte. 9 to Charles Town, left on Rte. 340; follow signs.*

11

17

6

21

PA

MD

6A

5

1

MD

WV

18

12

20

WV

VA

80

48

81

See
E–W book,
sec. 35.

See
E–W book,
sec. 35.

67 Luray Caverns

13.5 mi./20 min. East on Rte. 211. These vast, spectacular caverns were first viewed by candlelight in 1878 by two men who entered by letting themselves down on ropes. Today a 1¼-mile paved path and artfully naturalistic lighting make the caverns' 64 acres accessible to all.

Over the course of millions of years the dripping of mineral-rich water has created multicolored oddities in stone that resemble everything from bath towels to rows of hanging fish to fried eggs. Highlights of the 1-hour tour include the 195-foot-deep Pluto's Chasm, a flowstone shape known as the Frozen Fountain, and a 7-million-year-old formation called the Giant California Redwood Tree. Most impressive of all is the unique Stalacpipe Organ, which produces clear tones as the stalactite formations, tuned to the music scale, are struck by electronically controlled plungers. *Open year-round. Admission charged.* ⌂

57 Woodrow Wilson Birthplace, Staunton

2 mi./6 min. West on Rte. 250, right on Coalter St. America's 28th president was born in this Greek revival Virginia town house on December 28, 1856. Today, 12 beautifully restored rooms display a wide variety of original furnishings and family memorabilia. You'll see the Bible in which the Reverend Joseph Ruggles Wilson, a Presbyterian minister, recorded his son's birth; a period quilt; antique dolls; a rolltop desk and a typewriter desk from Wilson's study at Princeton University, where he served as president from 1902 to 1910; and two ornate brass oil lamps that he bought while he was a student at the University of Virginia. A lovely Victorian garden and a carriage house that contains Wilson's restored 1920 Pierce-Arrow presidential limousine add to the period atmosphere. A film about Wilson is shown regularly at the reception center. *Open daily Mar.–Dec.; Mon.–Sat. Jan.–Feb. except Thanksgiving Day, Christmas, and New Year's Day. Admission charged.* ♿

If You Have Some Extra Time: Shenandoah National Park

76 / 56 *Exit 76: 24 mi./35 min. Exit 56: 18 mi./25 min.* This awesomely beautiful park runs along the Blue Ridge Mountains for about 100 miles. Bisecting it from north to south is the Skyline Drive, where frequent overlooks afford spectacular views of the park's valleys, streams, cliffs, and waterfalls, as well as more distant vistas of the rolling Piedmont Plateau to the east and the Shenandoah Valley to the west. The park is particularly beautiful when the azaleas are in bloom in the spring, and in the autumn when the many varieties of hardwoods are ablaze with color.

A handy system of mile-markers along the drive makes it easy to locate such highlights as Shenandoah Valley Overlook, Thornton Gap, Big Meadows, Hawksbill Gap, and the Dickey Ridge Visitor Center. Several hiking trails lead to summits, including Stony Man, whose fairly easy trail takes you to sharp, rocky cliffs that provide an unobstructed view of the valley. The park's highest peak, Hawksbill, is the target of serious hikers, and Old Rag's boulder-strewn ridge can be reached after a strenuous climb.

The park's mountain streams, such as Jeremys Run, one of the most popular, offer excellent trout fishing. Gray foxes, black bears, raccoons, and skunks make their home here, along with a wide variety of birds, the monarch butterfly, and the luna moth. *How to get there: Exit 76, east on I-66, right on Rte. 340. Exit 56, east on I-64 to Exit 19, north on Skyline Dr. Open year-round. Admission charged.*

54 Cyrus H. McCormick Museum and Wayside

3 min. East on Rte. 606, left on Rte. 937. It's still not clear whether Cyrus McCormick invented the reaper that bears his name or simply adapted and marketed a prototype developed 20 years earlier by his father Robert. But Cyrus, now known as the father of mechanized farming, was a born entrepreneur. He expanded his horizons to the great American heartland by setting up business in Chicago and later became the millionaire founder-owner of the International Harvester Company. The blacksmith's shop in which the first reapers were built contains a replica of Cyrus's 1831 machine and models of some of his later inventions. *Open year-round.* ⌂

50 Natural Bridge

Exit 50: 5 min. South on Rte. 11. Exit 49: 5 min. North on Rte. 11. Natural Bridge is a single block of limestone—90 feet long, up to 150 feet wide, and 215 feet high—that straddles Cedar Creek and joins two mountains here in the

50–49. *The people in the picture help show the monumental size of the bridge.*

Blue Ridge country. The Monacan Indians named this striking natural phenomenon the Bridge of God, but geologists credit millions of years of erosion by the creek as its sculptor. On the southeast wall of the bridge are the initials G. W., carved by George Washington when he surveyed the site in 1750. It was once owned by Thomas Jefferson, who purchased it and 157 acres from George III for 20 shillings. Some of the trees are up to 1,000 years old. *Open year-round. Admission charged.* 🐟 ♿

42 Virginia Museum of Transportation, Roanoke

7 mi./11 min. South on I-581 to Exit 5, west on Williamson Rd., right on Salem Ave., right on 3rd St. The emphasis here is on railroading—the glamorous aspects as well as the nuts and bolts. You can stroll past locomotives and passenger cars and board a caboose on the tracks near an old freight-loading dock. Inside the museum you can browse among life-size dioramas of passenger car and sleeping car interiors, as well as photographs of passengers from a bygone era boarding trains, sitting in dining cars, and socializing in club cars. Another photo exhibit shows scenes from foundries and machine shops where trains are built.

Other modes of transportation are represented here too: there are some horse-drawn vehicles, automobiles, photographs of early local pilots, and models of spacecraft. Yet another exhibit, some 20 years in the making, shows a model circus with railroad cars, a bandwagon drawn by 40 horses, and a big top complete with elephants and trapeze artists. *Open Mon.–Sat. and P.M. Sun. except Thanksgiving Day, Christmas, and New Year's Day. Admission charged.* 🐟 ♿

39 Dixie Caverns

1 min. West on Rte. 460. Upon entering this cavern, you walk up into the hillside rather than down—a phenomenon shared with only a few other caverns worldwide. Discovered in 1856 by two U.S. soldiers and believed to be more than 100,000 years old, this site has several chambers; each contains bizarre formations created by continually dripping, mineral-bearing water. More than 70 weddings have been performed beneath the dome-shaped Wedding Bell. On the tour, you'll see shapes that resemble a paratrooper, a Portuguese man-of-war, and the Leaning Tower of Pisa. *Open daily except Christmas Day. Admission charged.* 🐟 ⛺ 🚐 🐟

26 Shot Tower Historical State Park

8 mi./11 min. South on I-77 to Exit 5, east on Rte. 69, left on Rte. 52. Thomas Jackson, an immigrant from England, built this park's fortresslike tower, with thick limestone walls, in about 1807. Using lead mined in the area, it produced shot for guns. Molten lead was poured through a sieve at the top and allowed to fall some 150 feet into buckets of cooling water in an underground shaft (it was believed that the fall molded the shot into its round shape). The park has lovely shaded picnic areas. About 100 feet from the tower is the midpoint of the New River Trail, with attractions such as an access point for fishing, a historic ferry site, and beautiful views of the New River. *Open daily late May–early Sept.; weekends late Apr.–late May and early Sept.–late Oct. Admission charged for tower.* 🐟 🚶 🐟

16 Mount Rogers National Recreation Area

5 mi./10 min. South on Rte. 16. More than 100,000 acres of picturesque varied terrain here encompass 60 miles of the Appalachian Trail and about 300 miles of other trails, as well as the three highest mountains in Virginia. High on Whitetop Mountain (the summit can be reached by car) you can enjoy spectacular views. A herd of ponies roams freely, nibbling on mountain grasses. Some of the picnic and camping areas have excellent trout streams. *Open year-round.* 🐟 ⛺ 🚐 🚶 🐾 🐟 ♿

2 Bristol Caverns

8 mi./15 min. South on I-381 (becomes Commonwealth Ave.), left on State St., right on Rte. 421. Imagine their surprise when, in 1864, settlers excavating for a root cellar discovered this wonderland of sculptured stone. The caves, however, were known to the Cherokees, who used them as a base for attacks on pioneer settlements. The caverns were first formed hundreds of millions of years ago by an underground river, and a subterranean stream still flows in the deepest parts. The rock formations are artfully lighted to accentuate their dramatic shapes and colors. *Open daily except Thanksgiving Day and Christmas. Admission charged.* 🐟

8 The Crockett Tavern Museum, Morristown

6 mi./12 min. North on Rte. 25, west on Rte. 11E; follow signs. Davy Crockett was only a boy of 10 when his parents built and ran a four-room log tavern here along one of the first roads that led west. The tavern was burned after the Civil War, but this reconstruction conveys the atmosphere of the original. The rope beds could accommodate up to six travelers, and the stone fireplace was used for cooking and heating. A loom room contains spinning wheels and other equipment for making cloth. All the furniture, the flintlock musket mounted on the wall, and the Conestoga wagon in the barn are authentic relics from the days when America was slowly pushing west. *Open Mon.–Sat. and P.M. Sun. May–Oct. Admission charged.*

52

See N–S book, sec. 36.

26 77

77

34

16

46

2 VA
—————
TN

8 See E–W book, sec. 41.

40

End I-81

41 The Alice T. Miner Colonial Collection

3 min. East on Rte. 191, right on Rte. 9. With a discerning eye, Alice T. Miner, wife of railroad tycoon William Miner, assembled a superb collection of china, glass, pewter, silver, and fine furniture of the colonial era. A magnificent Hepplewhite sideboard, a Queen Anne tiger maple lowboy, a 1775 rope-sprung marriage bed, and a rare set of miniature 18th-century furniture used as cabinetmakers' samples stand out as antique works of art. The house, built in 1824, was later enlarged to display the collection. *Open Tues.–Sat. Feb.–Dec. Admission free but donations encouraged.*

34 Ausable Chasm

5 min. East on Rte. 9N, left on Rte. 9. If you walk the trail beside the rushing Ausable River, consider that the flat stones underfoot were worn smooth in the Cambrian period some 500 million years ago. Stratified sandstone walls flanking the river soar to dizzying heights in an endless variety of sculptural forms with names such as Pulpit Rock, Elephant's Head, and Devil's Oven. Jacob's Well is a deep hole worn into the rock by stones spun in an eddy for eons of time. At Table Rock, you board a sturdy bateau modeled on those used by French explorers and float to the landing and the bus back to the parking lot. Allow 1½ hours for the tour. *Open daily mid-May–mid-Oct. Admission charged.*

28 Fort Ticonderoga

20 mi./30 min. East on Rte. 74. Ticonderoga, commanding a strategic point on the route from Canada to the middle Colonies, was first fortified by the French, then captured by the British, who held it until May 10, 1775, when Ethan Allen and his Green Mountain Boys took it in a surprise assault. Although the fort later fell to the enemy, the Americans captured some 50 cannons, more than 2,000 pounds of lead, and a number of muskets and flints that were dragged to Boston and used against the British. The fort's history can be relived by exploring this reconstruction. The museum displays muskets, cannons, uniforms, and other period memorabilia, including General Washington's razor and corkscrew. In July and August fife-and-drum programs and cannon firings are presented by troops in period uniforms. *Open daily mid-May–mid-Oct. Admission charged.*

20 19 Great Escape Fun Park

Exit 20: 2 min. South on Rte. 9. Exit 19: 1½ min. North on Rte. 9. The Steamin' (some call it Screamin') Demon roller coaster does complete loop-the-loops, and the 10-minute Raging River Ride plunges thrill seekers through real rapids and waterfalls. Under the big top, gravity-defying motorcyclists, trapeze artists, and elephants strut their amazing stuff. There's a ghost town, Jungleland, and a high-diving show, plus bumper cars, Ferris wheels, scare-a-second rides, games, musical shows, gift shops, and pavilions serving food of many lands. Fantasyland, scaled for young children, offers rides on miniature trains and mechanical animals—dragons, elephants, and mice. *Open Memorial Day–Labor Day. Admission charged.*

13 12 Saratoga Lake

Exit 13: 6 min. South on Rte. 9, left on Rte. 9P. Exit 12: 5 min. North on Rte. 9, right on Rte. 9P. A glimpse of this woodland idyll tells the story: tranquil waters and pine vistas against a dazzling blue sky. Because most of the lakeshore is privately owned, development has been minimal—just a few well-maintained camping areas and a lone sandy beach, where the pure water makes swimming a pleasure; a float offshore has a diving board. Anglers rate the largemouth-bass fishing among the state's best, with 12-pounders no rarity. Perch, pike, and crappie abound too. *Open year-round.*

23 Albany, NY 12207

Convention and Visitors Bureau, 52 S. Pearl St. (518) 434-1217; (800) 622-8464 outside NY. Settled in the early 1600's, chartered in 1686, and declared the capital city of New York State in 1797, Albany has a rich and varied history. The Dutch presence is recalled at the Van Rensselaer family home and the Ten Broeck Mansion. The Schuyler Mansion was built for a general in the Revolution, and the New York State Museum provides insights into local history. Empire State Plaza is a monumental modern-day architectural extravaganza. Boat trips on the Hudson reveal the city's importance as a shipping center.

21 Olana State Historic Site

5 mi./8 min. East on Rte. 23B, left on Rte. 23, across Rip Van Winkle Bridge, right on Rte. 9G. The renowned landscape painter Frederick Edwin Church, eminent in the Hudson River school, built this Persian-influenced stone-and-brick villa in 1870, naming it after an ancient Turkish treasure house/fortress. He saw it as his family's refuge as well as three-dimensional art, a harmonious blend of architecture and environment. His touch is everywhere: in forest and meadow tableaux framed by the windows, in hand-stenciled decorations enlivening various rooms, but chiefly in such masterly paintings as his "Autumnal View," "Bend in the River," the brooding sunset of "The Afterglow," and the extraordinary mystery of "El Khasne, Petra," painted after he had visited that ruined city. *Grounds open year-round. Tours of house given May–Labor Day. Admission charged for house.*

21 20 Catskill Game Farm

Exit 21: 11 mi./20 min. East on Rte. 23B, right on Rte. 23, then left on Rte. 32. Exit 20: 11 mi./20 min. West on Rte. 212, right on Rte. 32. A half-century of dedicated conservation work has created this home for 2,000 animals and birds, including many endangered species. Stroll the compounds and see what wonders we've almost lost: the wisent, or aurochs, a rare East European bison; the llamalike South American guanaco; the barasingha, or swamp deer, from India; the long-horned scimitar oryx from the Sahara; and the blesbok, white rhino, and sable antelope from southern Africa. In the spacious bird sanctuary, crowned cranes, flamingos, cockatoos, and other avian marvels display

21. *The Persian influence is richly exemplified in the Court Hall at Olana.*

their many colors. Deer and antelope wander freely. The prairie-dog village, daily animal shows, and a sand playground appeal to youngsters. *Open daily mid-Apr.– Oct. Admission charged.*

| 17 |
| 16 |

West Point Museum

Exit 17: 13 mi./25 min. East on Rte. 17, right on Rte. 9W, left on Rte. 218. Exit 16: 15 mi./30 min. East on Rte. 6, left on Rte. 293. right on Rte. 218. The collections here date from 1777, with armament captured when the British surrendered at Saratoga. In addition to weapons, you'll find paintings, dioramas, and other works of art depicting various aspects of military life. The West Point Room, American Revolution Room, World War I and II rooms, and other galleries include information and artifacts related to all the conflicts in which America has been involved. In the Weapons Room, the escalation of warfare, from the Stone Age to the atomic era, is dramatically portrayed. *Open daily except Christmas and New Year's Day. Admission free but donations encouraged.*

| 16 | ### Bear Mountain State Park

10 mi./15 min. East on Rte. 6, right on Rte. 9W. It is ironic that these spacious hillsides, softball fields, picnic grounds, and leafy nature trails were once the proposed site of a state prison. At Trailside many outdoor displays explain the local flora, fauna, and geology; and the attractions in the nearby museum and zoo range from turtles to bears to beavers at work on a cutaway dam. An excursion boat affords a look at the full beauty of the setting, the Hudson River, and the handsome Bear Mountain Bridge. Other summer diversions include swimming, boat rentals, and fishing; winter brings ice skating and sledding. *Open year-round.*

| 9 | ### Sunnyside, Tarrytown

4 min. South on Rte. 9. "I would not exchange the cottage for any chateau in Christendom," Washington Irving wrote in 1836, after remodeling the modest 17th-century stone house he called Sunnyside. He had recently returned from 17 years abroad, where he had written "Rip Van Winkle," "The Legend of Sleepy Hollow," and other works. Every feature of the house and its 24-acre wooded grounds reflects the joy of this internationally renowned American author at living in "this dear, bright little home" overlooking the Hudson's widest sweep. The original furnishings include Irving's writing desk and, in the parlor, the rosewood piano on which his nieces accompanied his flute recitals. His dressing gown and walking stick still rest in a large bedroom armoire. *Open year-round. Admission charged.*

| FDHM | ### The Bronx Zoo, New York Zoological Park

Fordham Rd. exit. 3 mi./12 min. East on W. Fordham Rd. and E. Fordham Rd. This 265-acre habitat ("zoo" seems so inadequate) contains one of the world's great displays of animal life. There's too much for a single visit, but you can start with Skyfari cable cars for an overview of cheetahs, giraffes, zebras, guanacos, and other African and South American mammals in natural settings, or the Bengali Express monorail for the rhinos, elephants, and tigers of Wild Asia. Special lighting in the World of Darkness permits a look at bats, owls, and other nocturnal creatures. The Holarctic Trail leads to Kodiak bears, red pandas, and snow leopards prowling the prairies and Himalayan highlands. The indoor World of Birds reproduces the lush splendors of a South American rain forest and other natural settings. There's much more here, including a children's zoo, where youngsters can be photographed holding animals. *Zoo open year-round; Children's Zoo and Wild Asia open May– Oct. Admission charged.*

9. *Decorative embellishments all but overwhelm Irving's modest cottage.*

| TRI | ### New York, NY 10019

Triboro Bridge exit. Convention and Visitors Bureau, 2 Columbus Circle. (212) 397-8222. The crowded diversity of the city can be overwhelming, but even a short visit will be rewarding if you decide in advance what you want to see. You might choose the spectacular views from the Empire State Building or World Trade Center, or stroll on Fifth Avenue past Rockefeller Center, St. Patrick's Cathedral, and intriguing shop windows. Central Park might beckon, or Chinatown, Greenwich Village, or the South Street Seaport. For museumgoers, the choices are a challenge: will it be the Metropolitan, Whitney, Guggenheim, Frick, or Natural History? Other temptations: a boat ride in the harbor, or to the Statue of Liberty, or around the island of Manhattan. Be forewarned, however: the city is a difficult—or expensive—place to park a car.

See E–W book, sec. 9.

90

23

28

21

13

20

41

17

15

16

34

9

16

See N–S book, sec. 47.

95

TRI

5

End I-87

8. *Saint-Gaudens's interest in sculptural forms extended to his garden, as indicated by the subtly related shapes in the landscape that the artist helped to design.*

25 Crystal Lake State Park

3 min. North on Rte. 16. Swimmers will enjoy the sparkling clarity of aptly named Crystal Lake as well as the relative warmth of these quiet, shallow waters. Poplar, ash, and white pine trees shade the picnic tables along the shore. To the east Mt. Wheeler, with its base of bare granite, its wooded slopes, and its rounded summit, dominates the skyline. Canoes, sailboards, and small rafts—but not motorboats—may be launched for offshore fishing and other aquatic recreation. Likely to be crowded on weekends. *Open daily late May–mid-Sept. Admission charged.*

16 Morse Museum, Warren

17 mi./30 min. East on Rte. 25 (becomes Rte. 25C at Piermont). As a boy growing up in a small farming community, Ira Morse dreamed of hunting big game in Africa. In 1926, having established a successful shoe business, he went on the first of six safaris to the Dark Continent. Among the trophies taken by him and his son are lions, hyenas, antelope, elephant tusks, and a group of artifacts including shields, a witch doctor's rattle, a tea set made from ostrich eggs, and Masai baskets so tightly woven that they hold water. A collection of over 200 pairs of shoes from around the world represents his business interests. *Open daily mid-June–Labor Day.*

10 Quechee Gorge State Park

6 mi./8 min. North on I-89, left on Rte. 4. In the tongue of the Abnaki Indians, *quechee* (pronounced *kwee*-chee) means "a deep gorge." Aptly named, the park parallels a scenic, mile-long stretch of the Ottauquechee River, a stream flowing some 160 feet below the bridge on Rte. 4. Anglers prowl on the river's reddish-gray slate banks to try for brown and rainbow trout. Mill Pond, north of the gorge, is favored for its northern pike and bass. A softball field and horseshoe pitch are further enticements in this delightful state park.

A 1-mile hiking trail connects the pond and the river, and two more trails join the main trail to a campground, which has secluded sites under tall pines. But hikers be warned: climbing the gorge walls is ecologically as well as economically unsound; violators will incur a $500 fine. *Open daily Memorial Day–Columbus Day. Admission charged.*

8 Saint-Gaudens National Historic Site

10 mi./20 min. East on Rte. 131, left on Rte. 12A. The world-famous sculptor Augustus Saint-Gaudens bought the estate he called Aspet in 1885. The site now includes his home, studios, gardens, and a 120-acre woodland. Many of the Queen Anne and Hepplewhite pieces that grace the house are Saint-Gaudens's original furnishings, but the main attraction is the sculptor's own work—more than 100 pieces in all. They include a reduction of his famous "Lincoln the Man," a copy of the massive "Puritan," and the bronze bust of Gen. William T. Sherman. In the gardens, which the artist helped design, are the Pan Fountain and a copy of the haunting Adams memorial in Washington, D.C.

Visitors may join a tour of the house and the Little Studio, where Saint-Gaudens worked, and walk along the wooded trails to Blow-Me-Up Brook or Blow-Me-Down Pond, where the sculptor loved to go wandering. *Open daily mid-May–Oct. Admission charged.*

6 Green Mountain Railroad, Bellows Falls

4 mi./6 min. South on Rte. 5, left on Canal St., left across bridge to Depot St. Buy your ticket at the 1925 Bellows Falls brick depot, wait on one of the wooden benches, and board one of the eight coaches built between 1891 and 1931. A first-generation diesel locomotive (circa 1951) pulls the train along a right-of-way that was by turns an Indian trail, pioneer path, military road, and stagecoach route. You'll see a rocky gorge and waterfall, open farmland, two covered bridges, and unspoiled New England villages. On weekends round trips are offered: two to Chester, each taking about 2 hours, and three to Ludlow, a 4½-hour run that stops at Chester Station and Chester South. *Open daily mid-June–Oct. Train fare charged.*

2 Brattleboro Living Memorial Park

1 min. West on Rte. 9, left on Guilford St. Extension. This award-winning park situated on a series of mountain plateaus is thoughtfully designed and immaculately maintained. It offers a wealth of diversions, including a beginners' ski run (open weekends and evenings only), playing fields, several short, easy nature trails through deep woodland, a swimming pool, horseshoe and shuffleboard courts, two outdoor tennis courts, and four indoor courts that convert into a skating rink in winter. A natural amphitheater is a perfect setting for concerts. *Open year-round.*

19 | Arcadia Wildlife Sanctuary, Easthampton

5 mi./13 min. West on Rte. 9, south on Rte. 10, left on Lovefield St.; follow signs. This ancient meander in the Connecticut River has filled in, creating a large marsh that supports small mammals, including muskrats and red foxes, as well as an impressive range of resident and migratory birds. Herons, wood ducks, great horned owls, northern orioles, cardinals, and bobolinks are among the scores of species you might see, if you are lucky, along the trails through fields, marshes, and woodlands and from the observation tower located beside Arcadia Marsh. The main building houses an auditorium for orientation films and lectures, a natural history library, and a gift shop. Seasonal checklists for bird-watchers are available at the main building. *Sanctuary open Tues.–Sun.; nature center open Tues.–Fri. Admission charged.*

45. *Conductor and motorman stand ready to welcome visitors for a nostalgic ride.*

3 | Riverside

5 mi./9 min. East on Rte. 57, left on Rte. 159. This pleasant site beside the Connecticut River has accommodated family outings since 1840, when it was a picnic grove. Now it is a 150-acre state-of-the-art amusement park, but it still retains some charming echoes of the past.

Along with a new Ferris wheel, tall as a 15-story building, the park has a high-speed roller coaster, a loop roller coaster, and one called the Thunderbolt, which is of classic wood design. There's a brand-new water rapids/water slide and, from another era, a hand-carved carousel.

There are old-style jugglers and puppet shows and a new pavilion theater. The midway games offer both the tried-and-true dime-pitch tests of skill and the latest video extravaganzas. The section for young children includes bumper cars, a mine train ride, magic shows, and a petting zoo. On Saturdays stock-car racing is the featured attraction. *Open daily Apr.–Sept. Admission charged.*

45 | The Connecticut Trolley Museum

2 min. East on Rte. 140. Along with the miracle of electricity came quiet, efficient trolleys, which provided interurban transportation during the time between the era of horsepower, produced by horses, and that of the internal combustion engine.

The trolleys were remarkable for their elegant design, as can be seen in the more than 30 examples here.

On the 3-mile ride offered, you might find yourself in the open Montreal Observation Car No. 4, with seats rising from front to back as in a theater, or a 1911 trolley from Rio de Janeiro, or perhaps in the classic 1901 open-style trolley car with etched glass panels beneath the roof. *Open daily Memorial Day–Labor Day; weekends and holidays Labor Day–Memorial Day. Fare charged for rides.*

31 | Hartford, CT 06103

Visitor Information Center, The Old State House, 800 Main St. (203) 522-6766. Two of the interesting buildings are here by virtue of Hartford's being a capital city. The Old State House is a classic designed by Charles Bulfinch, and the current capitol building is a study in architectural eclecticism. Both are included, along with 21 other highlights, on the Walk, a self-guiding tour. In addition, the Mark Twain House, whose gables and Victorian verandas reflect the famous author's whimsical

31. *America's first triumphal arch was dedicated to veterans of the Civil War.*

side, contrasts with the nearby home of Harriet Beecher Stowe, a model of restrained 19th-century design.

The Museum of Connecticut History has an outstanding collection of Colt firearms, and the Wadsworth Atheneum, one of the United States' first art museums, displays an overwhelming variety of treasures. In Bushnell Park the carousel, with its superb hand-carved mounts, stands on a sweeping lawn near the Corning Fountain, which is dedicated to American Indians.

1 | New Haven, CT 06510

Convention & Visitor Bureau, 900 Chapel St. (203) 787-8367. This city's classic New England green, laid out in 1638, still serves as common land and provides a setting for three handsome churches. Yale University, a major presence in the town, offers a variety of attractions. Connecticut Hall, constructed circa 1750, is the oldest building on the Yale campus. The Yale University Art Gallery has a wide-ranging and distinguished collection as does the Yale Center for British Art. The Yale University Collection of Musical Instruments presents some 850 pieces; the Peabody Museum of Natural History is noted for its exhibits in the Great Hall of Dinosaurs.

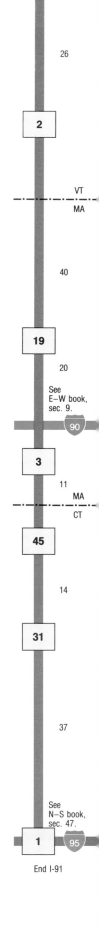

26

2

VT
MA

40

19
20
See
E–W book,
sec. 9.
90

3
11
MA
CT

45

14

31

37

See
N–S book,
sec. 47.

1
95

End I-91

FNP1. *The only sign of man's handiwork is the catwalk here in nature's rocky realm.*

42 | Forest Lake State Park

12 mi./20 min. North on Rte. 116; follow signs. Imposing views of 5,385-foot Mt. Monroe and 6,288-foot Mt. Washington add a special grandeur to this pleasant park. White pines, spruce, and paper birches shade the lakeside picnic area and provide a haven for downy woodpeckers, jays, and other woodland birds. In season, wildflowers add lovely splashes of color. For children there is a small playground. Although no boats may be launched from the narrow sand beach, fishing from the shore is permitted; the lake yields perch, bass, and trout. *Open daily late May–Labor Day. Admission charged.*

FNP2 | Cannon Mountain Aerial Passenger Tramway

Franconia Notch Pkwy., Exit 2. 1 min. A 5-minute aerial cable car ride to the 4,200-foot summit of Cannon Mountain reveals a spectacular panorama of distant valleys and the mountains of the Franconia Range. From the tram station, walk along Rim Trail, which will take you past rocky ledges and other fine views. The best vantage point for photographs is the summit observation tower, from which you can see five states and part of Canada.

You can go back down the mountain by tramway or take the 2-mile walking trail. *Open daily late May–late Oct., weather permitting. Admission charged.*

FNP1 | The Flume

Franconia Notch Pkwy., Exit 1. 1 min. This geological wonder is the result of ancient underground volcanic pressure, the surface erosion of frost, and the rushing water of Flume Brook. The ravine's narrow gorge, 800 feet long and 12 to 20 feet wide, has mossy walls extending as high as 90 feet. Along a boardwalk you can see verdant growths of ferns, mosses, and wildflowers. Four connecting paths lead to the Flume gorge and loop back past cascades, waterfalls, and huge glacial boulders. Allow about 1½ hours to complete this 2-mile walking circuit. Or you can take a bus, which crosses one of the oldest covered bridges in New Hampshire and leaves you within a 20-minute uphill walk of the gorge. *Open daily late May–late Oct. Admission charged.*

32 | Morse Museum, Warren

Exit 32: 17 mi./30 min. West on Rte. 112, left on Rte. 118, then right on Rte. 25C. Exit 26: 23 mi./35 min. West on Rte. 25, left on Rte. 25C. As a rural youth, Ira Morse dreamed of hunting big game in Africa. In 1926, having established a successful shoe business, he went on the first of six safaris to the Dark Continent. Among the trophies taken by him and his son are lions, hyenas, antelopes, elephant tusks, and a remarkable group of artifacts including shields, weapons, a witch doctor's rattle, a tea set made from ostrich eggs, and Masai baskets so tightly woven that they hold water. A collection of over 200 pairs of shoes from around the world recalls his business interests. *Open daily mid-June–Labor Day.*

24 | Science Center of New Hampshire

5 min. East on Rte. 25, left on Rte. 113; follow signs. Beginning in a wide meadow, a ¾-mile nature trail continues on to the fringes of the forest and across a marshy place where bridges traverse small waterfalls. Along the trail you'll get a close-up

18. *The inherent beauty of well-crafted functional objects is clearly depicted in these Shaker pieces exhibited in the meetinghouse. A child's chair is in the foreground.*

look at barred owls, porcupines, raccoons, bobcats, black bears, and white-tailed deer in their wooded enclosures. The Bear Facts House, a working beehive behind glass, and a community of voles are among other exhibits. *Open daily May–Oct. Admission charged.*　　　🪑 🚶 ♿

23　Endicott Rock

18 mi./24 min. East on Rte. 104, right on Rte. 3, left on Rte. 11B. In 1652 Gov. John Endicott of the Massachusetts Bay Colony carved his name, and four of his companions cut their initials, on this rock to mark the head of the Merrimack River and to set one boundary of their patent. These incisions remain clearly visible, and the rock is now protected by a granite structure (built in 1892). Nearby is an attractive public beach, with a broad expanse of sand, offering fine lake swimming. *Open year-round. Admission charged.*　　　🪑 🏊

18　Shaker Village, Canterbury

7 mi./14 min. Follow signs. "Put your hands to work and your hearts to God" is the Shaker creed embodied in this village dating from the end of the 18th century. Their buildings, furniture, tools, and household goods all share the distinctive elegance of pure function. Among their inventions are the first flat brooms, clothespins, and the circular saw. The 90-minute guided tours help to explain the Shaker beliefs and way of life. *Open Tues.–Sat., mid-May–mid-Oct. and holiday Mondays. Admission charged for tours.*　　　🪑 ♿

15W　Concord, NH 03301

Chamber of Commerce, 244 N. Main St. (603) 224-2508. In the New Hampshire Historical Society's museum you'll see a pristine model of the stagecoach that carried Concord's name throughout the West in the 1800's. Here, too, are period rooms and changing exhibits of historical interest. The Statehouse, impressively domed and porticoed, is the oldest in America in which a legislature has continuously met.

Concord's most famous citizen was President Franklin Pierce, and his restored mansion is much as it was in the 1840's, when he and his family lived there. Another beautifully restored dwelling is the Upham-Walker House.

Several examples of New England workmanship, treasured for its superb quality, are displayed at the League of New Hampshire Craftsmen.

4　The Robert Frost Farm

4 mi./8 min. East on Rte. 102, right on Bypass 28; follow signs. This 1884 clapboard house where Robert Frost and his family lived for 11 years was bought for

4. This comfortable upholstered chair was the poet's favorite place to sit and read.

him in 1900 by his grandfather, who was concerned by his seeming lack of a goal in life. Though Frost worked the land and raised some chickens, he milked his one cow late at night and again at noon to avoid early rising—to the consternation of his neighbors. In the barn, which is attached to the house, there are photographs of the family, excerpts from the poet's work, and videotapes that give additional insight into the life of the four-time Pulitzer Prize winner. A self-guiding nature trail reveals some of the environment that so influenced Frost's work. *Open daily Memorial Day–mid-Oct. Admission charged.*

44　Lowell National Historical Park and Heritage State Park

11 mi./16 min. South on I-495 to Exit 36, north on Lowell Connector to Exit 5N, right on Thorndike St., right on Dutton St. The history of this 19th-century mill town provides a fascinating overview of the Industrial Revolution. In the early 1800's Francis Cabot Lowell established a textile industry along the Merrimack River, where Pawtucket Falls could provide the power needed to drive the looms. Among the earliest workers were New England farm girls willing to conform to the strict company rules. Later on, immigrants from abroad came here to work. Excellent tours and exhibits help to explain the complex relationships among capital, waterpower, machinery, and the working people.

Across from the visitor center, the state park's museum—a former stove factory—now traces the story of waterpower in Lowell with displays and exhibits illustrating the history of the river, canal construction, machinery design, and mill architecture. On summer tours of the mills and more than 5 miles of canals, members of a living-history staff assume the roles and accents of a farm family and Irish immigrants of the era. *Open daily except Thanksgiving Day, Christmas, and New Year's Day.*　　　🪑 ♿

26　Boston, MA 02199

Convention & Visitors Bureau, Prudential Plaza. (617) 536-4100. Few places are so rewarding to explore on foot as the central section of this historic city. In a matter of a few hours one can savor the spacious tree-studded greensward of the Common, the cobbled streets and elegant homes on Beacon Hill, the maze of narrow streets in the North End, and the bustling Quincy Market. You can wander at will or take the Freedom Trail, a self-guiding walking excursion past 16 historic sites that starts at an information booth in the Common.

Among the many highlights beyond the city center itself are the Museum of Fine Arts, the charmingly idiosyncratic Isabella Stewart Gardner Museum, the Arnold Arboretum, the Franklin Park Zoo, and across the Charles River, Harvard Yard and the busy streets of Cambridge.

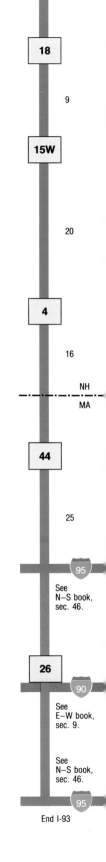

18

9

15W

20

4

16

NH
MA

44

25

95

See N–S book, sec. 46.

26

90

See E–W book, sec. 9.

See N–S book, sec. 46.

95

End I-93

62. *The covering to protect the timbers gives the old bridges their unique charm.*

62 | Watson Bridge

8 mi./12 min. North on Rte. 1 to Littleton, right on Carson Rd. Lush rolling farmland flanks the approach to this 190-foot covered bridge across the south branch of the Meduxnekeag River. The honest, careful workmanship shows in its heavy struts, latticed sides, and double-plank floor. Although no longer used, the bridge has been well preserved. An adjacent modern bridge now carries the traffic here. *Open year-round.*

59 | Lumberman's Museum

10 mi./15 min. West on Rte. 159. Logging is still big business in this northern region of Maine, and its colorful past is preserved here in 10 buildings. Dioramas and two life-size replicas of early logging camps (one built without nails), plus a blacksmith's shop, sawmills, a shingle machine, and a barrel-making exhibit, show how loggers lived and worked. Displays present the hand tools used in logging, including adzes and broadaxes, and the pike poles, peaveys, and swingdingles used to break up logjams in the river. There are two gigantic Lombard steam log haulers, one circa 1910, a national historic mechanical engineering landmark. You can also see more than 900 vintage photographs that document the early history of lumbering. *Open Tues.–Sun. Memorial Day–Labor Day; Mon. holidays July–Aug.; weekends early Oct. Admission charged.*

58 / 56 | Grindstone Falls

Exit 58: 16.5 mi./35 min. South on Rte. 11. Exit 56: 10 mi./24 min. West on Rte. 157, north on Rte. 11. Driving this scenic route that parallels I-95 adds about half an hour to your trip. Here in central Maine, surrounded by a seemingly endless panorama of dense forest, the Penobscot River and this small waterfall can be a welcome change from the forested landscape. Although the river drops only 2 feet, the riffle over a curious diagonal formation of slate is a refreshing sight and sound. Tall white pines shade the picnic sites. *Open year-round.*

52 / 51 | Indian Island

Exit 52: 5 min. Left on Rte. 43 to Davis Court, left over bridge. Exit 51: 4 mi./10 min. Right on Rte. 2A, left on Rte. 2. Home of the Penobscot Indians, this is one of about 200 islands that they own in the Penobscot River and its branches. The early Penobscots used an ideographic writing system similar in some ways to ancient Egyptian hieroglyphics. And when the earliest known European explorers arrived in 1524, this tribe was already part of a powerful confederacy. Today they continue to govern themselves and send a representative to the state legislature, making theirs the oldest uninterrupted government in North America. Visitors can drive through the town and explore the small museum and the craft shops, which sell moccasins and jewelry. *Open year-round.*

45A | Bangor, ME 04401

Chamber of Commerce, 519 Main St. (207) 947-0307. The 31-foot statue of Paul Bunyan, complete with ax and peavey, is a fitting memorial to the hardy loggers who worked the Maine woods in the 1800's. By 1842 Bangor was the second biggest lumber port in America. Lumber barons' mansions can be seen on a walking tour of the Broadway Historic District. The tools of the trade are on display at the Maine Forest and Logging Museum. The Bangor Historical Society's Greek revival museum features period rooms.

31 | Augusta, ME 04330

Chamber of Commerce, 1 University Dr. (207) 623-4559. The most imposing building in this city is the statehouse, rising grandly above Capitol Park. Constructed of granite from nearby Hallowell, it was designed by Charles Bulfinch, the gifted 19th-century Boston architect. The adjacent state museum is devoted to exhibits of Maine's heritage and natural history. Facing Capitol Park is the spacious home of James Blaine, a presidential nominee in 1884, which now serves as the state executive mansion. Fort Western Museum, built in 1754 to withstand Indian attacks, has rooms furnished with historical pieces.

27 | Peacock Beach State Park

3 min. South on Rte. 201. One of the few places in central Maine offering public access to the water, this park is named for the 1801 Peacock Tavern, a stagecoach inn and trading post that stands near the entrance and is now in *The National Register of Historic Places.* Pleasant Pond in the park is popular for swimming and some of the best largemouth bass fishing in central Maine. *Open daily Memorial Day–Labor Day. Admission charged.*

22 | Maine Maritime Museum, Bath

12 mi./15 min. North on Rte. 1 to Bath business district, right on Washington St. Visitors guide themselves around this restored turn-of-the-century shipyard, where apprentices still learn the trade of boat building. Dioramas of a hypothetical lobster village, a life-size 1880 cannery, and period boats lashed to an indoor wharf illustrate the history and technology of lobstering. A 142-foot Grand Banks fishing schooner can be boarded. During the summer the excursion ship *Dirigo* takes regular 40-minute trips down the Kennebec River. There's a mill and joiner's shop, a caulking shed, and a small-craft center. A new Maritime History Building, adjacent to the museum shipyard, documents more than 400 years of coastal life.

Two miles north on Washington Street, the 1844 Sewall House contains ship models, scrimshaw, navigational instruments, and a hands-on room for children. *Shipyard open late May–mid-Oct.; house open year-round. Admission charged.* 🚻 ♿

8 | Portland, ME 04101

Chamber of Commerce, 142 Free St. (207) 772-2811. Although they are now boutiques and restaurants, the original waterfront shops and warehouses of the Old Port Exchange still recall the age of sail, when Portland was a great port and a center for shipbuilding. The city's marine heritage is further emphasized by cruises on Casco Bay; Portland Head Light, one of the oldest lighthouses on the coast of the Atlantic that is still operating; the Portland Observatory, a 19th-century guide to navigation from which there is a spectacular view; and on a more intimate scale, the fine collection of Winslow Homer seascapes in the art museum. Other attractive echoes of Portland's past can be seen in the 18th-century Wadsworth-Longfellow House, the Tate House, and the Victoria Mansion, a 19th-century architectural extravaganza.

8. *Here at Portland Head is solid evidence that the "rockbound coast of Maine" is not just a cliché. The handsome lighthouse is considered to be a classic of its kind.*

7 | Two Lights State Park, Cape Elizabeth

9 mi./19 min. South on Rte. 1, left on Pleasant Hill Rd., left on Spurwink Rd. (Rte. 77), right on Two Lights Rd. A dramatic coastline, where huge waves crash onto odd rock formations called fissured slat slabs, makes this 41-acre park worth a visit in any weather. Slat-block staircases lead up a scenic trail flanked by bayberry and sumac; lady's slippers, columbines, and other blossoming wildflowers add color in the summer. *Open year-round. Admission charged in summer.* 🚻 🚶 🎣 ♿

7 | Crescent Beach State Park

7 mi./11 min. South on Rte. 1, left on Pleasant Hill Rd., left on Spurwink Rd. (Rte. 77). Here a mile-long sand beach with dunes and a gentle surf lies at the edge of a typical Maine wood. White pines, larches, and oaks shelter huge leather ferns and wildflowers; visitors may catch a glimpse of red foxes, woodchucks, and deer. *Open daily Memorial Day–Labor Day. Admission charged.* 🚻 🏊 ♿

If You Have Some Extra Time:

Acadia National Park

45A **43 mi./75 min.** In this vast preserve on Mt. Desert Island you will see, among other attractions, what is arguably the most dramatic conjunction of the Atlantic and New England's granite shore. Yet the surging sea and tide pools are but part of this watery realm of lakes, coves, ponds, and an impressive fjord.

The park's crowning glory is Cadillac Mountain, a great granite mass that rises 1,530 feet above the sea. From the summit in midsummer, you and your fellow early risers can be among the first persons in the United States to watch the sun come up. When daylight arrives, there are spectacular views of the indented shore, forested hills, rock outcrops, and low-lying islands far below in the seemingly endless sea.

At the visitor center, located at the park entrance just south of Hulls Cove, you can obtain detailed maps of the scenic Park Loop Road on the island and the 150 miles of trails for biking and hiking. Horse-drawn carriages and riding horses, which are available for rent, make good use of some 40 miles of carriage roads. You will find one of the most photographed lighthouses in New England at Bass Harbor Head, overlooking Blue Hill Bay on the southern tip of the island. *How to get there: east on Rte. 395, right on Rte. 1A to Ellsworth; continue on Rte. 1 and Rte. 3 to the park. Open year-round. Admission charged.*

45A

68

31

13

27

18

22

25

8

3

7

34

95

ME
NH 2

NH
MA

See
N–S book,
sec. 44.

93

See
E–W book,
sec. 9.

90 I-90

I-93

1 Fort McClary State Historic Site

7 mi./12 min. South on Rte. 236, left on Rte. 103. The first fort on the strategic heights of Kittery Point, above the Maine side of the entrance to the Piscataqua River, was built in 1715 to keep New Hampshire tax collectors from imposing heavy duties on ships from Massachusetts. The present hexagonal, 2½-story, granite and wood blockhouse, constructed about 1844 against possible attacks by the British, marks the transition from earth and timber forts to stone, as required to withstand the impact of more powerful artillery. This, the last blockhouse built in Maine, was never attacked, and it never fired a shot. Now in *The National Register of Historic Places*, it was named for Maj. Andrew McClary, who fell at Bunker Hill in 1775. *Open daily Memorial Day–Labor Day.*

7 Portsmouth, NH 03801

Chamber of Commerce, 500 Market St. (603) 436-1118. The people of Portsmouth have succeeded in preserving and reconstructing much of their cultural and architectural heritage. Rewarding evidence can be seen on a walking tour of six impressive houses, dating from 1716 to the 19th century (map and tickets available at the Chamber of Commerce). It can also be seen on a visit to Strawbery Banke, an ambitious restoration, begun in the 1950's, of a historic waterfront community. The 10-acre site accommodates some 35 buildings, mostly 18th-century houses with period furnishings, craft shops, a museum, gardens, and frequent special events.

2 Rye Harbor State Park

10 mi./20 min. East on Rte. 51, left on Rte. 1A. Known locally as Ragged Neck, this small rocky peninsula is a haven for birds and a good spot for a picnic and a swim at the adjacent mile-long sandy beach. Lobster boats attract herring gulls and terns to the nearby Isle of Shoals. Nearer shore you are likely to see egrets, blue herons, marsh hawks, snowy owls, and yellowlegs. In summer, sailboats bob in the lee of a jetty where fishermen cast for bluefish, mackerel, and a species of flounder that is known as blackback. *Open year-round. Admission charged weekends May–late June; daily, late June–Labor Day; weekends, Labor Day–Columbus Day.*

2 Hampton Beach State Park

6 mi./12 min. East on Rte. 51, right on Rte. 1A. This unspoiled, mile-long white sand beach stretching between some bluffs and the sea offers a peaceful environment for picnickers, swimmers, and surf casters. Bird enthusiasts will see sandpipers and cormorants, together with several species of gulls and terns. *Open daily Memorial Day–Labor Day. Admission charged.*

32. *The workers who brought prosperity to Lowell are memorialized here in bronze.*

58 Salisbury Beach State Reservation

4 mi./8 min. East on Rte. 110 and Rte. 1A. Campers, fishermen, swimmers, and wildlife coexist peacefully in these 520 acres of dunes. Deer, foxes, and raccoons forage among scrub pine, beach plum, and bayberry trees, while surf fishermen land striped bass, shad, bluefish, flounder, and cod along the 4-mile beach. Birders may see bald eagles, harlequin ducks, and piping plovers, a threatened species.

In the summer, programs are presented on marsh-bird identification, tide-pool life, and insect habits. First-come, first-served campsites are filled fast on holiday weekends. *Open daily Apr.–mid-Oct. Admission charged.*

54 Richard T. Crane, Jr., Memorial Reservation

12 mi./20 min. East on Rte. 133, right on Rte. 1A to Ipswich, left on Argilla Rd. In an inspiring example of sharing the wealth, the unusually fine amenities of this 1,400-acre preserve can now be enjoyed by the public. The 59-room Great House faces a half-mile swath of greensward leading to the sea and 4 miles of white sand beach. There's a sunken Italian garden, a rose garden, the Casino, and a bowling green. The natural history of Crane Beach and Castle Neck can be explored along the Pine Hollow Interpretive Trail, for which an illustrated guide is available. *Grounds open year-round; house tours four times a year. Admission charged.*

32 Lowell National Historical Park and Heritage State Park

15 mi./25 min. North on Rte. 3, right on Lowell Connector to Exit 5N, right on Thorndike St., right on Dutton St. The history of this 19th-century mill town provides a fascinating survey of the Industrial Revolution. In the early 1800's, Francis Cabot Lowell established a textile industry along the Merrimack River, where Pawtucket Falls could provide power to drive the looms. Among the earliest workers were New England farm girls willing to conform to the strict company rules. Later on, immigrants from many foreign lands came here to work. A variety of tours and exhibits explains the complex relationships that developed among capital, waterpower, machinery, and the working people.

Across from the visitor center the state park's museum was originally a stove factory. It traces the overall history of waterpower in Lowell with a number of imaginative displays and exhibits illustrating the river's history along with canal construction, mill architecture, and machinery design. The foresight and energy of these individuals whose vision turned Lowell into a thriving manufacturing center are also acknowledged. On summer tours of the canals and mills, members of a living-history staff assume the roles and accents of a farm family and Irish immigrants of the era. *Open daily except Thanksgiving Day, Christmas, and New Year's Day.*

I-93–I-90. Historic Faneuil Hall's market-place is a colorful accent in a busy city.

I-93
I-90 **Boston, MA 02199**

I-93 exit: 13 mi./20 min. I-90 exit: 12 mi./20 min. Convention & Visitors Bureau, Prudential Plaza (617) 536-4100. Few places are so rewarding to explore on foot as this historic city. In only a few hours one can savor the spacious tree-studded Common, the cobbled streets and elegant homes on Beacon Hill, the maze of narrow streets in the North End, and the bustling Quincy Market. You can wander at will through the city or take the Freedom Trail, a self-guiding walking excursion that starts at a booth in the Common.

Among the many highlights beyond the center of the city are the Museum of Fine Arts, the charmingly idiosyncratic Isabella Stewart Gardner Museum, the Arnold Arboretum, the Franklin Park Zoo, and across the Charles River, Harvard Yard and the busy streets of Cambridge.

7B **Bristol Blake State Reservation, Norfolk**

7 mi./12 min. North on Rte. 140, right on Rte. 115, left on North St. Known locally as the Stony Brook Nature Center and Wildlife Sanctuary, this 300-acre birders' paradise of woods, ponds, and marshland is partly owned by the Massachusetts Audubon Society. Among more than 150 bird species that you might see here are the American bittern, common snipe, great blue heron, and wood duck. A butterfly garden contains coreopsis, veronica, and other flowers that attract these flying jewels. A trail guide identifies plants and explains the ecology along a 1-mile walk. *Open year-round. Admission free but donations encouraged.*

6A **Watson Pond State Park, Taunton**

9 mi./12 min. South on I-495 to Exit 9, right on Bay St. Swimming, picnicking, and fishing are the order of the day in this attractive 14-acre park. The picnic tables are nicely dispersed beside the beach and on the rolling terrain, and some are shaded by handsome white pines. Fishermen try for the hornpout (catfish), pickerel, eels, and bass weighing as much as 7 pounds. Everyone keeps an eye out for snapping turtles, which are extremely dangerous. *Open daily Memorial Day–late Oct. Admission charged.*

21 **Providence, RI 02903**

Convention and Visitors Bureau, 30 Exchange Ter. (401) 274-1636. Roger Williams, who founded the town that later became Rhode Island's capital, is honored in a 4½-acre memorial park as well as a larger park just south of town. The imposing statehouse, one of the most beautiful in America, is topped by the world's second largest unsupported dome. Other attractions include the Arcade, built in 1828 (the country's oldest indoor shopping center), the Providence Athenaeum, where original Audubon illustrations can be seen, and the Rhode Island School of Design's art museum. Many of the city's landmarks on Benefit, Benevolent, and Meeting streets can be seen on tape-recorded walking tours.

5 **Arcadia Management Area**

5 mi./8 min. South on Rte. 102, south on Rte. 3, right on Rte. 165, left on Arcadia Rd. Miles of marked trails and dirt roads, superb fishing, and two swimming ponds are among the many attractions of this 12,000-acre area. Boats and canoes may be launched on Breakheart Pond and Wood River to pursue bass, salmon, and trout. Beach Pond has bathhouse facilities, while Browning Mill Pond offers rocky, shaded promontories for picnicking. A popular destination for hikers and backpackers is scenic Stepstone Falls. *Open June–Labor Day. Admission charged.*

90 **Mystic Seaport Museum**

2 min. South on Rte. 27. The artistry and resourcefulness of 19th-century New England shipbuilders as well as sailors are handsomely illustrated by the 40-odd museum buildings and the museum harbor. Along the bustling waterfront working coopers, shipsmiths, and sailmakers demonstrate the skills on which a great maritime tradition was built. Among the historic ships moored at the docks is the *Charles W. Morgan,* the last remaining whaler. In the reconstructed houses and other buildings are exhibits of scrimshaw, ship models and carved figureheads, paintings, and other marine artifacts. *Open year-round. Admission charged.*

90. Wooden sailing ships accentuate Mystic waterfront's 19th-century ambience.

82 Harkness Memorial State Park, Waterford

6 mi./17 min. South on Rte. 85, right on Jefferson Ave., right on Coleman St., left on Rte. 213. The broad lawns of the former estate of the philanthropist Edward Harkness attract picnickers, while strollers enjoy wandering through the formal Italian and Oriental gardens, informal rock gardens, and the large greenhouse, which is planted with cacti, ferns, and flowers. A vine-covered pergola offers visitors welcome shade on hot days. In the 42-room stone mansion, which will be closed until May 1990 for extensive renovations, a collection of watercolors of North American birds by Rex Brasher is featured. The furnishings are few, but photos reveal the opulence of the interior in the past. Servants' quarters will also be restored during the renovations. *Grounds open year-round; buildings open Memorial Day–Labor Day. Admission charged.* 🎋🐟♿

69. *The eccentric characteristics of the exterior are amply sustained on the inside.*

69 Gillette Castle State Park

18 mi./30 min. North on Rte. 9, right on Rte. 82; follow signs. The medieval-style castle was designed and built (1914–19) by William Gillette, the noted actor who portrayed Sherlock Holmes on the stage for more than 30 years. The massive fieldstone structure, with a two-story living room 50 feet long, stands on a ledge high above the Connecticut River. Gillette devised intricate, hand-carved wooden doors, handles, and locks, as well as furniture that moves on tracks. In the third-floor reproduction of Holmes's Baker Street study, all is ready for afternoon tea. The veranda offers a spectacular river view, and hiking trails follow the route of Gillette's miniature railway, long since moved to an amusement park. *Open daily Memorial Day–Columbus Day; weekends only Columbus Day–mid-Dec. Admission charged.* 🎋🚶

51 52 The Shore Line Trolley Museum, East Haven

Exit 51: 5 min. East on Rte. 1, right on Hemingway Ave., left on River St. Exit 52: 5 min. South on High St., left on Main St., right on Hemingway Ave., left on River St. A 3-mile ride on an antique trolley is a nostalgic reminder of how pleasant and efficient transportation by electric power can be. Stops include a carbarn where trolleys are housed and restored by master craftsmen. Among the prized examples you'll see a 1920 snow sweeper from the Third Avenue Elevated Line in New York City and a superbly refurbished 1911 open car designed for beach runs. *Open daily Memorial Day–Labor Day; weekends and holidays Sept., Oct., May; non-holiday weekends Dec.; Sun., Nov., Apr. Admission charged.* 🎋

47 New Haven, CT 06510

Convention & Visitor Bureau, 900 Chapel St. (203) 787-8367. The classic New England village green, laid out in 1638, still serves as common land and provides a setting for three handsome churches. Yale University, a major presence here, provides a variety of attractions. Connecticut Hall, circa 1750, is the oldest building on the Yale campus; the Yale University Art Gallery has a wide-ranging collection; and the Yale Center for British Art has a distinguished collection in a building designed by the noted architect Louis I. Kahn. The Yale University Collection of Musical Instruments includes more than 850 pieces, and the Peabody Museum of Natural History is noted for the imaginative exhibits in the Great Hall of Dinosaurs.

18 Sherwood Island State Park

2 min. South on Sherwood Island Connector. Sweeping lawns separate two beaches—totaling 234 acres—where the gentle surf and shallow waters make swimming ideal. Linden, juniper, mugho pine, and apple trees shade the picnic area. A stone jetty gives scuba divers access to deeper water. This is a good place to fly kites, play softball, toss a Frisbee, or lounge on the observation deck of the big pavilion. *Open year-round. Admission charged.* 🎋🏊

7 Stamford Museum and Nature Center

6 mi./20 min. Headed south: west on N. State St., right on Washington Blvd. (Rte. 137), left on High Ridge Rd., left on Scofieldtown Rd. Headed north: north on Washington Blvd.; proceed as above. The former estate of Henri Bendel, the department store founder, is now open to the public. Here you'll find a 19th-century working farm with goats, sheep, and cattle. The Tudor-style stone mansion houses a fascinating variety of natural history displays, an art gallery, and a North American Indian room. There are changing exhibits as well. The 20th century is also represented here by a planetarium (open on Sunday afternoons) and by an observatory that is equipped with a powerful telescope (open on Friday evenings). *Open year-round. Admission charged.* 🎋🚶♿

19 Rye Playland

3 min. South on Playland Pkwy. From 48 rides to fireworks, musical shows, and a seaside boardwalk, this venerable amusement park—now a national historic landmark—has something for everyone. After riding the roller coaster and bumper cars, you can stroll beside oak-shaded lawns lined with games of skill or chance. Young children enjoy the pony ride, the miniature railroad, and the carousel. Older ones can work off steam at a batting cage or with pedal boats and rowboats on the man-made lake. Swimming is available at a crescent-shaped beach and in a freshwater pool. *Open Tues.–Sun. mid-May–Labor Day. Admission charged.* 🎋🏊

New York, NY 10019

Convention and Visitors Bureau, 2 Columbus Circle. (212) 397-8222. The crowded diversity of the city can be overwhelming, but even a short visit will be rewarding if you decide in advance what you want to see. You might choose the spectacular views from the Empire State Building or the World Trade Center, or stroll on Fifth Avenue past Rockefeller Center, St. Patrick's Cathedral, and intriguing shop windows. Central Park might beckon, or Chinatown, Broadway, Greenwich Village, or the South Street Seaport. For museumgoers the choices are a challenge: will it be the Metropolitan, Whitney, Frick, or Guggenheim (all close to each other)? And there's also the American Museum of Natural History to consider. Other temptations are a boat ride in the harbor to Staten Island, or to the Statue of Liberty, or around the island of Manhattan. Be forewarned, however: the city is a difficult—or expensive—place to park a car.

13 Warinanco Park, Elizabeth

2 mi./7 min. West on Rte. 439 (Bayway Ave.), left on Rahway Ave. (Rte. 27). An oasis of greenery in the midst of Elizabeth's urban sprawl, this attractive park has unusually comprehensive facilities, which serve three adjacent communities and all of Union County as well. You'll find a pond stocked with catfish and bluegill, rental rowboats and pedal boats, a 2½-mile trail for jogging or biking, and a huge indoor skating rink. Whether your game is tennis, baseball, softball, cricket, horseshoes, or Frisbee, you'll find a field to suit your needs. Nature lovers can enjoy a stroll through the colorful flower gardens set amid tall oak, elm, and American beech trees. *Open year-round.*

8 Monmouth Battlefield State Park

10 mi./14 min. East on Rte. 33. During the Battle of Monmouth on June 28, 1778, the opposing commanders, Sir Henry Clinton and George Washington, personally directed their troops. The Continental Army, rigorously trained by Baron Friedrich von Steuben at Valley Forge, inflicted heavy casualties on the British. The legend of Molly Pitcher, who carried water to American soldiers and replaced her husband on a gun crew when he fell, originated here.

The 1,520-acre park includes the restored 18th-century house of John Craig, who participated in the battle. And at the visitor center audiovisual presentations and an illuminated diorama depict the day's action. Volunteers in period uniforms reenact the battle in late June each year. For the date call (201) 462-9616. There are trails for hiking, cross-country skiing, and horseback riding. Pond fishing is for children only. *Open year-round.*

CC Philadelphia, PA 19102

Center City exit: Visitors Center, 1625 JFK Blvd. (215) 636-1666. If you plan to stop in Philadelphia, don't be in a rush. Take time to do justice to Independence National Historical Park, which includes Independence Hall along with other historic structures on Independence Square. In the park you will view the Liberty Bell, Franklin Court, Carpenters' Hall, and several handsomely restored, period-furnished 18th-century houses, among other highlights on the 42-acre site. The Philadelphia Museum of Art and the Franklin Institute Science Museum are justly renowned. The city boasts a number of other museums, dedicated to such diverse subjects as Afro-American culture, Jewish history, antique toys, Wedgwood china, fire fighting, and the art of Norman Rockwell. There's also the American Swedish Museum, a medical museum, a Civil War museum, and the Please Touch Museum for Children.

CC Pomona Hall, Camden

Center City exit: 3 mi./10 min. West on Callow Hill St., left on 6th St.; cross Benjamin Franklin Bridge; continue on I-30, right on Kaighn Ave., left on Park Blvd. The elegant simplicity of the Quaker lifestyle is revealed throughout this handsome red brick Georgian house, built in 1726 by Joseph Cooper, Jr., a friend of Benjamin Franklin's. It was enlarged in 1788 and has recently been restored. The three-story building is furnished with some exquisite 18th- and 19th-century pieces, including a Hepplewhite sideboard, a Philadelphia tea table, Windsor chairs, a Garrett clock, and a Chippendale mirror. At the large kitchen fireplace, costumed guides demonstrate open-hearth cooking. *Open Sun.–Thurs. except Aug. Admission charged.*

CC. *A young citizen respectfully admires a venerable symbol of liberty for one and all.*

1B   See N–S book, sec. 42.

1A

0

NY

NJ

80

See E–W book, sec. 25.

24

13

New Jersey Turnpike

32

8

Headed south: to rejoin I-95, take NJ Tpk. Exit 7A; go west on I-195; then north on I-295.

Headed north: to rejoin I-95, go south on I-295; east on I-195; then north on NJ Tpk.

59

CC

76

See E–W book, sec. 32.

36

95

5

DE
MD

30

89

28

61

42

19

17

2

1

5 George Read II House and Garden, New Castle

4 mi./8 min. South on Rte. 141, left on Delaware St., left on 2nd St., right on Harmony St., right on The Strand. George Read II, lawyer and son of George Read, who was a signer of the Declaration of Independence and a framer of the Constitution, built this gracious brick mansion between 1797 and 1804 on the Delaware River. The house is a prime example of the federal style, with oversize doors and windows, wood carving, fine fireplaces and plasterwork, and fanlights. The 1840's garden, with winding brick paths, boxwood, and lilies, especially brings to mind a long-vanished time of elegance and charm. *Open Tues.–Sun. Mar.–Dec.; weekends only Jan.–Feb. Admission charged.*

89 Susquehanna State Park

6 mi./10 min. West on Rte. 155, right on Rte. 161, right on Rock Run Rd. "Heaven and earth seemed never to have agreed better to frame a place for man's commodious and delightful habitation," wrote Capt. John Smith when he came here in 1608. Many followed to settle the rich valley, leaving traces that can be seen today, among them the remains of a 45-mile canal dug in the late 1700's, a 1794 gristmill, and a tollhouse for the river bridge. At Steppingstone Museum—a cluster of shops and farm buildings in the park—craftspeople demonstrate many tools and skills common in earlier eras. *Park open year-round; museum open weekends May–Sept; mill open weekends and holidays Memorial Day–Labor Day. Admission charged for museum.*

61 Baltimore, MD 21202

Office of Promotion and Tourism, 34 Market Place, Suite 310. (301) 752-8632. The American institutions honored here with museums and displays include railroads, streetcars, volunteer fire departments, the flag, and the national anthem. Baltimore's marine heritage is recalled with the U.S. frigate *Constellation,* the oldest U.S. warship still afloat, and a maritime museum; there's also a superb aquarium. The renais-sance of Baltimore's inner harbor area is most notable in Harborplace, a large glass-enclosed complex of stores, markets, and restaurants. The Top of the World, which is also on the waterfront, has an observation deck from which there's a fine view of the harbor and surrounding region.

19 U.S. Naval Academy Museum, Annapolis

21 mi./25 min. East on Rte. 50, right on Rte. 70 (Rowe Blvd.), left on College Ave., right on King George St., left on Maryland Ave. The stirring story of America's naval achievements around the world is recounted with a wealth of displays in this dignified 1939 white brick building. On exhibit is the U.S.S. *Missouri*'s mess table, on which the Japanese surrender was signed in 1945. Collections include model ships, commemorative coins and medals, paintings, and more than a thousand battle prints of major naval engagements. Flags include Commodore Oliver Perry's 1813 "Don't Give Up the Ship" banner.

Be sure to take the self-guiding walking tour of the historic campus, concluding with a visit to the lovely domed chapel. Also explore the adjoining town of Annapolis, which is filled with centuries-old buildings. Among those open for tours are the elegant Georgian home of Declaration of Independence signer William Paca and the colonial-era state capitol, where George Washington resigned his commission as the commander-in-chief of the Continental Army. *Open daily except Thanksgiving Day, Christmas, and New Year's Day.* &

19 Washington, DC 20005

2 *Convention & Visitors Association, 1575 I (Eye) St. NW, Suite 250. (202) 789-7000.* The number of marvelous places to see here is so overwhelming that you should not begin without a plan. The three major centers are Capitol Hill, the Mall, and the White House area. The Capitol, the nation's greatest architectural monument, has evolved over 150 years to become the majestic building we see today; the interior is a vast treasure house of paintings and statuary. The Library of Congress, the Supreme Court, and the U.S. Botanic Garden are in the area.

Highlights on the Mall include the magnificent Lincoln Memorial, the Washington Monument, the National Gallery of Art, and the Smithsonian Institution, a complex of buildings that includes the Museum of Natural History, the Museum of American History, and the spectacular National Air and Space Museum. Near the White House you will see, along with the famous mansion itself, Lafayette Square, St. John's Church, the Octagon House, the Renwick Gallery, and the Corcoran Gallery, noted for its superb collection of American art.

1 Mount Vernon

56 *Exit 1: 9 mi./20 min. South on Mt. Vernon Memorial Hwy. Exit 56: 9 mi./16 min. East on Backlick Rd., left on Rte. 1, right on Mt. Vernon Memorial Hwy.* George Washington's home from 1754 until his death in 1799 is one of our

1–56. *The father of his country enjoyed a fine view of the Potomac from his front porch.*

country's most beloved shrines. The 11 meticulously restored original buildings include a smokehouse, a cookhouse, a stable, and the servants' hall. In the mansion, largely furnished with original pieces, the vibrant wall colors may come as a surprise, but they have been authenticated. Among the furnishings are a 1785 bust of the first president by Houdon and a porcelain tea service used by Martha Washington. Other highlights are the formal gardens, the tomb of Washington, and the museum. *Open year-round. Admission charged.* &

54 Gunston Hall

5 mi./10 min. North on Rte. 1, right on Gunston Rd.; follow signs. This is the elegant plantation mansion (circa 1755) of George Mason, one of our nation's most astute political minds. As author of the Virginia Declaration of Rights, father of the Bill of Rights, and one of the framers of the U. S. Constitution (among other notable tracts), Mason influenced many later documents in this country and abroad with his concepts of individual rights. His home reflects his intrinsic beliefs in order, balance, and proportion. It is noted for the beautiful 18th-century interior wood carvings. On the grounds you will find formal gardens, ancient boxwood—set out by Mason—a schoolhouse, a kitchen area, and a nature trail. *Open daily except Christmas. Admission charged.*

45 Fredericksburg, VA 22401

Visitor Center, 706 Caroline St. (703) 373-1776. The past is a palpable presence in this small town, which spawned heroes of the American Revolution and played a significant role in the Civil War. George Washington worked in the apothecary shop that is now a museum, and visitors may tour the house Washington bought for his mother in 1772. In the law office of his friend James Monroe you can see the desk on which the famous Monroe Doctrine was signed. Kenmore, the beautiful home of Washington's brother-in-law, has been restored, as has the Rising Sun, a popular 18th-century tavern. During the Civil War the town changed hands seven times.

45 Fredericksburg/Spotsylvania National Military Park

5 min. East on Rte. 3; follow signs. Spreading for miles on both sides of the interstate here is the greatest concentration of battlefields on the North American continent. Between December 1862 and May 1864, four savage engagements were fought in which Union attempts to crush Lee's Confederates ended in failure—at a combined cost of 100,000 casualties. It was here that Gen. Stonewall Jackson was by accident mortally wounded by his own men. To understand the sequence of the momentous events, begin at the visitor center in Fredericksburg. It requires a full day and a half to tour all the sites; there are interpretive trails to walk as well as a 100-mile auto route with numbered stops. Four historic buildings, including the Jackson Shrine, can also be visited. *Open daily except Christmas and New Year's Day.*

40 Kings Dominion

1 min. East on Rte. 30. It's five theme parks in one. Shock-Wave, the stand-up roller coaster, begins with a 95-foot drop, races in a 360° loop, and ends with a triple corkscrew—just one of the more than 40 rides here. The less intrepid can get their feet wet on one of several spectacular water rides; chime in for a sing-along; stroll, snack, and shop along International Street; mingle with Yogi Bear and pals; view some 50 species of wild animals from the Safari monorail; or look down on it all from atop a 330-foot-tall replica of the Eiffel Tower. *Open daily June–Labor Day; weekends late Mar.–May and mid-Sept.–mid-Oct. Admission charged.*

10A Richmond, VA 23219

10 *Convention and Visitors Bureau, 300 E. Main St. (804) 782-2777.* Although the imperatives of today are stylishly acknowledged at Shockoe Slip and the Sixth Street Marketplace, proud memories of the Old South are found throughout this state capital, once the Confederacy's capital. The capitol building is a handsome classic design selected by Thomas Jefferson. On Monument Ave., paved with hand-

If You Have Some Extra Time:

Colonial Williamsburg

11 **50 mi./70 min.** In this first and finest restoration of an early American town, one can come as close as is possible in the 20th century to experiencing the scope and character of colonial life in the 1700's. The main thoroughfare is the mile-long Duke of Gloucester St., which runs from the Capitol to the College of William and Mary (this country's second oldest college). Throughout this 173-acre community, shops, taverns, homes, public buildings, and a royal governor's palace are authentically restored. Wheelwrights, blacksmiths, cabinetmakers, candlemakers, bakers, bootmakers, gunsmiths, weavers, and many other shopkeepers and artisans in colonial dress explain their trades. Live sheep graze on the village green. In the blissful quiet the rhythmic clip-clop of carriage horses reinforces the illusion of a less complex and crowded time. *How to get there: east on I-64, right on Rte. 132; follow signs. Open year-round. Admission charged.*

laid brick, statues of Confederate heroes vie with stately houses for attention. Other historic highlights are St. John's Church, the Wickham-Valentine House, and the John Marshall House. Attractions of more recent vintage include the Virginia Museum of Fine Arts, the Richmond Children's Museum, the Museum of the Confederacy, and the Science Museum of Virginia, all excellent examples of their kind.

3 Centre Hill Museum, Petersburg

2 min. West on E. Washington St., right on N. Adams St. Several distinct architectural periods are reflected in this 1823 brick mansion. The original owner, English tobacco planter Robert Bolling, favored the federal design. His son added Greek revival features in 1850, and the third owner, Charles Davis, included colonial revival touches at the turn of the century.

Guided tours of the first and second floors are given. Early photographs of its owners and of the mansion's interior (also an exterior shot by Mathew Brady) are on display on the first floor. Spacious, beautifully appointed and maintained second-floor rooms attest to Davis's appreciation of the better things of life—including a shower stall with 13 heads. *Open daily except holidays. Admission charged.*

3 Old Blandford Church, Petersburg

2 min. East on Wythe St., right on Crater Rd. Completed in 1735 and enlarged in 1752, this simple brick church served as a Confederate hospital during the siege of Petersburg, and some 30,000 soldiers were buried in the adjacent cemetery. In 1901 a group of local women were delegated to develop a fitting tribute. They wisely commissioned Louis Comfort Tiffany to design a set of 14 memorial windows of stained glass; as his personal contribution, Mr. Tiffany added a 15th window. This exquisite grouping, a rare American treasure, remains a luminous memorial to a tragic time. *Open daily except holidays.* &

3 Petersburg National Battlefield

5 min. East on Rte. 36. Union general Ulysses S. Grant attacked Petersburg (a rail center important to the Confederates) in June 1864 and succeeded in cutting two rail lines. Gen. Robert E. Lee realized that if Petersburg fell, Richmond and the South were doomed. For 10 months the Confederate forces withstood the longest siege on American soil, but Petersburg finally fell in April 1865, forcing Lee to surrender a week later at Appomattox. Today you can explore the earthworks and battle-scarred

3. *A battlefield medical tent and table are ready to fold and move on short notice.*

terrain along a numbered auto route. History comes alive as uniformed soldiers re-enact daily life in a typical Union camp, or a fast-moving gun crew brings a cannon into action and opens fire. *Open daily except Thanksgiving Day and Christmas. Admission charged for museum.* 🌲 &

168 Historic Halifax State Historic Site

5.5 mi./9 min. East on Rte. 903, left on Pittsylvania Ave., left on Norman St., right on Rte. 301. Founded in 1760, the river port of Halifax soon became a social and commercial center for the Roanoke Valley; it was the scene of significant political events during the American Revolution and also served as a supply depot and recruiting center during that war.

Of the remaining original buildings, the circa 1760 Owens House is the oldest; it contains several antiques of the period, including a local 1760 Halifax County corner chair. The federal-style Sally-Billy House (c. 1808) and the late 18th-century Eagle Tavern can also be seen, along with the excavated foundation of a 1762 Georgian house, which is now enclosed and protected within a museumlike structure. A museum at the visitor center displays artifacts and dioramas that document the changing fortunes of the town. *Open daily Apr.–Oct.; Tues.–Sun. Nov.–Mar.* 🌲 &

150 Medoc Mountain State Park

11 mi./15 min. West on Rte. 44, right on Rte. 48, left on Rte. 1002. Here on the edge of the piedmont plains, a granite ridge resisted the glacial action that scoured out the lowlands to the east. A number of trails wind through the 2,300-acre park and reveal vegetation and wildlife indigenous to both ecosystems. On the 3-mile Summit Trail, loblolly and other pines are seen beside oaks and chestnuts. Pink lady's slipper, trailing arbutus, mountain laurel, and several other shrubs and flowers flourish. Among the many resident and migrating birds are red-tailed hawks, great horned owls, indigo buntings, and goldfinches. Fishermen come primarily for pickerel, bass, catfish, and gar. *Open year-round.*
🌲 ⛺ 🚐 🚶 🎣

138 Rocky Mount Children's Museum

5 mi./10 min. East on Rte. 64 bypass, right on Rte. 64 (business), left on Beal St., left on Bryant St., left on Gay St. Live animals, dioramas of the local environment, a planetarium, and a botanical garden are combined here to help children and others gain a better understanding of science, history, and ecology. Evidence of the Tuscarora Indian presence is presented with arrowheads and other artifacts. Highlights include some of Thomas Edison's inventions and miniature horse-drawn vehicles. *Open daily mid-Mar.–mid-Oct., Mon.–Fri. mid-Oct.–mid-Mar. except holidays.* &

107 Charles B. Aycock Birthplace State Historic Site

13 mi./18 min. North on Rte. 301, right on Rte. 222, right on Rte. 117, left on Rte. 1542. This modest unpainted building was the birthplace and early home of a farm boy who grew up to become a progressive and respected governor of North Carolina. The kitchen fireplace and parlor, and the barn with granary, tools, and equipment, help to illustrate life on the farm a hundred years ago. Living-history programs with the original tools and methods re-create how crops were planted and harvested, food prepared, and cloth spun and woven. *Open Tues.–Sun. Nov.–Mar.* 🌲

55 | Fort Bragg, Fayetteville

40 *Exit 55: 10 mi./20 min. West on Rte. 301 (I-95 business), right on Rte. 24, left on Randolph St. Exit 40: 15 mi./30 min. North on Rte. 301 (I-95 business), left on Owens Dr. (becomes All-American Frwy.), right on Gruber Rd., left on Rte. 24, left on Randolph St.* Named after Confederate general Braxton Bragg, the post was established in 1918 to train artillery troops for World War I. In 1942 a new kind of soldier, the paratrooper, was trained here. Today the post accommodates the headquarters of the XVIII Airborne Corps, including the 82nd Airborne Division. It is also the home of the Special Forces (the Green Berets). From the visitor center a self-guiding tour passes 14 stops with signs interpreting this vast installation. A museum honors the 82nd Airborne Division; and unconventional means of war, from the Revolution onward, is the unusual theme of the JFK Special Warfare Museum. *Base open year-round; Special Warfare Museum open Tues.–Sun. except Thanksgiving Day, Christmas, and New Year's Day; Airborne Div. Museum open Tues.–Sun. except federal holidays.* ♿

193 | Little Pee Dee State Park

13 mi./20 min. East on Rte. 57, left on Rte. 1722. In this park, which is named for the Pedee Indians, who once lived in this area, a 54-acre lake provides swimming in a designated area. On the half-mile nature trail through various kinds of pine and oak, bird fanciers may spot the endangered red-cockaded woodpecker and many other species. Rental boats are available. *Open daily mid-Mar.–mid-Oct., Thurs.–Mon. mid-Oct.–mid-Mar.* ⛵ ⛺ 🚐 🚶 🏊 🎣 ♿

170 | Florence Air and Missile Museum

8 mi./10 min. South on Rte. 327, right on Rte. 76; follow signs. A World War II V-2 rocket, a B-26 flown by U.S. airmen in three wars, and an F-11F retired from service with the Blue Angels (the navy's precision flying team) are among the more than three dozen combat aircraft and missiles to be seen here. Exhibits trace developments in aviation and space from the beginning of U.S. air warfare in France in 1918 to the space voyages of the Apollo project and the *Challenger* tragedy. *Open year-round. Admission charged.* ♿

164 | Florence Museum of Art, Science, History

4 mi./12 min. South on Rte. 52, left on Rte. 76 (W. Palmetto St.), left on Graham St. to Spruce St. A 26-room former residence in the international style houses an unusual collection that started in the 1920's with 78 pieces of Hopi Indian pottery. Over the years the museum has added Greek and Roman antiquities, textile, ceramic, and bronze items from several Chinese dynasties, African folk art, and American works of art. The South Carolina Hall of History and the museum grounds feature articles that are of particular significance in local history; these include the old town bell and the propellers from a Confederate cruiser. *Open Tues.–Sat. and P.M. Sun. except Aug. and holidays.*

164 | NMPA Stock Car Hall of Fame, Darlington

8 mi./11 min. North on Rte. 52, left on Rte. 34/151. Located at the Darlington Raceway, this collection of stock cars and trophies won by the men who drove them provides an overview of life on the race track and glory at the finish line. In the museum—the dream of a famous driver, Little Joe Weatherly—you'll see record-breaking engines as well as illegal parts of cars that were found to be not "stock." Of all the displays, the most thrilling is a race simulator, where you sit in the driver's seat of a stock car and screech through two filmed laps of an actual race flashing on a screen just beyond your hood. *Open daily except Thanksgiving Day and Christmas. Admission charged.* ♿

146 | Lynches River State Park

24 mi./35 min. South on Rte. 341, continue on Rte. 403, left on Rte. 541, left on Rte. 52, left on Rte. 21/147. Part of a 19th-century stagecoach route has become a 2-mile nature trail in this forest of longleaf and loblolly pines and scrub oaks where deer and raccoons may be seen. An Olympic-size swimming pool and softball field invite more active pursuits. *Open daily beginning of daylight saving time–mid-Sept., Thurs.–Mon. rest of year. Admission charged for pool.* ⛵ ⛺ 🚶 🏊 🎣 ♿

193. *Considering the relative size of the craft and the fisherman, it would seem that only catches of a modest size are to be expected in the Little Pee Dee River near the park.*

40 — See E–W book, sec. 42.

55

15

40

49

NC
SC

193

23

170

6

164

18

20 — See E–W book, sec. 47.

146

11

95

135 ## Woods Bay State Park

12 mi./17 min. East on Rte. 378, left on Rte. 301, left on Woods Bay Rd. The park includes one of the Carolina bays, egg-shaped geologic depressions that occur on the South Atlantic coastal plain. Some of the bays are dry, but this one is flooded and supports a wide variety of wildlife and vegetation. The Mill Pond, adjoining the bay, has a nature trail through stands of oak, pine, tupelo, dogwood, sweet gum, and cypress. Warblers, ducks, herons, woodpeckers, and fish-eating anhingas inhabit the area. A cypress swamp, where alligators live, can be investigated from the safety of a boardwalk or a rented canoe. *Open Thurs.–Mon.*

135
122 ## Williams-Brice Museum/ Archives, Sumter

Exit 135: 16 mi./27 min. West on Rte. 378 and Rte. 76 (becomes Liberty St.), right on N. Washington St. Exit 122: 20 mi./30 min. North on Rte. 521 and Rte. 15, left on Liberty St., right on N. Washington St. More than 200 years of county history are celebrated here. In a 19th-century mansion you'll find paintings and artifacts from the Revolutionary days, including a 1796 Rembrandt Peale portrait of a local hero, Gen. Thomas Sumter, along with Confederate muskets, knives, and other trophies, as well as chandeliers, fine furniture, ornate moldings, and Oriental rugs. In the garden a log cabin, built circa 1760, reveals a more humble way of life. *Museum open Tues.–Sat. and P.M. Sun.; archives open Wed.–Sat. Admission free but donations encouraged.*

135
122 ## Swan Lake Iris Gardens, Sumter

Exit 135: 18 mi./29 min. West on Rte. 378 and Rte. 76, (becomes Liberty St.). Exit 122: 14 mi./26 min. North on Rte. 521 and Rte. 15, left on Liberty St. Graceful swans glide along the ebony swamp waters of a lake surrounded by colorful plantings of Japanese irises; cypress trees rise from the water, and the sweet-scented breeze rustles the leaves. Six of the world's eight swan species live here: the black Australian, mute, whooper,

black-necked, coscoroba, and trumpeter. The peak flowering season is in late May, when the city of Sumter holds its annual Iris Festival; but taking a slow stroll on the sandy path beside the water in this 125-acre garden is a sensuous delight at any time of the year. *Open year-round.*

98 ## Santee State Park

5 min. West on Rte. 6; follow signs. The fishing in Lake Marion, which is fed by the Santee River, is world-renowned, and state records were set here with a 55-pound striped bass and a 73-pound blue catfish. Bream, crappie, and rockfish also provide good sport, and you can rent a boat and buy bait and tackle in the park. Enticements for non-fishermen include tennis, swimming, and boating. Pedal boats and bicycles are for rent, and there's a 4-mile bike path. Three nature trails invite walkers into the wooded realm of rabbits, squirrels, deer, and birds of many kinds. A nature center offers daily activities in summer. *Park open year-round; day-use area open mid-Mar.– mid-Oct. Admission charged in summer.*

98. *Some rather impressive equipment has been employed in capturing this bass.*

68 ## Colleton State Park

5 min. East on Rte. 61, left on Rte. 15. The Edisto River is the dominant feature in this 38-acre park. There's no swimming, but fishing is allowed. In the summer the programs for children include talks on river ecology, astronomy, reptiles, and the identification of plants. There are hiking trails beneath a dense canopy of sweet gums, live oaks, tupelo gums, and pines. Here you might see raccoons and deer. Listen for the jungle cry of the pileated woodpeckers, which nest here along with barred owls, cardinals, Carolina wrens, and jays. *Open daily Apr.–late Oct.; Thurs.–Mon., late Oct.–Mar.*

57 ## Tour of Historic Walterboro

4 min. South on Rte. 64 and Rte. 15 to Chamber of Commerce, 213 Jefferies Blvd. In 1784 low-country rice planters began building summer cottages here. A driving tour offers views of some 50 structures dating from the early 1800's to 1931. Look for the 1824 Glover-McLeod House with camellia gardens, carriage house, slave cabin, and stable. There are four churches and three municipal buildings open to the public, including the Old Colleton County Jail, which looks like a miniature castle, and the Colleton County Courthouse, both in *The National Register of Historic Places. Open daily except holidays.*

17 ## Savannah, GA 31499

Visitors Center, 301 W. Broad St. (912) 944-0456. The citizens of Savannah are justly proud of their city and their success in preserving, maintaining, and improving a remarkable heritage. The Historic Landmark District, the largest such area in the United States, includes the orderly grid of streets and squares originally laid out by Gen. James Oglethorpe in 1733. More than 1,000 historic homes grace this area and the adjacent Victorian district. Among them the visitor will find superb examples of Georgian, Regency, federal, Greek revival, Gothic revival, and Victorian architecture. Mapped tours are available for driving or walking, and bicycles can be rented.

15 Fort McAllister State Historic Park

10 mi./14 min. East on Rte. 144 and Spur Rte. 144. Ft. McAllister, a restored Confederate earthwork fort, is the centerpiece of this 1,700-acre park on the Ogeechee River. In 1863 the fort withstood a series of bombardments by Union ironclads, but in 1864 General Sherman took it from the land side, thus ending his march to the sea and causing the fall of Savannah. On a self-guiding tour you can see earthworks, a hot-shot furnace (used for heating cannonballs, which could create fires when they hit wooden ships), powder magazines, and three cannons. A museum exhibit includes a movie recounting the history of the fort. *Open year-round. Admission charged.*

10 Fort King George State Historic Site

4 mi./7 min. East on Rte. 251, right on Rte. 17, north on Rte. 99, left on McIntosh Rd. From 1721 until 1727 a small garrison of British soldiers occupied a cypress blockhouse that was built here to discourage the Spanish and French from colonizing the land along the Altamaha River. In addition to the site of the fort, visitors can see the locations of a large Indian village and a Spanish mission and the ruins of three sawmills. The museum recaptures the variety of events here with Indian artifacts, dioramas of daily life, and sawmill displays. *Open Tues.–Sat. Admission charged.*

6 Fort Frederica National Monument

17 mi./31 min. East on Rte. 84, left over bridge to Rte. 17. In 1736 Gen. James Oglethorpe started to build a fort on St. Simons Island to keep the Spanish from the colony he had established in Georgia. The fort, designed for the wilderness, was named for George II's only son. It briefly supported a thriving walled town, but in 1749, 7 years after the Spanish were repulsed, the garrison was disbanded. The town declined, and after a fire in 1758 it all but disappeared. An introductory film and a museum, as well as self-guiding and guided tours, help to explain the story of

95. *The oldest house has seen the flags of Spain, Britain, the U.S., and the Confederacy.*

this frontier post, now reduced to foundations and ruined barracks. *Open daily except Christmas. Admission charged.*

2 Crooked River State Park and Tabby Sugar Works

8 mi./13 min. to park, 6 mi./8 min. to sugar works. East on Rte. 40 to park signpost, east on unmarked road to second park signpost, left on Spur Rte. 40. A wooded 500-acre park along the Crooked River includes a nature trail with a boardwalk over an Indian kitchen midden. There's a swimming pool and a miniature golf course, and birders are asked to help add to an already extensive list of birds sighted in the area. Nearby is the ruin of a pre–Civil War sugar mill built of tabby—an early building material composed of lime, sand, and water. *Open year-round.*

117 Jacksonville, FL 32202

Convention & Visitors Bureau, 33 S. Hogan St. (904) 353-9736. The bend in the St. John's River here has been a crossing place and focal point since prehistoric times. Today the river can be enjoyed from either side. Jacksonville Landing, on the north side, has stores, markets, and restaurants. Riverwalk, on the opposite side, features

restaurants, entertainment, and a boardwalk that is more than a mile long.

The Cummer Gallery of Art, the Jacksonville Museum of Arts and Sciences, the Jacksonville Art Museum, the Jacksonville Fire Museum, and the Lighthouse Museum provide a wealth of objects for perusal.

95 St. Augustine, FL 32084

Chamber of Commerce, 52 Castillo Dr. (904) 829-5681. When the United States purchased Florida in 1821, St. Augustine had been under Spanish rule for 2½ centuries—a legacy that is still being preserved and enhanced. The most dramatic original structure is the Castillo de San Marcos (1672–95). Although the stone fortress has been attacked and besieged, its massive walls have never been breached.

St. Augustine also boasts America's oldest house and store. The latter is a museum with a reputed 100,000 antique artifacts. In the old Spanish Quarter with its narrow streets and walled gardens there are 10 restored 18th-century houses and a blacksmith's shop that can be visited.

The Lightner Museum is remarkable for its collections of American, European, and Oriental art, cut crystal, Tiffany glass, and mechanical musical instruments.

93 Marineland of Florida

91 *Exit 93: 14 mi./17 min. East on Rte. 206, right on Rte. A1A. Exit 91: 17 mi./25 min. East on Rte. 100, left on Rte. A1A.* Playful otters, penguins, flamingos, and electric eels are among the entertainers at this imaginative attraction. But dolphins dominate the show as they jump through hoops, pitch balls to batters, score baskets, and even bring their books to school. Many marine species, including sharks and turtles, can be viewed and photographed through windows at two oceanariums. A nature walk, marina, boardwalk, and a seashell shop and museum are also featured here, along with an innovative play area for youngsters. *Open year-round. Admission charged.*

92 Faver-Dykes State Park

3 min. North on Rte. 1, right on Faver-Dykes Rd. This 752-acre recreation area and wilderness preserve, still unspoiled and seemingly remote, retains the tranquillity of a virgin forest. It stretches along the marshy shores of Pellicer Creek, a stream popular with fishermen, who come here to try for trout, redfish, flounder, and blue crabs. A boat ramp is provided. Several nature trails wind through stands of longleaf pines, palmettos, and live oaks, which provide shelter for deer, wild turkeys, foxes, and even bobcats, and offer shade along the marsh, inhabited by waterfowl, wading birds, and alligators. *Open year-round. Admission charged.*

88 Ormond Beach and Tomoka State Park

Beach: 5 mi./11 min. Park: 8 mi./13 min. East on Rte. 40, left on N. Beach Rd. The 400-year-old live oaks of Tomoka have witnessed the rich history of this peninsula. When the Spanish arrived here in 1605, they found a Timucuan Indian village. In 1763, when Florida became British, an indigo plantation was founded at this spot; the ruins can still be seen. Today, as nature covers the footprints of the past, visitors can enjoy camping, fishing, and boating. The brackish water of the Tomoka River yields speckled trout, sea bass, and snook.

In autumn manatees, endangered marine mammals weighing up to 2,000 pounds, come here to browse on underwater vegetation. Nearby Ormond Beach attracts both swimmers and surfers. *Open year-round. Admission charged.*

84 New Smyrna Sugar Mill Ruins State Historic Site

5 min. East on Rte. 44, right on Mission Dr. The high price of sugar, the low price of Florida land, and slave labor led New York businessmen William Depeyster and Henry Cruger to this spot in 1830, where they established a sugar plantation and mill. The mill and outbuildings were destroyed in 1835 in the first action of the Second Seminole War. The plantation and the East Coast sugar industry never recovered from the Indians' revenge for the taking of their land. Today the ruins' weathered walls and elegant arches made of coquina—a local stonelike formation of sand, shells, and corals—are all that remain. Plaques throughout the ruins describe the various steps in the demanding process of making sugar and molasses in the 19th century. *Open year-round.*

79. *These space age artifacts have a strange and compelling sculptural beauty.*

79 Kennedy Space Center

12 mi./15 min. East on Rte. 50, right on Rte. 405; follow signs to Spaceport USA. The first stop at this huge complex is Kennedy Space Center's Spaceport USA, a villagelike area that provides an introduction to the wonders of space travel. (In case you forgot your camera, you may borrow one without charge at the information center.) Guided tours include the Gallery of Spaceflight Museum and Galaxy Center, where you will see examples of space launch hardware and various films, including *The Dream Is Alive*, which re-creates the sights and sounds of spaceflight on a screen 5½ stories high. The Rocket Garden displays earlier rockets and launch vehicles.

A bus tour takes visitors to the Mercury and Gemini launch sites at Cape Canaveral Air Force Station; another tour visits Kennedy Space Center itself. *Open daily except Christmas. Admission charged for some programs.*

71 Brevard Zoo, Melbourne

2 min. East on Rte. 192. Feed for birds and mammals is available at this small but well-cared-for zoo, and the apes and monkeys, including gibbons, capuchins, and stumptailed macaques, put on an especially good show to attract their fair share. Among the big cats to be seen are lions, a panther, a leopard, and a jaguar. The huge brown Kodiak bear dwarfs his black-furred cousin, which is also in residence here. The abundance of birds includes peafowl, which roam at large, ostrichlike rheas, African crowned cranes, and a sizable assortment of parrots and parakeets. *Open year-round. Admission charged.*

69 McLarty/Sebastian Inlet State Recreation Area

Visitor center: 16.5 mi./20 min. East on Rte. 512, right on Rte. 510, left on Rte. A1A. Some artifacts from a Spanish fleet that was wrecked in the shallows here in 1715 are displayed in the visitor center. Today the incoming breakers attract surfers; fishermen come for redfish, sharks, pompano, and bluefish, and clamming is also popular. The 576-acre recreation area,

If You Have Some Extra Time: Walt Disney World Resort

86 / 79 — *Exit 86: 41 mi./55 min. Exit 79: 38 mi./55 min.* To walk through the turnstile is to enter a world as you would like it to be—immaculately clean, beautifully landscaped, perfectly maintained, safe, orderly, and filled with happy people. In the Magic Kingdom, an enchanting Cinderella Castle is surrounded by Frontierland, Tomorrowland, Adventureland, Fantasyland, and more. Fifteen minutes away by car or monorail is Epcot Center, with Future World and World Showcase. Future World has pavilions, exhibits, and rides with an educational or futuristic accent. World Showcase, situated around a beautiful wide lagoon, represents a dozen different countries with its buildings, reproduced street scenes, shops, and restaurants. Unlike traditional park rides, the rides at Disney World transport you into new worlds of imagination.

For a representative sample try the Magic Kingdom's Space Mountain, Pirates of the Caribbean, or The Haunted Mansion—all three can be seen in half a day. At Epcot Center you can walk into a replica of Beijing's famed Temple of Heaven, or take a ride through the greenhouses of The Land pavilion and see remarkable agricultural innovations. At the Magic Eye Theater three-dimensional images that are incredibly realistic leap off the screen.

Disney World can be crowded, and some attractions have long lines, but for the most part its 20,000 employees make it work like a well-oiled machine. It takes 4 days for a visitor to feel reasonably satisfied, but even if you have only a day it will be unforgettable. *How to get there: Exit 86, west on I-4 to Orlando; follow signs. Exit 79, west on Rte. 50; follow signs. Open year-round. Admission charged.*

---

1 Vizcaya, Miami

3 min. Follow signs. James Deering, the co-founder of International Harvester, built this lavish villa from 1914 to 1916 as a winter residence. The name, meaning "elevated place," is from the Basque language of northern Spain, but the architecture is Italian Renaissance in style. The interior of the magnificent 34-room villa is a veritable museum. Surrounding the central courtyard are rooms resplendent with statuary, furniture, paintings, tapestries, carpets, and decorative objects in the Renaissance, baroque, rococo, and neoclassical styles.

The 28-acre grounds include a forest of hardwood hammock, a mangrove shoreline, and the studied elegance of 16th- and 17th-century Italian gardens replete with formal plantings, statuary, and water fountains. On the seaward side is the Great Stone Barge, a breakwater in the shape of a ship that created a small harbor for waterborne guests. *Open daily except Christmas. Admission charged.*

---

24 Topeekeegee Yugnee Park, Hollywood

2 min. West on Sheridan St., right on N. Park Rd. The name means "gathering place" in the Seminole Indian language, and this quiet park surrounded by a busy urban area still serves that purpose. People come here to relax and enjoy the wide shaded lawns, the picnic tables and grills, or to take advantage of the park's 40-acre lake and athletic facilities. There's a filtered and chlorinated swimming lagoon boasting a wide sand beach, and a nearby 50-foot-high water slide provides excitement with 700 feet of turns, drop sections, and occasional tunnels. There's a volleyball net, a basketball court, and playing fields; paddleboats, sailboats, sailboards, and canoes are available for rent. *Open year-round. Admission charged.*

---

64 Savannas Recreation Area, Fort Pierce

5 mi./10 min. East on Rte. 712. This marshy wilderness, once a reservoir for the city surrounding it, has long been popular with fishermen. The waters contain bass, bluegills, and catfish; and flat-bottomed johnboats, pedal boats, and canoes are available for rent. The marsh provides a haven for a variety of wildlife, including alligators, which often break the surface like partially submerged logs. A petting farm, with pigs, rabbits, and other gentle animals, is popular with children. *Open year-round. Admission charged.*

---

60 / 59 Jonathan Dickinson State Park

Exit 60: 8 mi./15 min. East on Rte. 708, right on Rte. 1. Exit 59: 15 mi./20 min. East on Rte. 706, left on Rte. 1. The park is named for Jonathan Dickinson, a Quaker who with his wife and infant child was shipwrecked near here in 1696. With some 10,000 acres of scrub pines, palmettos, and mangrove swamps, it stretches along the Loxahatchee River, which looks much as it did in Dickinson's day. The varied environment here supports sandhill cranes, scrub jays, bald eagles, and other woodland and marsh birds. The brackish waters of the river are home to sand sharks, snooks, sheepsheads, and manatees (an endangered species). A 9½-mile trail for backpackers leads into ever more remote territory. The Trapper Nelson Interpretive Site, which is nearby, was once the home of a colorful local recluse whose interest in plants and animals is still evident. *Open year-round. Admission charged.*

on a long barrier island between Indian River and the Atlantic, is less than a mile across at its widest point, and includes an inlet, coves, a coastal hammock, and mangrove swamps. More than 150 bird species have been spotted here, and there are great congregations of herons. *Open year-round. Admission charged for visitor center.*

Index appears in East–West volume.

Credits and acknowledgments

The editors gratefully acknowledge the assistance of the many individuals, chambers of commerce, tourist bureaus, and state and local park, highway, and police departments that helped make this book possible.

Driver-reporters (and the routes they drove)
Gregory Archbald (I-5), Thomas Barr (I-5, I-15, I-25), Noreen Church (I-5, I-15), Kent and Donna Dannen (I-15, I-25), Don Earnest (I-25), Cory Kilvert (I-26, I-75, I-77, I-81, I-87, I-91, I-93, I-95), Robert Lancaster (I-35, I-55), Norman Mack (I-35), Susan Macovsky (I-25), George Marsden (I-57, I-65, I-69, I-75, I-77, I-79), Richard Marshall (I-25, I-29, I-35, I-43, I-55, I-69, I-75), Barbara Roether (I-5, I-55, I-65)

Picture credits

The numbers in **bold type** below refer to the section numbers at the bottom of each page. The positions of the photos are indicated thus: (l) left; (m) middle; (r) right; (t) top; (b) bottom.

Cover Robert Frerck/Odyssey Productions, Chicago. **Introduction** Jay Maisel. **1** (l) © Pat O'Hara; (m) Randy Wells; (r) © David Muench Photography 1988. **2** (l) Ron Kimball/Wildlife Safari; (m) Michael Dunn; (r) R. Krubner/H. Armstrong Roberts. **3** (l) John F. Reginato/Shasta-Cascade Wonderland Association; (m) Audrey Gibson; (r) E. Cooper/H. Armstrong Roberts. **4** (l) Alan Pitcairn/Grant Heilman Photography; (m) Deborah Long/PhotoBank, Inc.; (r) © David Muench Photography 1988. **5** (l) © David Muench Photography 1988; (r) David Hiser/Photographers Aspen. **6** (tl) Tom and Pat Leeson; (bl) Jeff Gnass; (r) Rickers Film Productions. **7** (l) E. Cooper/H. Armstrong Roberts; (tr) © David Muench Photography 1988; (br) Royce L. Bair/The Stock Solution. **8** (l) © David Muench Photography 1988; (r) Manley Photo/Shostal Associates. **9** (l) Kent and Donna Dannen; (r) Lee Foster. **10** (l) Wyoming Travel Commission; (r) Jeff Gnass. **11** (tl) A. Bilsten/H. Armstrong Roberts; (bl) © David Muench Photography 1988; (tr) R. Krubner/H. Armstrong Roberts; (br) Eduardo Fuss. **12** (l) Eduardo Fuss; (r) Willard Clay. **13** (l) Clayton Wolt; (r) South Dakota Tourism. **14** Paul Horsted/South Dakota Tourism. **15** (l) Audrey Gibson; (r) Bob Glander/Shostal Associates. **16** (l) R. Hamilton Smith; (r) Positive Reflections. **17** (l) Iowa Department of Natural Resources; (r) Mike Whye. **18** (l) Mark E. Gibson; (m) Positive Reflections; (r) Bob Taylor. **19** (l) Positive Reflections; (r) Richard Stockton/The Stockhouse. **20** (l) Bob Daemmrich/Light Images; (tr) Kent and Donna Dannen; (br) Lee Foster. **21** (tl) Ken Dequaine; (br) George R. Cassidy/Third Coast; (br) Willard Clay; (tr) Ray F. Hillstrom/Hillstrom Stock Photo. **22** (l) James P. Rowan/Hillstrom Stock Photo; (m) Mark E. Gibson; (r) Frank Oberle/Six Flags Over Mid-America. **23** (l) Ken Dequaine; (r) Robert Jordan/The University of Mississippi. **24** (l) Florewood River Plantation; (tr) Don Warren; (br) Garry D. McMichael/Southern Images. **25** Greg Laun/Hillstrom Stock Photo. **26** (l) Charles Westerfield; (tr) William Strode; (br) Charles Westerfield. **27** (l) Ed Malles/Photo Options; (r) Raymond G. Barnes:Click/Chicago. **28** (t) Mark E. Gibson; (b) Grant Heilman/Grant Heilman Photography. **29** Positive Reflections. **30** (l) Ken Dequaine; (r) Larry West. **31** (l) Positive Reflections; (r) Joseph P. Messana. **32** (l) © David Muench Photography 1988; (r) Thomas Peters Lake. **33** Tourist Division, Georgia Department of Industry and Trade. **34** (l) Florida Division of Tourism; (m) Jungle Larry's Safari Park, Naples, FL; (r) M. Landre/H. Armstrong Roberts. **35** (tl) Elsie Ziegler; (bl) Mark E. Gibson; (r) Wolfgang Weber. **36** (tl) B. Cory Kilvert, Jr.; (bl, r) Arnout Hyde, Jr. **37** (l) Bruce Roberts; (r) © David Muench Photography 1988. **38** (l) H. Edelman/View Finder; (r) Arnout Hyde, Jr. **39** (l) The 1890 House Museum and Center for the Arts; (r) Zmiejko Photographics/Hillstrom Stock Photo. **40** (l) © David Muench Photography 1988; (r) M. Woodbridge Williams. **41** (l) © David Muench Photography 1988; (r) Ken Dequaine. **42** (l) Olana State Historic Site/Friends of Olana, Inc.; (r) Guy Gillette. **43** (l) Thomas Ames, Jr.: f/Stop Pictures; (m) James A. McInnis; (r) Fred M. Dole: f/Stop Pictures. **44** (tl, bl) John R. Wells; (r) © 1988 Joseph St. Pierre. **45** (l) John R. Wells; (tr, br) © David Muench Photography 1988. **46** (l) B. Cory Kilvert, Jr.; (tr) Eric Carle/Shostal Associates; (br) Clyde H. Smith. **47** (l) Eric Carle/Shostal Associates; (r) J. Nettis/H. Armstrong Roberts. **48** (l) G. Ahrens/H. Armstrong Roberts; (r) W. Bertsch/H. Armstrong Roberts. **49** (l) B. Cory Kilvert, Jr.; (r) Jack Dermid. **50** (l) Max and Bea Hunn/Shostal Associates; (r) W. Bertsch/H. Armstrong Roberts. **51** (l) Luis Casteñeda/The Image Bank; (r) Dave Forbert/Shostal Associates. **Back cover** (tl) J. Nettis/H. Armstrong Roberts; (bl) Eric Carle/Shostal Associates; (r) Arnout Hyde, Jr.

Library of Congress Cataloging in Publication Data

Reader's Digest Association.
On the road, U.S.A.

Includes index.
Contents: v. 1. North–South routes—v. 2. East–West routes.
1. United States—Maps, Tourist. 2. United States—Description and travel—
Guide-books. I. Title.
G1201.E635R4 1989   912'.73   88-675238
ISBN 0-89577-318-X (set)
ISBN 0-89577-316-3 (v. 1)
ISBN 0-89577-317-1 (v. 2)

Reader's Digest Fund for the Blind is publisher of the Large-Type Edition of *Reader's Digest*. For subscription information about this magazine, please contact Reader's Digest Fund for the Blind, Inc., Dept. 250, Pleasantville, N.Y. 10570.